German thought

This book provides an introduction to the complex genesis of Germany's intellectual identity, focusing on themes of a cultural, historical, philosophical and literary nature.

As Goethe and Schiller noted in 1796, 'Germany? But where does one find her? [...] Where her learning begins, her politics end'. German identity has always been a problem, which has come to the fore once again with German unification and with Germany's role in Europe and the wider world.

Whilst many academic courses focus on the twentieth century, this book provides a much wider perspective on Germany's cultural past. Topics include the legacy of the medieval Holy Roman Empire; German Protestantism; the German response to the Enlightenment; nationalism and the *Sonderweg* debate; the significance of education for social development; and the emergence of a German bourgeoisie.

Key figures in philosophy, history, politics and literature are introduced, and each chapter is supplemented by an *Arbeitsteil* of annotated texts in German, followed by further material for individual study. An essential text for foundation courses in German studies, it also provides valuable source material for more advanced students.

H.-J. Hahn is Head of German at Oxford Brookes University.

H.-J. HAHN

German thought and culture

FROM THE HOLY ROMAN EMPIRE

TO THE PRESENT DAY

Manchester University Press

Manchester and New York

distributed exclusively in the USA and Canada

by St. Martin's Press

Published by Manchester University Press
Oxford Road, Manchester M13 9NR, UK
and Room 400, 175 Fifth Avenue, New York, NY 10010, USA

Distributed exclusively in the USA and Canada
by St. Martin's Press, Inc., 175 Fifth Avenue, New York,
NY 10010, USA

British Library Cataloguing-in-Publication Data
A catalogue record for this book is available from the British
Library

Library of Congress Cataloging-in-Publication Data applied for
Hahn, Hans J. (Hans Joachim)
German thought and culture : from the Holy Roman Empire to the
present day / H.J. Hahn.
p. cm.
Includes bibliographical references.
ISBN 0–7190–4191–0.—ISBN 0–7190–4192–9 (pbk.)
1. Germany—Intellectual life. 2. Germany–Civilization—
Philosophy. 3. Enlightenment—Germany. 4. Literature and society—
Germany—History. I. Title.
DD61.H27 1995
943—dc20 95-3504
CIP

ISBN 0 7190 4191 0 *hardback*
0 7190 4192 9 *paperback*

First published 1995
99 98   10 9 8 7 6 5 4 3 2

Printed in Great Britain
by Biddles Ltd, Guildford and King's Lynn

Contents

Illustrations

Preface

A visitor from Germany who happened to watch the 'last night of the Proms' might be forgiven for expressing some astonishment at the almost boundless exhilaration displayed in the singing of *Rule Britannia* or at the exuberant display of the Union Jack in a variety of ingenious guises. Our visitor would undergo a similar experience of patriotic celebration in the United States on Independence Day or in France on Bastille Day. Although enthusiastic participants in numerous local *Fests*, the Germans, having suffered the shameful disgrace of National Socialism, followed by forty years of division, are still struggling to find their national identity. This uncertainty over the German national character is neither particularly recent nor is it restricted to political issues. Two hundred years ago Goethe and Schiller felt compelled to observe:

Deutschland? Aber wo liegt es? Ich weiß das Land nicht zu finden.
Wo das gelehrte beginnt, hört das politische auf.[1]
(Germany? But where does one find her? I do not know how to find this country.
Where her learning begins, her politics ends.)

For most of its long history Germany has been a divided country, often searching for its identity, even at times when, to the more superficial observer, the country seemed to be one strong and united force. There are many other quotations which would support Goethe's and Schiller's observation, but two more will suffice. Karl Marx noted a dichotomy between the German world of philosophy and poetry and that of 'real' politics and economics:

Wie die alten Völker ihre Vorgeschichte in der Imagination erlebten, in der *Mythologie*, so haben wir Deutschen unsere Nachgeschichte im Gedanken erlebt, in der *Philosophie*. [...] Die Deutschen haben in der Politik *gedacht*, was die anderen Völker *getan* haben.[2]

(Just as the ancient peoples have experienced their pre-history in their imagination, in *mythology*, so have we Germans experienced our later history in thought, in *philosophy*. [...] Germans have *thought* in politics what other nations have *enacted*.)

It can be argued that there has been more than enough action by Germany in this century and even today, Germany gives the impression of an industrious, striving nation. Much of this activity, on closer inspection, appears to be the result of a volatile fear of imagined or real dangers, be they political, environmental or economic. Friedrich Nietzsche, writing at the end of the nineteenth century, observed this volatile character at a time, when many thought Germany had at last found her true place in the concert of nations:

[Die Deutschen] sind von vorgestern und übermorgen, sie haben noch kein heute.[3]

([The Germans] are from the day before yesterday and from the day after tomorrow, they have not yet reached today.)

This book is based on over two decades of teaching on an undergraduate first-year course. It was devised as a remedy, to fill a gap in most A-level syllabuses and to supplement an increasing number of undergraduate courses which concentrate on twentieth century Germany, some even exclusively on developments since 1945. Imagine just for one moment that your knowledge of your own country was limited to events spanning only the last two or three generations and that such knowledge was further restricted to either the literary or political sphere, and you will concede that such a blinkered view is quite unacceptable. This book will attempt to provide a survey, a bird's eye view of Germany's development since the early Middle Ages, but should not be read as a history of Germany. It could best be compared to a kaleidoscope: the individual chapters forming certain pictures, consistent in themselves, but not to the exclusion of other, similarly consistent pictures. As a native of Germany, having spent half my life teaching in Britain, I have selected topics which, in my view, can contribute towards a better understanding between the two countries. The seven chosen themes will relate to aspects of German history, society, literature, culture and education, and I have attempted to bring all these topics together in the final Chapter, which looks at Germany in our time.

My own studies have been indebted to eminent masters who have attempted similar tasks throughout the years and have, no doubt, been far more successful in presenting Germany to the world outside. I have particularly in mind Heinrich Heine's analysis of Germany (1833), originally written for his French audience and, despite its fragmentary character, still a most exhilarating, witty guide to German philosophy and literature up to his time.[4] I, myself, was much influenced by Helmuth Plessner's *Die verspätete Nation*,[5] first published in 1935, but not generally known until its 1959 edition and, later, by Hans Kohn's *The Mind of Germany* (1960).[6] Both works are no longer easily accessible, either in print or in the way in which they approach the subject-matter. Germany has by now joined the Western family of nations and has developed her own stable democratic system, has become integrated in alliances and committed to a catalogue of values which is very much that of the Western world. And yet, in times of crisis, such as the unification process of the early 1990s, we can still catch the occasional glimpse of an earlier age and of bygone traditions, and it is these vistas into the past which this book sets out to explore.

The individual Chapters are organised in a loosely chronological order; they are also graded, so that the first two are easier to understand and shorter than the subsequent ones. In each case, I have tried to create links with our own century in order to demonstrate the relevance of the subject-matter.

Each Chapter consists of three parts: an introduction to the topic in English, prefaced by a synopsis which is meant to map out the argument, illustrated by a collection of 'Textual studies' in German and supported by a commentary and list of vocabulary. At the end of each Chapter are 'Topics for further study', intended both as revision, but also as the basis for discussion in class or for the individual investigation into a particular issue. The 'Brief survey of major historical data' and the 'Brief survey of major cultural periods/events' are intended as a guide to the historical background and to the numerous technical terms which it was necessary to include.

Experience gained from teaching such a course has shown that the subject-matter is not easy to grasp; an element of apparent confusion and contradiction should not deter the reader from further pursuing the subject. Indeed, in truly German fashion, I believe that a degree of bafflement may be a necessary intermediate stage before clarity and comprehension can set in, and even then, given the nature of the topic, our discourse will not come to an end, but will continue to complement our studies.

My approach has been an interdisciplinary one and I can well imagine that subject specialists will find it easy to take me to task for not having covered the latest publication on a given topic or for indulging in a somewhat personal account of a complicated issue. I feel no need to apologise for this approach: the book is meant for undergraduate students; there is no wish to conceal a personal approach and, indeed, the hope is to capitalise on the individual experience of someone who – for professional and personal reasons – has spent the greater part of his life explaining the peculiarities of Germany to British students. The current climate of post-modern parochialism and of growing nationalism has made this task more difficult than expected, but I do not wish to be taken as an ambassador for my country. Many of the existing prejudices against Germany contain, at the very least, a grain of truth; I have no wish to refute them, but rather hope to explain them and put them into a modern, critical perspective.

Finally, I wish to thank my teachers and my students for having helped and guided me in my own studies; the former for arousing my interest in the history of ideas in general and the subject of German in particular, the latter for their patience, their astute challenge of positions assumed by me and for encouraging me to produce a book on this topic. Writing this book in English was, in itself, a study of cultural divergence; I am grateful to all those who read individual Chapters, but most of all to my wife who endured the perusal of several versions and who questioned many a logical eccentricity and reined in my rather Germanic propensity to speculate and theorise, often at the expense of clarity and logic of progression.

Oxford, September 1994

Notes

1   Schiller, *Sämtliche Werke* (Säkularausgabe), Vol. 2, Stuttgart/Berlin, 1904; p. 103 (Xenie 85).
2   K. Marx, 'Die Rückständigkeit der Deutschen', *Deutsch-Französische Jahrbücher*, Paris, 1844; p. 237.
3   F. Nietzsche, *Jenseits von Gut und Böse, Friedrich Nietzsche, Werke in drei Bänden*, K. Schlechta (ed.), 2nd edn, Munich: Hanser, 1962; p. 706.
4   H. Heine, *Zur Geschichte der Religion und Philosophie in Deutschland*, Paris, 1834 and *Die romantische Schule*, Paris, 1833.
5   H. Plessner, *Die verspätete Nation, Über die politische Verführbarkeit bürgerlichen Geistes*, Stuttgart: Kohlhammer, 1959.
6   H. Kohn, *The Mind of Germany, the Education of a Nation*, London: Macmillan, 1960.

1

The Holy Roman Empire, the tradition of the *Reich* and German particularism

The continuing medieval structure of the Empire prevented Germany's development into a modern state; its Christian mandate and the subsequent rivalry between pope and emperor delayed the concept of national identity and encouraged the fragmentation of Germany.

Introduction

Before we can enter a serious discussion on the emergence of the Holy Roman Empire, a number of wider issues deserve clarification. The end of classical antiquity is conventionally dated by the final collapse of the decaying West-Roman Empire (476), when its Emperor was deposed by the barbarian leader Odoacer. A succession of events led to the fall of the Roman Empire; these together resulted in the great migration of Celtic and Germanic tribes which could no longer be halted at the imperial borders. We are used to seeing these changes as a chronicle of disasters and of describing them as the end of the civilised world. And yet, civilisation is made of stronger stuff than many historians would have us believe, undergoing renewal to re-emerge into new states and socio-political orders. The Roman historian Tacitus, and before him Caesar, had extolled the virtues of the Germanic enemy in a manner reminiscent of the description of the 'noble savage' in Dryden's time. The apparent 'vandalism' of the various Germanic tribes laid the foundations for a renewal of civilisation and for the emergence of modern individualism:

The great service that the barbarians rendered was a service of destruction. In doing so they prepared the way for a return to the past. Their first efforts in reconstruction were also valuable, since the difficulty of the work and the clumsiness of the product revived the respect of men for the superior skill of Rome. In the end the barbarians succeeded in that branch of constructive statesmanship where Rome had failed most signally. The new states which they founded were smaller and feebler than the Western Empire, but furnished new opportunities for the development of individuality, and made it possible to endow citizenship with active functions and moral responsibilities.[1]

Today's reader might not quite agree with the optimistic tone of the quotation, and it certainly took a long time for the concept of individuality to re-emerge. However, throughout the Middle Ages an awareness of antiquity survived,[2] even if the love of beauty and sensitivity was lost under the over-arching impact of Christian asceticism and metaphysics.

The concept of the 'Middle Ages' itself is anything but clear. It evolved to describe the period between the end of antiquity and the conquest of Byzantium by the Turks (1453). It is obvious that a period of some thousand years cannot be comprehended in universal terms, the concepts of the Empire as well as that of papal authority changing significantly, as did the general social, political and moral order. Long regarded as a dark period or a time of transition, the Middle Ages were ultimately to come into their own thanks to the positive way they were viewed in the German literary revival of the eighteenth and nineteenth centuries.

The development of the Holy Roman Empire
The Carolingian tradition: The coronation of Charlemagne gave recognition to a statesman who could continue the tradition of the Roman Empire but who irrevocably changed the face of western and central Europe. Already king of the Franks and Lombards and acquiring through conquest a realm

which was a worthy successor to the Roman Empire, he bestowed upon himself the title *Imperator*. Crowned by the Pope in Rome on Christmas Day 800, Charlemagne became protector of the Christian faith, thus reviving the Western Empire as 'holy' as well as 'Roman'. His father, Pepin, had already fatefully allied the Franks with the Papacy by guaranteeing the Papal patrimony in Italy and awarding the Pope territories conquered from the Lombards.

The Empire under Charlemagne, was soon to reveal its problematic nature, symbolised by the rule of sword and cross and illustrated by the two imperial centres of Aachen, the seat of Charlemagne and Rome, the Holy See. Whilst the rule of sword was based largely on Germanic/Frankish practice of loyalty to the king and on oral tradition, administration and communication within the vast Empire increasingly relied on the clergy who looked to the authority of Rome. The physical division between Rome and Aachen, Pope and Emperor, would sow the seeds for the emerging power struggle between these two forces which was a major factor in the eventual disintegration of the Empire.

The Carolingian realm barely survived its founder. Soon after Charlemagne's death (814) the ideal of the Empire had to give way to the political reality of the Germanic tradition of inheritance: by the Treaty of Verdun (843) the Empire was divided up amongst his three warring grandsons. The titular Emperor Lothar was awarded the Middle Empire, today's Benelux countries, Alsace Lorraine,[3] Burgundy, Provence and Northern Italy. The remainder was divided into the West-Frankish and East-Frankish kingdoms. This settlement was important in that it laid the foundation for the emergence of the nations of Western Europe, reflecting 'the nascent and lasting linguistic, economic and racial divisions of the continent'.[4] The West-Frankish kingdom, later to develop into France, was not only blessed with natural borders on three sides, it had also inherited through its imperial past, a more sophisticated administration, a superior road system and an already highly developed Romance civilisation. The East-

Frankish Empire, the actual home of the German lands, had few natural borders, had scarcely been under the influence of the Roman Empire and was occupied by many warring Germanic tribes, each with its own war lord.[5] The historical development of the next four to five centuries would result in the strengthening of political rule in the West-Frankish Empire, finally leading to political unification under a strong dynasty and with a clearly defined capital. The East-Frankish Empire, by contrast, would achieve few brief moments of political power, would continue and increase its decentralisation and would fail to establish a clearly defined capital. We shall return to the reasons for this development later.

Throughout this period, however, another Christo-Imperial tradition remained alive. The East-Roman emperor Constantine (fourth century) came to be seen as the first truly Christian Emperor, protecting the Church against heretics and heathens. This tradition found its base in the Augustinian philosophy of the Christian Church with its two realms, the earthly (*civitas terrena*) and the heavenly realm (*civitas dei*). Throughout the Middle Ages, history is understood as *historia divina*, (*Heilsgeschichte*), and in accordance with this view, the Roman Empire was conceived as a divinely inspired masterpiece, providentially created to receive Christ and to spread the knowledge of Christianity across the world. The twelfth century *Kaiserchronik* maps out the history of the Roman Emperors and celebrates Charlemagne as the great renewer, concentrating on the transfer of authority from Rome to 'Germany', in the person of Charlemagne:

> Karl der Pippînes sun,
> der sæligen Perhtun,
> der gwan den namen scône,
> daz er der êrste kaiser wart ze Rôme
> von Diutisken landen. . . .[6]

(Karl [Charlemagne], son of Pepin, of blessed Bertha, gained the name in the rightful manner, so that he became the first emperor in Rome of German lands. . . .)

The emerging concept of *Reich*: The word *Reich* derives from *regnum*, rule, reign. It can be applied both to the Germanic concept of rule as practised by the Frankish kings and to the tradition of the Roman Empire, considered the last of the four realms, as interpreted by medieval Biblical scholars.[7] Following Augustinian philosophy, Pope and Emperor rule over *sacerdotium* and *imperium*, the heavenly and the earthly realm. The close relationship between emperor and pope is seen as a symbol of the victory of God over Satan, each emperor is judged in relation to his service to the Church.

In the intervening years between the last Roman Emperor and Charlemagne the belief arose that the imperial crown was kept on St. Peter's altar in Rome thus viewing the position of the Emperor clearly from a Christian perspective. The coronation of the Emperor by the Pope is an important symbolic act, not necessarily signifying the superior position of the latter, but demonstrating that the emperor occupies his position in the service of the church, as the protector of Christianity. The emblem of the eagle, to this day associated with Germany, may well also have its origin in the Christian-Roman tradition. Originally a bird sacred to Jupiter, it became an ancient symbol of power and victory, represented on the standards of the Roman legions, and in medieval times also seen as a symbol of Christ's ascension.[8] During the latter part of the Middle Ages it became associated with the Empire rather than the Emperor, and an illustration of 1511 shows clearly the combination of its sacred and worldly role (Figure 1).

With the Saxon king Otto the Great the imperial crown came into the possession of the East-Frankish Empire. His defeat of the Hungarian armies at the Battle of the Lech (955) made him saviour of the Empire and the Christian world. Otto's empire was now separated from the West-Frankish realm. He continued the Carolingian tradition with his coronation as king of the Franks in Aachen and subsequently gained the Imperial Crown. Historians in the nineteenth century therefore named it the Holy Roman Empire of the

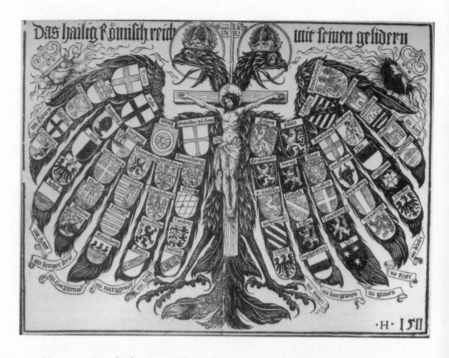

Figure 1: *Das heilig Römisch reich mit seinen gliedern* (1511). Note the combination of Imperial eagle and cross. The heraldic shields on the wings seem to suggest no particular order, except that the more important countries are in the top row and along the body of the eagle. The scrolls at the tip of the wing from top left to top right read: und Bauern, und Städte, und ehrbare Freie, und Burggrafen, und Markgrafen, und Seiler, und Vikare (Geistliche), und Landgrafen, und Grafen, und Ritter, und Dörfer, und Burgen. (Printed with the kind permission of *Germanisches Nationalmuseum Nürnberg*)

German Nation, but the name can be misleading since it never was intended as a nation state, nor was its 'German' nature firmly established. The name *deutsch* was applied increasingly from the eleventh century on, it is derived from West-Frankish 'theodisk', itself probably a translation from Latin *vulgaris*, referring to a people who do not speak the official language (Latin) and may well be of pagan and Barbarian origin.[9]

From Otto's reign onwards, the political and military involvement in Italy became an important tradition for the German king, culminating in the coronation as Emperor in Rome. As a consequence of the Emperor's involvement in Italy tensions developed between him and the Pope, frequently involving other forces, such as German rivals of the Emperor, Italian princes or cities or even the French king. From a papal point of view the question at issue was the emancipation of the clergy from secular authority, following on from the ecclesiastical reforms of the *Cluny* movement.[10] From a monarchic viewpoint royal authority was at stake with individual kings seen as the anointed of the Lord empowered to invest bishops with ring and staff. Collectively, these conflicts are known as the Investiture Contest (*Investiturstreit*) and led to a significant weakening of both the papal authority and, in particular, the position of the Emperor. Nineteenth century German historians interpreted this conflict in a nationalistic light as the struggle of an embattled German emperor against the latinate tradition of Italy and France; today's scholars interpret the issue less emotionally as an inevitable process of modernisation with the Roman church insisting on the investiture of bishops, and the German king or Emperor upholding the traditional custom of installing the bishops who fulfilled worldly functions in his realm. The conflict began in 1070, when Henry IV invested the Bishop of Milan against the wishes of the Pope and ended with the Concordat of Worms (1122). Its aftermath was felt throughout the reign of the Staufen dynasty (1138–1254) and not only affected inner-German rivalries, but actually ended the traditional role of the Emperor as protector of Christendom. It is therefore one of the major reasons for the debilitation of the Holy Roman Empire which, having lost its protective role over Christianity, was never to establish a new, meaningful function such as the claims to national leadership in France and Britain.

The Concordat of Worms distinguished strictly between spiritual (*spiritualia*) and temporal (*temporalia*) functions of authority, with the former executed by papal rule and the latter by royal command. However, since the bishops also performed secular duties within the Empire, the Concordat contributed significantly towards the weakening of the Emperor's status. Further examination of the Empire's feudal order will elucidate this matter; firstly, a brief glance must be given to the position of the German king, frequently also Emperor or at least Emperor designate.[11]

The position of the German king, though often not distinguished clearly from that of the Emperor, differed nevertheless in that it was based on Frankish and Saxon tradition. His election by 'the people' meant, in fact, that he was supported by the dukes of the Germanic tribes (*Stammesherzogtümer*) of Franconia, Saxony, Swabia, Bavaria and Lotharingia and by the archbishops of Mainz and Cologne. On the occasion of Otto's election as king the archbishop of Mainz raised his right hand and, turning to the assembly, proclaimed that he presented them with Otto, chosen by God, nominated by his father Henry and now declared king before all the dukes.[12] The four dukes of Swabia, Bavaria, Franconia and Lotharingia served symbolically at his ceremonial meal and the archbishop of Mainz adorned him with the royal insignia of sword, cloak, staff and sceptre. The royal duties primarily comprised the spreading of the Christian faith, the preservation of peace and the war against the enemies of Christ. The essence of *regnum* in this earlier phase of the Middle Ages was based on a complicated relationship between the king and his subjects: royal service by the individual dukes was based on mutual recognition and a state of peace and the whole order was based on the principle of the *familia*, a peaceful community where each person exercised certain functions according to rank. Throughout this time, and despite the change from a law based on oral tradition to written legal forms and the development away from a purely agrarian society to a more urban structure, the preservation of the peace (*Landfrieden*) remained one of the major functions of the German king.

From feudalism to particularism: The feudal order of the Empire can be discussed here only to the extent that it shaped the realm and contributed towards the development of German particularism. The word feudalism derives from Latin *foedum*, meaning a pact or personal relationship. The German term is *Lehenswesen* related to *leihen*, implying that the power, ultimately in the hands of God, has been passed down to Emperor and king and via several stages of 'loan' to the lowest of free men who in turn rule over serfs. Modern German historians refer to the Empire's feudal system as a *Personenverband*, indicating that the administration of the realm was based on a relationship of personal loyalty between ruler and ruled,[13] where office was chiefly seen as service. The vassal owes service to his lord, but the lord can rely on this service only if he himself has kept his side of the bargain, and peace exists between him and his vassal. This European feudal system was to last from the eighth to the thirteenth century.

From the thirteenth century on the feudal order developed into a corporate state with the personal relationship becoming more formal, and vested in various corporations. This type of rule was itself largely abolished by absolutist governments towards the end of the sixteenth century, except for the Imperial government itself, which continued its corporate order until its demise in 1806. The establishment of the *Reichsfürst*, the dynastic quarrels between Guelfs and Ghibellines,[14] the dispute between pope and emperor all contributed to the continuous weakening of the Empire and the concomitant strengthening of its individual states, leading to its ultimate destruction with the emergence of particularism.

The position of *Reichsfürst* was established by the end of the twelfth century. The title refers to a prince who is authorised to carry out imperial duties within a given territory, in particular the preservation of the peace (*Landfrieden*) and judicial functions. Amongst this group of *Reichsfürsten* were some of the dukes of the traditional *Stammesherzogtümer*, secular nobility and also bishops and abbots. The creation of the *Reichsfürst* marks an early stage in the transition from a feudal order to a corporate state in that, so far as these princes were seen as a group in their own right, it paved the way to later particularism. Of special significance for the emergence of the seven electors was the feudal order of the *Heerschild* (see Figure 1) as described by Eike von Repgow in his thirteenth century legal code, the *Sachsenspiegel* (Text 1). This code was conceived at a time when the feudal system was coming under attack as it tried to conserve an hierarchical order, justified for the purpose of *Reichsdienst* or imperial service. This service led in turn to the creation of the *Ministeriale*, a new social class which was to perform special services within the Empire, as administrators, merchants or mounted soldiers, effectively turning them into noble knights (*Ritter*). Joachim Bumke describes their social position and sees them as forerunners of the lower nobility with whom they had merged by the fourteenth century:

> As the heads of the central court administration in the emerging territories, as the guardians of their sovereign's castles, as the princes' representatives in the cities, the ministerial played a crucial role in the expansion and organisation of territorial sovereignty. [...] Although there were great social differences within the ministerial class, we can say that as early as around 1200, the leading ministerial could hardly be distinguished from the old nobility in regard to their lifestyle.[15]

One of the most famous of the ministerials was the poet Walther von der Vogelweide (*c.* 1168–1228), an astute commentator on the political issues of his time to whom we shall return at the end of this Chapter (Text 2).

The position of the emperor weakened considerably towards the end of the Staufen dynasty. Whilst Henry VI, perhaps the most powerful Staufen emperor, had managed to bring the kingdoms of Germany, Burgundy, Italy and Sicily under his control in an attempt to change the Empire into a dynastic realm, his early death in 1197 effectively brought to an end attempts to create a powerful, centralised state. A coalition of forces hostile to his plans, consisting of Italian princes, the Pope and some German princes gained the upper hand and forced the election of the Guelf Otto as a contender to lay claim to the Imperial crown. Old rivalries between the Staufen dynasty of Ghibellines and their opponents, the Guelfs, re-emerged, lasting for more than ten years and bringing to an end the efforts of Henry VI and his father, Emperor Barbarossa, to create a modern state, comparable to those of the Western neighbouring states of France and England, where strong central governments were being established. With the end of the *Thronstreit*, the Staufen dynasty had effectively lost control over the Empire: Frederick II ruled almost exclusively from Southern Italy, with his sons delegated to keep the peace in Germany. The execution of his sixteen year old grandson Conradin, by the French prince Charles of Anjou, later king of Sicily, in alliance with the French Pope Clement IV, marked the end of the Staufen dynasty (1268). The death of Conradin's father had already signalled the beginning of the *Interregnum*, a period of nearly twenty years where no clear leader emerged and foreign princes, amongst them Richard of Cornwall, laid claim to the Imperial throne. As a result, the German princes had increased their powers, resorting to international intrigue for private gain, thus working towards the practical extinction of the Empire which was to continue under the Hapsburgs in name only.

We have already seen how various popes found themselves in complete opposition to the Holy Roman Emperor and we can interpret this schism as the inevitable struggle between a modernised church, seeking an international and independent position, and a conservative Empire. The reform movement of Cluny in the mid-eleventh century had established the authority of the church over the worldly order. Pope Gregory VII saw his office as omnipotent and infallible. He believed it to be within his power to drive dissenting worldly princes from their thrones and withholding from them the sacraments of the church, thus severing them from the allegiance of their subjects. Papal claims of absolute power over the investiture of all bishops and territorial right over their worldly estates had to be challenged by the Emperor, still insisting on the old feudal order. This confrontation came to a head with the excommunication of Emperor Henry IV. He was left with no alternative but to cross the Alps on foot in the dead of winter (1077), to seek out Pope Gregory in the mountain fastness of Canossa and do penance in order to be received back into the Christian community. The Emperor's action might have been statesmanlike in that he forced the Pope to reinstate him, but the symbolism of this pilgrimage was potent enough to weaken the Emperor's position for ever. Later Emperors, in particular Barbarossa, tried to re-establish Imperial dominance over the Papacy, but their attempts had no lasting effect and by the middle of the thirteenth century the Emperor, no longer invested with the Imperial crown in Rome, was effectively restricted to the German lands and his own dynastic seat.

The *Goldene Bulle* (Golden Seal) of 1356 effectively limited the authority of the Emperor and ended any claim by the Holy Roman Empire to be a central power. The law established the election of the Emperor by seven electors on a majority principle. The three archbishops of Mainz, Cologne and Trier represented the papal interests and the four princes of the Palatinate, of Brandenburg, Saxony and later of Bohemia represented secular interests. From then on the candidate to the Imperial crown was at the mercy of these electors and paid large bribes in order to gain the crown, thus weakening the central influence even further. The Holy Roman Empire had become a particularist state with far-reaching special rights transferred to the individual princes. Special Diets (*Reichstage*) took over constitutional and even executive matters and with the Peace of Westphalia (1648) the central power had merely a symbolic significance: the *Reich*, in effect, had become an illusion, unable to prevent internal warfare or coalitions of individual German states with foreign powers working against the interests of the central power. By the end of the Middle

Ages 'Germany' consisted of some 300 individual autonomous states, which had gained territories at the expense of the ever shrinking *Reich* (Figure 2). The particularist system prevented the development of a German nation state at a time when other European states were forming their national identities and were soon to spread their influence into distant continents, eventually forming their own colonial empires. The slow political and socio-cultural decline of the Empire must be seen against the background of rapid development towards national identity in the rest of Europe. By the end of the sixteenth century France and Britain were completing the process, Spain was developing in the same direction, whereas Germany was further away than ever from becoming a nation state and was in fact in danger of losing even its cultural identity. Plessner's concept of Germany as *verspätete Nation* must be seen in this context.

The 'Barbarossa myth' and its historical reflection in nineteenth century Germany

Emperor Frederick I (1121–1190), named 'Barbarossa' after his red beard, although not the most powerful of the Staufen emperors, had a strong missionary vision of the office of Emperor as head of Christendom. Influenced by his uncle, the Bishop of Freising, author of a history of the Roman Empire, Barbarossa went back to the Augustinian concepts of the four Biblical empires and of the divine state.[16] Barbarossa also tried to re-establish the old Frankish tradition of rule. He secured the sanctification of Charlemagne, brought about peace between Guelfs and Ghibellines, attempted to regain control of the Northern Italian cities, tried to arbitrate between rival popes and sought to reassert the primacy of the Emperor as the first lord of Christendom. Such traditional Frankish aspirations met with the opposition not only from the Pope and the Italian cities, but also from the Englishman, John of Salisbury, who questioned the authority of the German as arbiter over other nations.[17] This opinion demonstrated that there was already a conflict between the emerging

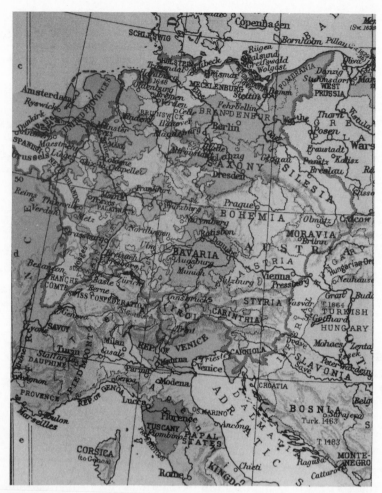

Figure 2: Map of the Holy Roman Empire from 1795, illustrating the particularist nature of Germany. In total, Germany in 1789 consisted of 1789 individual territories. (Printed with kind permission of London Geographical Institute)

14   *German thought and culture*

concept of nation states and the more traditionalist views of Barbarossa. His idealised concept of chivalry and courtly life manifested itself in the famous Court Feast at Mainz, the *Mainzer Hoffest* (1184), which was to symbolise imperial splendour and trans-national chivalry. Contemporary chroniclers saw it as the greatest court feast ever held in Germany, allegedly attended by some seventy thousand knights, 'not counting the clerics and the people of other orders'.[18] The Duke of Bohemia alone was said to have been accompanied by two thousand knights. Princes from all over Europe attended the festivities; many tents were erected outside the city; a wooden palace was constructed and it was said that wine flowed from the city's many fountains. The festivities began with the crowning of the Emperor and Empress, followed by the coronation of their son Henry VI as King of Germany. The festival itself became the standard for poetic feast descriptions as in Heinrich von Veldecke's *Aeneas*. True to his idealistic vision, Barbarossa brought the festivities to a conclusion by taking the cross and announcing another crusade to the Holy Land. Before reaching his destination he drowned in the river Saleph in Asia Minor.

Such was the impact of Barbarossa's reign and the sudden loss of this charismatic figure that, by the fifteenth century, a legend had grown up around him. He was portrayed as asleep inside a mountain (possibly the *Kyffhäuser* mountain in Thuringia (Figure 3)), waiting to emerge as Germany's saviour in times of danger, leading his people into the glory of a new golden age. There are similarities here with the *Tannhäuser* myth, where a Christian knight is seduced by the goddess Venus in her mountain and, in a wider sense, the Barbarossa myth also relates to the central Christian dogma of Christ's death and resurrection. The nineteenth century saw the revival of the Barbarossa myth in the writings of the brothers Grimm (1816)[19] as well as in several later poems. Heinrich Heine's version in *Deutschland, ein Wintermärchen* (1844) polemicises against reactionary forms of German patriotism: whilst not hostile towards the Barbarossa figure and

Figure 3: Left: Photograph of the Kyffhäuser Memorial, built between 1890 and 1896. It is located near the legendary *Barbarossahöhle* in an area where there had been a large fortification which, after its destruction in 1118 was rebuilt by Barbarossa in 1152. The *Kyffhäuser Denkmal* was intended as a memorial to Kaiser Wilhelm I, the first emperor of the new 'Second' *Reich*; it was also politically symbolic, relating the Prussian Hohenzollern dynasty to Barbarossa, the most famous emperor of the Staufen dynasty. Right: A popular cartoon by Karl Arnold, portraying Hitler as a new Barbarossa, his elongated moustache firmly embedded in the marble table before him, beating the drum to awaken Germany. Karl Arnold was a famous cartoonist in the Weimar Republic; the cartoon itself appeared in the satirical magazine Simplizissimus on 21st August 1932. (Printed with the kind permission of K. Arnold, *Drunter, drüber, mittenmang. Karikaturen aus dem Simplicissimus*, Munich/Vienna: © Carl Hanser Verlag, 1974; p. 123)

the Middle Ages, Heine objects to its exploitation in the service of patriotic, anti-French propaganda and to the analogy between the Hohenstaufen and the Prussian Hohenzollern dynasties.[20] From the 1830s onwards, poets such as Emanuel Geibel and Felix Dahn employed the Barbarossa myth to promote their own concept of a German nation state which would develop differently from the rest of Western Europe,

16   *German thought and culture*

basing this vision on some vague, Romantic concepts of *Volk*, *Reich* and military glory. The historian Johann Gustav Droysen encapsulated these literary ideas in the formula: 'To the Hohenzollern belongs the place which has been empty since the days of the Hohenstaufen'.[21] Time does not allow for a thorough analysis of the revival of the Middle Ages in nineteenth and twentieth century Germany. However, the naming of a second and third *Reich* clearly harks back to medieval traditions,[22] alien to an enlightened modern understanding of the idea of the state, as does a yearning for a hidden saviour. Even Hitler's perverse revival of German colonisation in Eastern Europe, culminating in a military campaign against the Soviet Union, codenamed 'Operation Barbarossa' (1940), can be seen in this context.

In conclusion, we return once more to the Middle Ages and the concept of the 'Holy Roman Empire'. It is clear that its idealistic character and its inability to adjust to the newly emerging concepts of nationhood and the modern state prevented the development of Germany as a nation. The Hundred Years War (1337–1453) gave France and Britain some early notion of national identity, the final defeat of the Saracens (1492) achieved the same for Spain. By the end of the Middle Ages, the German-speaking territories had lost their political identity and had torn each other apart. They made no contribution to the great discoveries and military conquests which introduced the new age of the Renaissance. The French, Spanish and English monarchies were setting up political systems which would establish law and order, and above all prosperity for their citizens, laying the foundation for the birth of a middle-class culture, for the development of liberalism and democracy and, ultimately, for the industrial age. In contrast, German knights and soldiers had lost their lives in conflicts between rival princes, German energies being dissipated in wars against the popes and the Italian cities. Paying allegiance to an increasingly illusory Holy Empire, Germany could develop no capital, no focal point for the formation of nationhood.

And yet, the course of events in Germany also had its advantages. German particularism led to a far greater dissemination of culture, and this widespread development of learning and craftsmanship saw the flowering of many provincial cities. Germany never encountered the phenomenon of one dominant capital, expanding at the expense of the provinces, neglected and starved of cultural resources. German particularism led to a decentralisation of art and scholarship, encouraging the rise of scores of smaller capital cities, each one establishing its own university, theatre and opera house, art gallery and other cultural centres. Thus, the historical development of Germany laid the foundation for a flourishing cultural life, fostering the careers of a multitude of composers, musicians, scholars and artisans. Being the centre of the Holy Roman Empire also encouraged the development of much theological thought and of philosophical speculation. Religion has always occupied a central role in Germany, even prior to the Reformation, a subject-matter which will preoccupy us in the next Chapter.

Notes

1 H. W. C. Davis, *Medieval Europe*, 2nd edn, Oxford: OUP, 1960; p. 19.
2 J. Huizinga, *The Waning of the Middle Ages*, London: Pelican, 1955; pp. 18, 331ff.
3 The German *Lothringen* still illustrates this historic division.
4 J. Bowle, *A History of Europe*, London: Secker and Warburg/ Heinemann, 1979; p. 173.
5 The German *Herzog* still refers to the original meaning.
6 *Kaiserchronik*, verses 14815ff, in E. F. Ohly, *Sage und Legende in der Kaiserchronik*, Darmstadt: Wissenschatliche Buchgesellschaft, 1968; p. 228.
7 cf. Book of Daniel, Chapter 2, verses 31ff. The four realms were seen to be the Babylonian, the Carthaginian, the Macedonian and the Roman Empires. The importance of this view is illustrated by Notker the German (from St. Gallen monastery): 'zům ersten sol men wissen, das menig künigrich ist gewesen in der welte, aber under den allen so sint vier grosze und rehte rich oder keisertům gewesen.' ('Psalter', 98,9, after J. und W. Grimm, *Deutsches Wörterbuch*, Vol. 8, Leipzig, 1893; col. 574.)

8 J. Hall, *Dictionary of Subjects and Symbols in Art*, New York: Harper and Row, 1974.

9 J. und W. Grimm, *Deutsches Wörterbuch*, Vol. 6, Neubearbeitung, Leipzig: S. Hirzel, 1983; col. 811–19.

10 Monastery, founded in 910 by William I of Aquitania, became a centre for the Christian reform movement which distanced the Church further from worldly rulers.

11 Two different concepts of leadership: the German king was elected according to Germanic custom, the *Kaiser* stood in the tradition of the Roman Empire. As a rule both titles were held by the same prince.

12 H. Vollrath, 'Deutsche Geschichte im Mittelalter', in M. Vogt (ed.), *Rassow, Deutsche Geschichte*, Stuttgart: Metzler, 1987; p. 1.

13 *ibid.* p. 13

14 Known in German as *Staufer* and *Welfen*: two rivalling noble families, repeatedly rivalling for the possession of the Imperial Crown during the twelfth century.

15 J. Bumke, *Courtly Culture, Literature & Society in the High Middle Ages*, Berkeley: University of California Press, 1991; p. 35.

16 cf. note 7. Barbarossa did this in order to strengthen the Christian mission of his leadership and to reaffirm his position of leader over Christianity.

17 Vollrath, 'Deutsche Geschichte im Mittelalter', p. 82.

18 Bumke, *Courtly Culture*, p. 204.

19 J. und W. Grimm (eds), *Deutsche Sagen*, Vol. 2, 3rd edn, Berlin: Nicolaische Verlagsbuchhandlung, 1891; pp. 105, 208.

20 H. Heine, *Deutschland, ein Wintermärchen*, Kaput 14–17, in particular Kaput 17.

21 H. Kohn, *The Mind of Germany, the Education of a Nation*, London: Macmillan, 1960; p. 5.

22 cf. N. Elias, *Studien über die Deutschen. Machtkämpfe und Habitusentwicklung im 19. und 20. Jahrhundert*, Frankfurt a.M.: Suhrkamp, 1992; p. 416.

Suggestions for further reading

Bumke, J., *Courtly Culture, Literature & Society in the High Middle Ages* (transl. by Th. Dunlap), Berkeley: University of California Press, 1991.

Conze, W., *The Shaping of the German Nation*, London: George Prior, 1979.

Kohn, H., *The Mind of Germany, the Education of a Nation*, London: Macmillan, 1960; Chapter 1.

Mayer, Th., 'Die Ausbildung und Grundlagen des modernen deutschen Staates im hohen Mittelalter', pp. 284–331, in H. Kämpf (ed.), *Herrschaft und Staat im Mittelalter*, Darmstadt: Wissenschaftliche Buchgesellschaft, 1972.

Vogt, M. (ed.), *Deutsche Geschichte*, Stuttgart: Metzler, 1987; pp. 1–143.

Textual studies

1. Eike von Repgow, *Sachsenspiegel* (*c.* 1225)

In des keisers kore sal der erste sin der bischof von Menze,
der andere der von Trire, der dritte der von Kolne. Unter den
leienvursten ist der erste der palenzgreve von dem Rine, des
riches druczesse, der andere der hertzoge von Sachsen, der
5 marschalk, der dritte der markgreve von Brandenburg, der
kemerer. Der schenke des riches, der konig von Behemen,
der en hat keinen kure umme daz, daz er nicht dutsh iz. Sint
kiesen des riches vursten alle, phafen unde alle leien. Die zu
deme ersten an der kore benant sint, de en sollen nicht kesen
10 nach irem mutwillen, sunder wen de vursten unde alle zu
koninge erwelen, den sollen se keisen.
(Cl. Frhr. von Schwerin (ed.), *Sachsenspiegel* (*Landrecht*),
Stuttgart: Reclam, 1953; p. 124.)

(At the Emperor's election the first shall be the Bishop of
Mainz, the other the Bishop of Trier, the third the Bishop of
Cologne. Amongst the worldly princes the first is the Count
Palatine of the Rhine, the steward of the Empire, the other
the Duke of Saxony, marshall, the third the Margrave of
Brandenburg, the chamberlain. The cupbearer of the Empire,
the King of Bohemia, has no voting right, since he is not
German. All the princes of the realm can choose, whether
clerical or worldly. Those named the first at the election, they
must not choose arbitrarily, but him whom the princes all
together have chosen as their King, him they must elect.)

Commentary: (numbers in parentheses refer to line numbers
in the text)
The passage is taken from Book 3, Chapter 57.2. Note the
relationship of 'kore' (1) with 'Kurfürst', elector, and of the
verb 'kesen' (9) with 'to choose'. Note also the special position of the King of Bohemia (6) who later was counted
amongst the German princes. The text also suggests some
misgivings (7f): why do we need these electors when every

prince is involved in the election? The traditional position of the *Heerschild* is still alluded to, with the seven electors representing the seven Biblical ages, being the theological justification of feudalism. Finally, no mention is made of the Pope; the election of the Emperor in *c.* 1220 may already have put the Pope's position in this matter into dispute.

2. Walther von der Vogelweide, from: *Reichssprüche* (1198?)

Ich sach mit mînen ougen	I saw with my eyes
mann unde wîbe tougen,	man and wife secretly
daz ich gehôrte und gesach	What I heard and saw
swaz iemen tet, swaz iemen sprach.	Was what this one did and that one spoke.
5 ze Rôme hôrte ich liegen	In Rome I heard lies uttered
und zwêne künege triegen.	And the betrayal of two kings
dâ von huop sich der meiste strît	This caused the greatest dispute
der ê was oder iemer sît,	Which ever was or will be,
dô sich begunden zweien	There they began to fall out
10 die pfaffen unde leien.	the clergy and the laity.
daz was ein nôt vor aller nôt:	This was the worst evil of all evils
lîp unde sêle lac dâ tôt.	Body and soul lay dead.
die pfaffen striten sêre:	The clergy fought hard:
doch wart der leien mêre.	But the lay people were in the majority.
15 diu swert diu leiten si dernider,	They laid down the swords,
und griffen zuo der stôle wider:	and took up again the stole:
sie bienen die si wolten,	They excommunicated whoever they liked
und niht den si solten.	and not those whom they should have.

dô stôrte man diu goteshûs.	The churches were thus disrupted

20 ich hôrte verre in einer klûs	I heard far away in a hermitage
vil michel ungebaere:	A great deal of wailing:
dâ weinte ein klôsenaere,	There a hermit cried,
er klagete gote sîniu leit,	He confessed his grief to God,
'owê der bâbest ist ze junc: hilf, hêrre, dîner kristenheit.'	'Dear God, the Pope is too young; Lord, help your Christian Church.'

(Carl von Kraus (ed.), *Die Gedichte Walthers von der Vogelweide*, 12th edn, Berlin: de Gruyter, 1955; p. 11.)

Commentary: (numbers in parenthesis refer to line numbers in the text)

(5), (10), (12), (17f) Antipapal sentiments: a devious Rome, references to the *Investiturstreit*, to clerical policies at the expense of spiritual and physical wellbeing. Excommunication is used as a political weapon.

(6) The two kings are Philip of Swabia (Ghibelline) and Otto IV (Guelf)

(20–24) In contrast the Christian hermit, symbol of true piety, referring to an inexperienced Pope (Innocence III, crowned just recently in 1198) who was ill-equipped to adjudicate in this situation. These lines also link back to the beginning (1–4), emphasising the contrast between private and public matters.

The Barbarossa cycle

3a. Friedrich Rückert (1788–1866), Barbarossa (1815?)

Der alte Barbarossa,	5 Er ist niemals gestorben
Der Kaiser Friederich,	Er lebt darin noch jetzt;
Im unterirdschen Schlosse	Er hat im Schloß
Hält er verzaubert sich.	verborgen

Zum Schlaf sich hingesetzt.

Er hat hinabgenommen
10 Des Reiches Herrlichkeit,
Und wird einst
wiederkommen,
Mit ihr, zu seiner Zeit.

Der Stuhl ist elfenbeinern,
Darauf der Kaiser sitzt:
15 Der Tisch ist
marmelsteinern,
Worauf sein Haupt er
stützt.

Sein Bart ist nicht von
Flachse,
Er ist von Feuersglut,
Ist durch den Tisch
gewachsen,
20 Worauf sein Kinn ausruht.

Er nickt alswie im
Traume,
Sein Aug' halb offen
zwinkt;
Und je nach langem
Raume
Er einem Knaben winkt.

25 Er spricht im Schlaf zum
Knaben:
Geh hin vors Schloß, o
Zwerg,
Und sieh, ob noch die
Raben
Herfliegen um den Berg.

Und wenn die alten Raben
30 Noch fliegen immerdar,
So muß ich auch noch
schlafen,
Verzaubert hundert Jahr.

(*Friedrich Rückerts gesammelte poetische Werke in 12
Bänden*, [Heinrich Rückert ed.], Vol. 1, Frankfurt a.M.:
Sauerländer's, 1882; p. 108)

Commentary: (numbers in parentheses refer to line numbers
in the text)
From *Zeitgedichte*, written in the patriotic spirit of the wars
against Napoleon. Essentially an accurate rendering of the
myth, but with emphasis on Barbarossa's 'second coming'
when the time is 'right'. (10) refers to the Holy Roman Empire
which he will re-establish (12). (26) *Zwerg* refers to *Knabe*,
the ravens (29) are traditionally linked with royalty.

Vocabulary:
unterirdisch = subterranean; verborgen = secretly; Herrlichkeit (f) = glory; elfenbeinern = of ivory; marmelsteinern

= of marble; Flachs (m) = flax; Kinn (n) = chin; alswie = as if; zwinken = to blink; Raum (m) = period; winken = to beckon; Knabe (m) = page; Rabe (m) = raven; immerdar = still.

3b. Emanuel Geibel (1815–1884): *Friedrich Rothbart* (c. 1835)

Tief im Schoße des
 Kyffhäusers,
bei der Ampel rotem Schein,
sitzt der alte Kaiser Friedrich
an dem Tisch von
 Marmorstein.
[...]
Auf dem Helm trägt er die
 Krone
und den Sieg in seiner
 Hand;

Schwerter blitzen, Harfen
 klingen,
wo er schreitet durch das
 Land.
Und dem alten Kaiser
 beugen
sich die Völker allzugleich,
und auf's neu zu Aachen
 gründet
er das heil'ge deutsche
 Reich.

(From *Jugendgedichte*, in W. Stammler (ed.),
Geibels Werke, Vol. 1.2, Leipzig:
Bibliographisches Institut Leipzig [1918]; p. 84.)

Commentary:
In comparison with Rückert much more militant, further removed from the myth, anticipating German world rule through war, but based on the early medieval concept of Charlemagne.
Kyffhäuser: mountain in Thuringia, associated with Barbarossa myth and crowned by a monument to Barbarossa and Kaiser Wilhelm I, the first emperor of the Second Empire (1871–1918) (cf. Figure 3).

Vocabulary:
Ampel (f) = hanging lamp in church; Marmorstein (m) = marble stone; Harfe (f) = harp; schreiten = to stride across; beugen = bending of knee, paying homage to; gründen = to found.

3c. Felix Dahn (1834–1912), *Siegeslied der Deutschen beim Einzug in Mailand unter Barbarossa*

Nun lasset die Posaunen tönen, nun breitet froh die Fahnen aus,
Laßt durch Lombardenlüfte dröhnen des Deutschen Sieges Jubelbraus:
Denn unser Kaiser Barbarossa, der Held, that einen großen Schlag: —
Seit jener Nacht in Schloß Canossa ist dies der erste deutsche Tag.
5 Das Lied soll durch die Alpen klingen bis Deutschland, ein Triumph-Orkan.
Und drohend an das Ohr soll's dringen dem Bischof dort im Lateran.
Nun auf, des welschen Lorbeers Reiser frohlockend schlingt, um Helm und Speer
Und jauchzend folgt dem großen Kaiser im Schritte des Triumphs das Heer.
Das Schwert gezückt, die Faust zur Seite, durch Staub und Blut, durch Schutt und Stein,
10 Stolz, in des Hasses Prachtgeleite, so reiten wir in Mailand ein.
Zu lange ließ't den Herrn zu pochen am Thor, du Stadt voll Widerstand:
Da hat in Trümmer dich zerbrochen die zorn'ge kaiserliche Hand.
[...]

(*Felix Dahns Gedichte*, Leipzig, 1906; p. 26f.)

Commentary: (numbers in parentheses refer to line numbers in the text)
A variation on the Barbarossa theme. Barbarossa is depicted as victorious over the Lombard city states, culminating in the peace treaties of Venice (1177) and Konstanz (1183), in reality much less glorious for Barbarossa than is suggested here. The poem is of a very general nature, recalling German

hostility to medieval Italian treachery and also an anti-Papal expression.
(4) Canossa (1077): Emperor Henry IV had to cross the Alps on foot to sue for peace with Pope Gregory VII. This was generally seen as a humiliation of the emperor.
(6) Lateran: then papal residence in Rome.

Vocabulary:
Posaune (f) = trumpet; Lombardendüfte (m) = the air of Lombardy; dröhnen = to roar; Jubelbraus (m) = exultant shouts; Schlag (m) = blow; Triumph-Orkan (m) = thunderous triumph; welsch = Italian; Lorbeers Reiser (m) = laurel branch; frohlockend = jubilant; gezückt = drawn; Schutt (m) = ruins; des Hasses Prachtgeleite = in the splendour of hateful escort.

Topics for further study

1. Summarise the main findings of Chapter 1 under six headings.
2. Give geographical, historical and political reasons for the rise of particularism in Germany.
3. List ten German cities and examine their historic cultural institutions.
4. Examine the 'Barbarossa Myth' and analyse its importance for Germany in the nineteenth century. (You may wish to make use here of the poems by Rückert, Geibel and Dahn, but you should also read 'Caput' xv and xvi in Heine's *Wintermärchen*.)

2

German Protestantism and the relationship of Church and State

This Chapter will seek to define 'Protestantism', in its wider sense, as a typically German form of Christianity. It will also examine its effects on German philosophy and literature and will explore to what extent it influenced the development of a distinctively German brand of political culture.

The peculiar nature of German Protestantism

We have learned in the previous Chapter how the Catholic Church remained firmly orientated towards Rome and how it resisted any attempts to integrate it further into the 'German' Empire. Catholicism, indeed, developed into a world-wide, trans-national movement, closely defined by church laws and dogmas. Its orthodox, almost rational nature brought it nearer to the Latinate than to any German tradition; it strove to preserve its orthodox nature, based on the body of a firmly established Church.

The Protestant movement has always found itself in opposition to this form of established orthodoxy, an opposition which expressed itself in the rejection of Latin and the adoption of the vernacular. Right from its inception, Protestantism profoundly influenced the development of the German language and might well have supported the development of a nation state, had the ravages of the Thirty Years War and the subsequent fragmentation of the *Reich* not halted such tendencies. By translating the Bible from the original Greek and Hebrew into German, Luther (1483–1546) had attempted 'to make Moses so German that no one would suspect he was a Jew'.[1] Luther's Bible rapidly came to occupy a central role in the evolution of German literature and thought. A brief glance at Germany's premier dictionary of quotations, Georg Büchmann's *Geflügelte Worte*, will demonstrate the impact of Luther's German: nearly thirty per cent of all German quotations are taken from Luther's Bible translation.[2] The translation itself served to limit the authority of orthodox Rome by making the Bible accessible to a wider lay movement. Such movements abounded in the latter part of the Middle Ages, particularly in France and the Netherlands,[3] but their lasting effect on Germany was perhaps more profound. Walther von der Vogelweide testified to the importance bestowed on the hermit who 'far off in his cell', seemed closer to God than was the Pope, surrounded by secular splendour and political intrigue.

Similar sentiments were expressed by the German mystics, a lay movement, based not on rational scholasticism, but on an emotional, irrational form of knowledge. Their aim was to achieve the *unio mystica*, a feeling of actual absorption into the deity, giving direct access to God. This highly individualised form of religion, bypassing dogma and church institution began in Germany in the twelfth century (Hildegard von Bingen) and flourished in the convents of the thirteenth century, reaching its high point with Meister Eckhart (*c.* 1260–1327) and Johannes Tauler (*c.* 1300–1361). It was deeply influenced by Augustinian philosophy, which gave it a new, strongly personal and emotional basis, and in this form it had a profound influence on Luther. He was particularly drawn to Tauler whose influence was also strongly felt in the German pietist movement of the seventeenth century.[4]

Women played an important part in German mysticism and, excluded from the study of Latin and Greek, they struggled to find German equivalents to the Latinate terminology in order to grasp the ultimate truth of the Christian gospel. Mystics tried, furthermore, to overcome the dogmatic orthodoxy of the Latin terminology; they attempted to attain a depth of experience which could hardly be expressed in words and at the very least needed some new approach.

The language of the mystics gained a new dynamic and ecstatic vigour. Meister Eckhart expressed this in one of his sermons: 'Swaz eigentlich gewortet mac werden, daz muoz von innen her ûz komen und sich bewegen von innerer forme und niht von ûzen her în komen, mêr: von inwendic sol ez her ûz komen.'[5] (What actually can be put into words, that must come from within and must move outward from within and not inwardly from outside; indeed, it must move from within outwardly.) We notice the verbal derivative 'worten' and the emphasis on 'inner' and 'outer', with the direction from inward to outward gaining prime importance. Today's German owes many of its most emotional and moving expressions to the mystical tradition, words such as *Einfluß, Eindruck, Eingebung, einleuchten, begreifen, bildlich, anschaulich, wesentlich*; many nouns ending in *–heit* and *–keit* reach back to the mystical tradition. Most of these words are translations of Greek and Latin concepts, and through their 'trans-lation' they have been revitalised and gained a life of their own. German philosophy would be unthinkable without such 'word-creations'.

It may well have been this mystical, irrational aspect of German Protestantism which affected the Lutheran attitude towards work and worldly matters. Max Weber's famous study *Die Protestantische Ethik und der Geist des Kapitalismus*, first published in 1904–5, is still of some importance for our understanding of the Lutheran form of *Beruf* (calling) and goes some way to explain, why Luther's form of protestantism failed to promote capitalism, discounting any form of predestination and with it the need for self-realisation by focusing instead on divine grace and personal faith. For Luther the divine calling concentrates on the fulfilment of worldly duties as willed by God, 'and hence every legitimate calling has exactly the same worth in the sight of God'.[6] In a very similar vein, *Arbeit* (work) is not measured by its material success or achievement, as seems the case with Jean Calvin (1509–1564),[7] but must be seen as a means towards self-fulfilment. There is thus a certain analogy between God's divine creation and our everyday creative work. Work has to be creative, be it the artisan at his work bench or the philosopher in his study. Both *Arbeit* and *Beruf* contain a strong element of professionalism, reflecting a very personal attitude towards one's occupation, 'no matter what that occupation may be'.[8] Weber demonstrates how Luther's attitude to 'calling' and 'work' represents a step forward from the traditional Catholic viewpoint, in that it frees the individual from the intervention by priest or sacrament and removes him/her from any notion of penance. However, the Lutheran stance, with its emphasis on divine grace, is still traditionalist in comparison with Calvinism. For Calvin, personal gain and prosperity will result from our labour and both are seen in a positive light as assurance of individual salvation, provided they were secured in an ascetic frame of mind which prevents their exploitation through idleness or extravagance. If we condense the difference between Luther and Calvin into an oversimplified formula, we might suggest that Calvin views the gain from our labours as evidence of our self-realisation whereas Luther defines work in terms of duty towards God by sinful man. Weber's comparison of Luther and Calvin demonstrates different attitudes towards economic and political issues as illustrated in the history of Germany on the one hand and that of England and America on the other.

It cannot be our task to pursue these differences between Luther and Calvin, but rather to concentrate on the specific nature of German Protestantism. Its mystical nature sustained a form of individualism which turned inward, became sentimentalised and spiritualised the world. The uniquely German term *Weltfrömmigkeit* is evidence of such a development. Helmut Plessner continued Weber's work by analysing the origins of Lutheran *Weltfrömmigkeit*, suggesting that it arose out of an incongruous relationship between individual piety and a newly emerging state-church. Personally conceived religious fervour, soon stifled by the emerging state-churches, sought compensation in *Weltfrömmigkeit* by transforming its personal religiosity into those 'secular' concerns close to philosophy and literature, while excluding the public sphere of politics which was surrendered to the authority of the state.[9] Thus, the German Lutheran movement relied on absolutist princes in the various territorial states to gain independence from Rome and the Empire and saw any form of rebellion against the government of the day as sinful misuse of power.[10] In contrast, Calvinism in its Western European strongholds found itself in collision with absolutist state power. It came to accept the right of resistance to despotic regimes and embraced the developing ideas of human rights.

Plessner also refers to a specifically German concept of *Kultur*, embedded in a secularised form of Lutheranism and emphasising its creativity. The German language distinguishes clearly between *Kultur* and *Zivilisation*, endowing the former with an actively creative, artistic and individualised character and restricting the latter to mere technical achievement, more related to comfort and therefore of only secondary importance. A modern dictionary of philosophy demonstrates these differences even today:

> Der Unterschied zwischen Kultur und Zivilisation besteht im deutschen Sprachgebrauch darin, daß Kultur der Ausdruck und der Erfolg des Selbstgestaltungswillens eines Volkes oder eines Einzelnen ist, während Zivilisation das Insgesamt der Errungenschaften der Technik und des damit verbundenen Komforts ist.[11]
> (The difference between *Kultur* and *Zivilisation* in German usage consists of *Kultur* being the expression and achievement of the will of a nation/individual in defining the Self, whereas *Zivilisation* is the totality of technical achievements and its related material comfort.)

This strong emphasis on individuality and creativity is also seen in much of German philosophy which has always demonstrated a certain scepticism towards Western forms of positivism. Indeed, the stereotypically perceived lack of a German sense of humour and a serious approach to art and culture may well stem from this German Protestant brand of

Weltfrömmigkeit. Any confinement to the private sphere necessarily restricts the development of humour, which feeds off the public sphere and emphasises the relativity of the human domain, whereas 'jene dem Deutschen eigentümlich gewordene Tiefe verweltlichter Frömmigkeit [...] ihren Ursprung in dem Verhältnis des Luthertums zu weltlicher Arbeit und Berufstätigkeit hat.'[12] (that depth of secularised piety peculiar to the Germans [...] has its origin in the relationship of Lutheranism towards secularised work and occupation.)

The impact of Luther's Protestantism on German philosophy and literature is undeniable. The significance of the German *Pfarrhaus* (vicarage) as birthplace to a host of German writers (Lessing, Lenz, Mörike, Hesse), philosophers and scholars (Hegel, Schelling, Nietzsche, Heidegger, Schweitzer), and the importance of the Tübingen theological *Stift*[13] in the emergence of German idealism, bear witness to the connection between Protestantism and German culture. The influence of Luther on German pietism (*c.* 1650–1780) has been amply documented[14] and the rebirth of German literature in the eighteenth century was based to a considerable degree on the language, emotions and sensitivity of the pietist movement. The verse of Klopstock, the poetry of the young Goethe, the literary works of the Romantic movement are all deeply indebted to the Pietist tradition. Furthermore, several sociological studies have demonstrated that a far higher proportion of Protestants sent their children on to higher education, which remained the case until the mid 1960s, when politicians defined young Catholics as part of a hitherto untapped source of potential talent (*Begabungsreserve*).[15] These observations on the peculiar nature of German Protestantism will conclude with the reminder that its particular form of *Weltfrömmigkeit* is historically rooted in an ultimately uneasy relationship between Lutheran individual piety and emerging Protestant state-churches. Plessner took great care to emphasise that this particularly German *Weltfrömmigkeit* may not outlast the decline in traditional middle-class social mores. Our final Chapter will try to establish how much of German Protestantism has survived to the end of this century.

Luther's Reformation and the German concept of freedom

It is hardly necessary to remind ourselves that Luther's Reformation was not the first attempt in the history of the Church to bring about a rejuvenation. A powerful precursor to Luther in the latter part of the fourteenth century was the Oxford cleric John Wycliff, as was his Prague colleague John Hus. Luther succeeded where both reformers failed. There were several good reasons for Luther's success: Germany was more affected by the Roman Curia than other countries, in particular its corrupt practices met with strong condemnation, as seen in the *Gravamina* of 1456, a catalogue of complaints issued at a diet of German princes in Frankfurt. In addition, Johannes Gutenberg's invention of mechanical printing (*c.* 1468) allowed for the swift and relatively cheap dissemination of opinion at a time when Germany was experiencing a renewed interest in culture and learning, evident in the foundation of some eight new universities. Printing became known as 'the German art'[16] with important publishing houses established in the newly Protestant cities of Mainz, Strasbourg, Nuremberg, Frankfurt and Leipzig.

Most important, however, was the general feeling of an impending new age, closely associated with Humanism and the Renaissance, and a new emphasis on the individual (Figure 4). Nothing embodied the advent of individualism more than the Florentine generation of Michelangelo and Leonardo da Vinci. When Italy fell under the domination of Spain (1540), the Inquisition sought to suppress this fertile intellectual life. Some of its most precious energies crossed the Alps to settle in central Europe, relatively untroubled by wars and dynastic rivalries. Flanders and the Netherlands in particular began to flourish; Erasmus of Rotterdam (1467–1536) held pride of place among the intelligentsia, editing the

Figure 4: Self-portrait of Albrecht Dürer in his 30th year. If compared with medieval portraits, we recognise immediately the new sense of realism and individuality. Dürer assumes here the pose of Christ, allegedly in his last year on earth. This was not an act of blasphemy, but a literal interpretation of Genesis I, 26: 'And God said, let us make man in our image'. The picture symbolises the new spirit of individualism, a hallmark of the 'new' age (Renaissance). (Printed with kind permission of *Alte Pinakothek*, Munich)

Greek New Testament and advocating the translation of the Scriptures, in many ways laying the foundation for Luther's own translation.

Luther's impact on Germany is best understood if we see him at the very threshold of this new age, sharing its interest in spiritual renewal. His aim was a rejuvenation of the Catholic Church, at the heart of which was man's personal relationship to God, freeing the individual from any patronage by Pope, Emperor, saint or priest. He questioned the very existence of a separate clergy, 'for all Christians are truly part of the clergy so that there is no difference in office as such'.[17] He insisted that man's soul had direct access to God and thus the Church's role lost in importance and faith became a very personal matter. The concept of salvation through faith alone formed the essence of Luther's Christianity, with God no longer seen as judge over our sins, but instead as the forgiving father in whom man puts all his trust. Man now had to recognise that no amount of good deeds, nor any form of mediation by saints could contribute towards personal salvation.

Luther's Address to the Christian Nobility of the German Nation, *An den Christlichen Adel deutscher Nation* (1520), as well as other early statements evince a genuinely revolutionary character. They were an attempt to emancipate his fellow Christians from domination by the clergy, demonstrating the equality of all men before God and aspiring to liberate Germany from any form of interference by Rome. His comments on the Holy Roman Empire and its dependence on the Roman Curia deserve special attention:

... da wir vermeinet, Herrn zu werden, sein wir der allerlistigesten Tyrannen Knecht worden, haben den Namen, Titel und Wappen des Kaisertums, aber den Schatz, Gewalt, Recht und Freiheit desselben hat der Papst; so frißt der Papst den Kern, so spielen wir mit den lebendigen Schalen.[18]
(when we thought we had become masters, we had in fact become servants of the most cunning tyrants, we were in

possession of the name, title and coat of arms of the imperial might, but wealth, power, justice and freedom were in the hands of the Pope; thus the Pope kept the fruit and let us play with the peelings.)

There are comparisons here to the demands of the leaders of the French Revolution of 1789: liberation of the laity from the influence of the clergy, a new sense of patriotism and a desire for self-determination are all present in Luther's address.

And yet, Luther was not interested in political reform. His attitude towards freedom demonstrates a most peculiar personal dichotomy: whilst not lacking the personal courage and individualism of the modern revolutionary, his political understanding remained steeped in medieval thought. His *Letter on a Christian's Freedom* (Text 1) bestows on us absolute freedom, while at the same time denying this freedom when matters of worldly interest are at stake. One important reason for Luther's political backwardness may lie in his Augustinian monastic training. St. Augustine, fifth century bishop of Hippo, postulates in his main opus, *De Civitate Dei*, a bitter struggle between the realms of God and the Devil. Whilst man's soul is of divine origin, belonging to the divine realm (*civitas dei*), man's body and all his earthly goods are part of the worldly or Satanic realm (*civitas terrena* or *diaboli*). Man is seen as an impure union of body and soul and it is vital for a Christian's development that the soul returns to its divine origin, freed from imprisonment in the body. Based on this Augustinian philosophy, Luther's concept of freedom is embedded in a mystical belief that freedom means only freedom to believe and that earthly matters are important only in so far as they might serve to impede this freedom.[19] His earlier, more political utterances against the practice of indulgence, against simony and other forms of profiteering, all promote the aim of returning man's soul to God. He is in favour of civil disobedience only as far as the first three Commandments are concerned, affecting man's relationship to God and the keeping of the Sabbath. Failing to recognise the wider issue of freedom of conscience, he ignores the need for any degree of social equality and political emancipation in order to attain spiritual freedom. He would not have understood that spiritual freedom could be undermined by lack of education or that other, more subtle forms of political suppression might bar people from access to the Holy Word.

Luther's attitude towards freedom is well illustrated by his response to the Peasants' Rebellion (1524/25). His pamphlet *Against the Murdering, Thieving Hordes of the Peasants* (Text 2), advocated their severest punishment and exonerated the authorities from any blame in the vicious suppression of the uprising. Freedom, according to Luther, was a matter for the soul alone, no other aspect being worthy of its defence.

The rebellion itself is now generally recognised as the largest mass movement in German history,[20] an uprising not only of the peasants, but of the common people in town and country. By 1500 the economic situation had deteriorated, so that many farmers were restricted to living off their smallholdings. At the same time the nobility and the clergy were increasing their pressure: serfdom became even more oppressive, the use of the common land, of fishing and hunting was forbidden, compulsory service to the landlord and taxation were on the increase, legislation became ever more despotic and the *jus primae noctis* was widely practised.[21]

Given such provocation, the peasants reached eagerly for the new freedom as proclaimed by Luther. They insisted on the 'Divine Right', i.e. the literal application of the Gospel and published their 'Twelve Articles'. These demanded the right to choose their own minister, the use of the corn tithe to support him and the poor within the community, the abolition of serfdom, the reduction of their crushing taxes, the guarantee of a few rudimentary legal rights, the democratic control of the clergy with reduced salaries and titles (Text 3). These demands were moderate and the articles were rapidly disseminated throughout southern and central Germany; printing ran to twenty-five editions. In the summer of 1525 the peasants met at *Frankenhausen*, at the foot of the *Kyffhäuser* mountain, their gathering possibly a symbolic act intended to link them with Barbarossa, perceived by now not only as a national leader, but also as a champion of the people.[22] Their vicious massacre by the troops of the princes of Hesse and Saxony, allegedly committed whilst they sang hymns prior to the battle, marked the inevitable end of the rebellion, in the course of which some 75,000 peasants were killed. Emperor Charles V's new criminal law of 1532, the *Carolina*, ensured that the lives of the survivors were even harsher and signalled the end of a free peasantry in southern and central Germany.

Many of Luther's contemporaries were more advanced in their thinking. Ulrich Zwingli (1484–1531) recognised that a Christian also has worldly obligations and considered political reform a Christian obligation. To some extent, Zwingli's stance prepared the various cantons of Switzerland for their secession from the Holy Roman Empire and put them on the path towards democracy. Thomas Müntzer (*c.* 1490–1525) followed a similar line. Opposing Luther's 'fanatical belief' in St. Augustine,[23] he preached instead that, far from turning their backs on the world, Christians had the responsibility of rendering the world a Christian domain. His main concern was the poor, and seeing the princes of Saxony as God's executors in this world, he beseeched them to take up the sword against a perverted clergy and to weed out God's vineyard at this time of harvest.[24] Finding himself opposed by Luther and abandoned by his worldly protectors, he finally turned political revolutionary and played a leading part in the uprising at Mühlhausen (1525) where the townspeople overthrew their patrician council to join the peasants in their revolt against the nobility. Müntzer's new revolutionary doctrine showed a political concern for the underprivileged and went well beyond anything Luther ever advocated: 'Die herren machen das selber, das in der arme man feyndt wirdt. Dye ursach des auffrůrß woellen sye nit wegthůn, wie kann es die lenge gůt werden? So ich das sage, můß ich auffrůrisch sein, wohl hyn.'[25] (It is the fault of the nobility that the poor man becomes their enemy. They do not wish to get rid of the cause of the rebellion, how then can there be improvement in the long run? As I say this, I have to be rebellious, so be it.)

While Luther's lack of experience in political matters might have preserved his own Protestant reforms from opposition by the German princes, it certainly had an adverse effect on the development of political culture in Germany. The devastating defeat of the peasants' uprising, together with Luther's stance towards worldly authority worked to the benefit of the individual *Landesfürsten* and paved the way for a relationship between Church and State that was to affect Germany for centuries.

The relationship of Church and State in Germany
Luther's 'moderate' attitude during the Peasants' uprising earned him the support of many of the Empire's princes. By 1530 a majority of states and free cities had joined the Reformation movement whilst, at the same time, contriving to distance themselves from Luther's proclaimed attitude towards freedom and politics. Obedience towards the Emperor was no longer automatic, coalitions with France and Denmark were concluded against the Emperor's authority. Even in church matters the authority of the Prince became unassailable: within the individual protestant states the prince acted as *Notbischof*, *de facto* head of the church, with overall control of the protestant clergy. The investiture issue, in the Middle Ages a source of bitter rivalry between Emperor and Pope, was now settled, the individual prince investing the clergy within his own territory. Church property, too, came under state control and was used for secular purposes, such as the founding of new universities.

The new alliance of Throne and Altar made the state the protector of the Church, eliminating the latter as an independent force for authority or opposition and thus strengthening the position of the individual prince. The position of the clergy was virtually that of a civil service, with the state raising a special tax to cover their salaries and maintain church property.[26] The Peace of Augsburg (1555) formulated the famous conclusion of *cujus regio, ejus religio*,[27] thus making the secular ruler the final arbiter of his subjects' religion. The fight for religious freedom was now minimal, taking matters back by centuries to an almost medieval theocracy.

By the beginning of the nineteenth century almost all the princes of the Empire were Protestant. This Protestant church became increasingly allied with contemporary politics and with a newly developing nationalism. Ignoring the social questions which arose in the wake of the Industrial Revolution, it involved itself in a new interpretation of history: Luther had assumed the role of standard bearer for a national identity and this became even more pronounced after the formation of the Second Reich:

> Kein Zweifel kann sein, daß nach 1871 relativ schnell der entschiedene Nationalismus in die Kirche einströmt, der 'Pastorennationalismus', die Identifizierung von evangelischer und nationaler Gesinnung, von Kaiser, Reich und Protestantismus.[28]
>
> (There can be no doubt that relatively soon after 1871 a decisive form of nationalism entered the [Protestant] church, 'pastoral nationalism', the identification of the Protestant with the national persuasion of *Kaiser*, *Reich* and *Protestantism*.)

This trend towards an undemocratic and, at the same time, national Lutheran Church can be illustrated by the following three examples. While it would be unreasonable to blame Luther for this peculiarly German type of Protestantism, it must, nevertheless, be recognised that Luther's Augustinian attitude towards freedom and secular affairs profoundly affected the relationship between Throne and Altar in Germany.

The Development of Prussia: The Grand Master of the Brandenburg Teutonic Order was one of the first to adopt the new faith; he transformed his territory into a secular dukedom (1525) with dynastic rights of inheritance, which became the nucleus of the Prussian state, characterised by its Lutheran Protestantism. Prussia, however, did not develop into a great European power until the end of the eighteenth century and its success was the result of several factors. Never having been an integral element of the Holy Roman Empire, it possessed a territorial independence and modernity and was blessed with a succession of enlightened leaders. And yet, both its military and economic success and its efficient administration breathe the spirit of Luther's Protestantism. There was little significant opposition to the dynastic leader. Those very Prussian virtues of a sense of duty and loyalty, and the associated military qualities of unquestioning obedience and discipline, flourished in the new state and can be related to Lutheran ethics. The Prussian civil servant outshone his counterparts elsewhere in conscientiousness, incorruptibility and service to the state. In accordance with Lutheran views on the relationship between faith and state, neither the mores nor the authority of the latter were ever questioned. Plessner comments on this Lutheran aspect of unquestioned service to state, family and *Beruf*: 'Für den lutherischen Christen fallen die Grenzen der Pflichten gegen Gott nicht mit denen der Kirche zusammen, weil Staat, Familie und Beruf die gottgegebene Sphäre der Werke des Glaubens bedeuten.'[29] (For a Lutheran Christian, man's duties towards God do not coincide with his duties towards the Church, since state, family and profession have for him come to mean the God-given sphere of faith.) In other words: state, family and profession are God-given, their validity and integrity are not open to question, duty to state and family are aspects of service to God.

When the religious component declined, as happened during the Enlightenment, a time which coincided with Prussia's ascent to military power, these energies were channelled into scholarship and discipline. The secularised Prussian brand of Protestantism found its most distinguished representative in Hegel (1770–1831) who interpreted the Lutheran belief in authority as unquestioned obedience towards the State, a state based on a monarchic principle and on a system of government administered by an impartial elite of civil servants. This would eventually lead to a change of direction in Germany's history, away from Vienna and its international Roman Catholic orientation, towards Berlin, a young city outside the sphere of the Holy Roman Empire, a garrison town looking more towards the North and East than towards the West.[30]

The *Kulturkampf* under Bismarck (1870–78): This brief survey cannot do justice to Bismarck (1815–1898) and his inner-German policy, nor can it give a full account of his fight against the Roman Catholic Church. We shall restrict ourselves to a discussion of the *Kulturkampf* in the light of the Lutheran tradition. The conflict began with the Doctrine of Papal Infallibility (1870), mistakenly interpreted as a Vatican claim to world domination which led to a split within the German Catholic Church. Bismarck, backed by the Liberals, also enjoyed the support of some European statesmen such as the British Prime Minister Gladstone in his campaign to diminish the influence of the Catholic Church in German political life.[31] Bismarck's real campaign was directed against the newly formed Centre Party (*Zentrum*) which sought to represent Catholic interests in a by now predominantly Protestant state. A closer study of Bismarck's interior policy would demonstrate a similarly Machiavellian attitude to other political parties, but it was his Lutheran background which made him take exception to the ecclesiastical influence of an independent 'Roman' church over the state (Text 3).[32] Hostile to the influence of the Church in matters of education, he abolished the Catholic Section within the Ministry of Education and placed the management of primary schools under state control. He also banned the Jesuit Order and broke off diplomatic relations with the Holy See. The 'May Laws' stipulated that all members of the clergy had to be German citizens, their education and appointment to be supervised by the government. The *Kanzelparagraph*, abolished only in 1953,[33] specified that priests were forbidden to make political observations from the pulpit on the grounds that they were likely to endanger public peace. Civil marriage became the only legally accepted form of marriage. Whatever Bismarck's motives in his fight against the Catholic Church, they demonstrate a staunchly Protestant conviction, reflecting Luther's interpretation of *Matthew* 22.21 that 'the things which are Caesar's' govern all worldly affairs and that it is not the business of the Church to get involved in such matters.

The Relationship of Church and State under Hitler (1933–45): The dilemma of German Protestantism under Hitler and the wider historical implications of the position of the Church under National Socialism cannot be discussed here in detail. A fuller analysis would demonstrate that the churches were not alone in their ambivalent attitude towards Nazi tyranny. With the demise of the German monarchy, the alliance between the Protestant Church and the State underwent a crisis. Under the Weimar Republic the churches viewed the social policies of the various governments with some unease. The Concordat between Hitler and the Vatican in July 1933, while remaining one of the more shameful chapters of Roman Catholicism, was no more than a *Zweckbündnis*, an attempt to salvage as many rights as possible for the Catholic Church in Germany. The position of the Lutheran church, whilst by no means uniform, was more supportive in its attitude to National Socialism. Its *völkisch* wing welcomed the self-styled national uprising (*nationale Erhebung*) as a source of religious renewal, 'Vollendung der deutschen Reformation aus dem Geist des Nationalsozialismus'[34] (completion of the German Reformation in the spirit of National Socialism). Hitler was seen as a God-given leader and he himself, without prior consultation with the Lutheran Church, appointed Ludwig Müller as *Reichsbischof*. The *Deutsche Christen*, in the main, supported National Socialism and gained convincing majorities in synod elections in July 1933 (Text 5).[35] Almost a year elapsed before a splinter opposition group emerged (May 1934), the *Bekennende Kirche*, supported by the First

World War hero Martin Niemöller and by Dietrich Bon-
hoeffer who was later implicated in the ill-fated assassination
attempt against Hitler, and allied to the existentialist ('dialec-
tic') theology of Karl Barth. And yet, even the *Bekennende
Kirche*, despite its brave opposition to Hitler, was steeped in
Lutheran aversion to political involvement, emphasising the
deep division between God and world.[36]

After the collapse of National Socialism, the Lutheran
churches recognised the errors of the *Deutsche Christen*,
embodied in the *Stuttgarter Schulderklärung* (1945) which
states:

> Mit großem Schmerz sagen wir: Durch uns ist unendliches
> Leid über viele Völker und Länder gebracht worden. [...]
> Wohl haben wir lange Jahre hindurch im Namen Jesu
> Christi gegen den Geist gekämpft, der im nationalsozial-
> istischen Gewaltregiment seinen furchtbaren Ausdruck
> gefunden hat; aber wir klagen uns an, daß wir nicht mutiger
> bekannt, nicht treuer gebetet, nicht fröhlicher geglaubt und
> nicht brennender geliebt haben.[37]
>
> (We state with great sorrow: infinite suffering has been
> inflicted upon many peoples and countries because of us.
> [...] Although we have fought for many years in the name
> of Jesus Christ against the spirit which found its frighten-
> ing expression in the National Socialist system of terror;
> we ourselves stand accused of not having witnessed with
> greater courage, of not having prayed with greater zeal, not
> having believed with greater joy and not having loved with
> greater fervour.)

This declaration of guilt deserves special recognition, since it
represents the only declaration of its kind which was made
by any church, organisation or institution with regard to their
implication in Third Reich policies. Without in any way belittling this exhortation of the spiritual power of faith, hope
and love, we still see within it the spirit of Luther in its somewhat vague acknowledgement of the political involvement of
the Church as a public organisation. A closer examination of

the history of the declaration would reveal serious divisions amongst individual church leaders and an overwhelmingly negative, even hostile response from congregations. A certain naivety in secular matters is also evident in the Church Council's response to the letter from the Archbishop of Canterbury to the German people, particularly with reference to the Council's condemnation of Polish and Russian 'territorial greed'.[38]

Karl Barth's *Ein Wort an die Deutschen* (1945) also elicited a revealing response. In welcoming the Stuttgart Declaration, Barth advises his brothers and sisters in Germany to enter into a mood of soberness of mind and to recognise that a simple return to the pre-1933 spirit would lead only to a politics of restoration while ignoring the roots of National Socialism. Professor Helmut Thielicke's critical response to this was not conducive to a changed attitude by the Church towards secular matters. Blaming the Versailles Treaty for the rise of Hitler gave him an excuse for extending the issue of guilt beyond Germany to its former enemies and for reducing the whole question to the basic issue of original sin.[39]

We shall discuss in the final Chapter the extent to which the Protestant Church in recent decades has managed to overcome this Lutheran heritage and whether it has by now become an integral part of public life.

Notes

1 B. Dobson, 'German History 911–1618', in M. Pasley (ed.), *Germany, a Companion to German Studies*, London: Methuen, 1972; p. 182.
2 G. Büchmann, *Geflügelte Worte. Der Zitatenschatz des deutschen Volkes*, 25th edn, Berlin: Verlag der Haude und Spenerschen Buchhandlung Max Paschke, 1912. (The number of quotations from the Luther Bible in recent editions has decreased to *c.* twenty-five per cent.)
3 J. Huizinga, *The Waning of the Middle Ages*, London: Pelican, 1955; pp. 153–228.
4 J. Quint (ed.), Meister Eckhart *Die Deutschen Werke*, Vol. 1, Stuttgart: Metzler, 1958; p. 66.
5 A. Langen, 'Pietismus', in *Reallexikon der deutschen Literaturgeschichte*, Vol. 3, Berlin: Kohlschmidt und W. Mohr/de Gruyter, 1977; p. 106.

6   M. Weber, *The Protestant Ethic and the Spirit of Capitalism* (transl. by R. H. Tawney), London: Allen and Unwin, 1974; p. 81.

7   Johannes [Jean] Calvin, Swiss reformer and representative of the theory of predestination, according to which the individual's fate after death has been determined by God at birth.

8   Weber, *Protestant Ethic*, p. 194 (translator's note).

9   H. Plessner, *Die verspätete Nation*, Stuttgart: Kohlhammer, 1959; p. 61.

10 F. Fischer, 'Der deutsche Protestantismus und die Politik im 19. Jahrhundert', in H. Böhme (ed.), *Probleme der Reichsgründungszeit 1848–1879*, Cologne: Kiepenheuer and Witsch, 1968; p. 49f.

11 G. Schischkoff (ed.), *Philosophisches Wörterbuch*, 22nd edn, Stuttgart: Kröner, 1991; p. 407. For a more detailed study cf. N. Elias, *Über den Prozeß der Zivilisation. Soziogenetische und psychogenetische Untersuchungen*, Vol. 2, Munich: Suhrkamp, 1969.

12 Plessner, *Verspätete Nation*, p. 65.

13 Seminary for Protestant Theology, founded in sixteenth century; gained fame during Reformation as seat of Luther's friend Melanchton. In the late eighteenth and early nineteenth centuries seat of many famous German philosophers and poets (Hegel, Schelling, Hölderlin, Mörike and others).

14 A. Langen, *Der Wortschatz des deutschen Pietismus*, 2nd edn, Tübingen: Niemeyer, 1968; p. 390f.

15 G. Picht, *Die deutsche Bildungskatastrophe*, Olten: 1964. Some statistical figures will shed further light on the dominant position of Protestants in German public life: in 1907, eighty-three per cent of officers and some eighty-six per cent of university teachers were Protestant (cf. U. Ruh, *Religion und Kirche in der Bundesrepublik Deutschland*, Munich, judicium, 1990; p. 11). In Chapter 5 the matter will be discussed further.

16 H. A. L. Fisher, *A History of Europe*, Vol. 1, London: Eyre and Spottiswoode, 1936; p. 468.

17 S. und C. Streller (eds), *Hutten, Müntzer, Luther, Werke in zwei Bänden*, Vol. 2, p. 19 [Luther, 'An den Christlichen Adel deutscher Nation'] Berlin/Weimar: Nationale Forschungs- und Gedenkstätten der klassischen deutschen Literatur in Weimar.

18 *ibid.* p. 94f

19 *ibid.* p. 120 [Luther, 'Von der Freiheit eines Christenmenschen']

20 U. Lange, 'Deutschland im Zeitalter der Reichsreform, der kirchlichen Erneuerung und der Glaubenskämpfe (1495–1648)', in M. Vogt, *Deutsche Geschichte*, Stuttgart: Metzler, 1987; p. 172.

21 F. Engels, *Der deutsche Bauernkrieg*, Berlin O.: Dietz, 1989; p. 43. *Jus primae noctis*: the right of the master to spend the first night with his servant's bride.

22 E. Badstübner, *Das alte Mühlhausen*, Leipzig: Koehler und Amelang, 1989; p. 169.

23 S. und C. Streller (eds), *Hutten, Müntzer, Luther*, Vol. 1, p. 262; [Müntzer, 'Hochverursachte Schutzrede'].

24 *ibid.* p. 207 [Müntzer, 'Die Fürstenpredigt']
25 S. und M. Liebe, *Mühlhausen*, Leipzig: Brockhaus, 1989; p. 14.
26 The institution of the church tax still exists in Germany today, it amounts to between seven and ten per cent of the personal income tax and is collected by the state on behalf of the church. Ruh, *Religion und Kirche*, p. 81.
27 He who reigns shall determine the religion of his subjects.
28 Th. Nipperdey, *Religion im Umbruch. Deutschland 1870–1918*, München: Beck, 1988; p. 94.
29 Plessner, *Verspätete Nation*, p. 65.
30 cf. W. Röhrich, *Die verspätete Demokratie. Zur politischen Kultur der Bundesrepublik Deutschland*, Cologne: Diederichs, 1983; p. 23.
31 F. Hertz, *The German Public Mind in the Nineteenth Century*, London: Allen and Unwin, 1975; p. 346.
32 He also resented the fact that many of the Catholic minorities were situated in border regions close to Poland (Silesia), Austria (Bavaria) or France (Alsace-Lorraine).
33 H. M. Müller, *Schlaglichter der deutschen Geschichte*, Mannheim/Vienna/Zurich: Bibliographisches Institut, 1986; p. 187.
34 W. Hofer (ed.), *Der Nationalsozialismus, Dokumente 1933–1945*, Frankfurt a.M.: Fischer, 1957; p. 132.
35 Ruh, *Religion und Kirche*, p. 50.
36 K. Barth, 'Der Christ in der Gesellschaft', in Ruh, *Religion und Kirche*, p. 49.
37 M. Greschat (ed.), *Die Schuld der Kirche. Dokumente und Reflexionen zur Stuttgarter Schulderklärung vom 18./19. Oktober 1945*, München: Kaiser, 1982; p. 102.
38 *ibid.* pp. 106–9, 126–9
39 *ibid.* pp. 160–72

Suggestions for further reading

Conway, J. S., *The Nazi Persecution of the Churches*, London: Weidenfeld and Nicolson, 1968.
Craig, G. A., *Germany, 1866–1945*, Oxford: Oxford University Press, 1978.
Engels, F., *The Peasant War in Germany* (introduction by D. Riazanov, transl. by M. J. Olgin), London: Allen and Unwin, 1926.
Mann, G., *The History of Germany since 1789*, Harmondsworth: Penguin, 1968.
Mullett, M., *Luther*, London: Methuen, 1986.
Rupp, E. G. and Drewery, B., *Martin Luther*, London: Open University Book, E. Arnold, 1970.
Scribner, R. W., *The German Reformation*, London: Macmillan, 1986.
Taylor, A. J. P., *Bismarck, the Man and the Statesman*, New York: Hamish Hamilton, 1955.
Wehler, H. U., *Krisenherde des Kaiserreichs 1871–1918*, Göttingen: Vandenhoeck and Ruprecht, 1970.

Textual studies

1. Martin Luther, *Von der Freiheit eines Christenmenschen* (1520)

[...] Damit wir gründlich können erkennen, was ein Christenmensch sei und was es sei um die Freiheit, die ihm Christus erworben und gegeben hat, davon Sankt Paulus viel schreibt, will ich diese zwei Sätze aufstellen:

5 *Ein Christenmensch ist ein freier Herr über alle Ding und niemand untertan.*

Ein Christenmensch ist ein dienstbarer Knecht aller Ding und jedermann untertan.

[...] Um diese zwei einander widersprechenden Sätze von 10 der Freiheit und der Dienstbarkeit zu verstehen, sollen wir bedenken, daß ein jeglicher Christenmensch ist von zweierlei Natur, geistlicher und leiblicher. Nach der Seele wird er ein geistlicher, neuer, innerer Mensch genannt, nach dem Fleisch und Blut wird er ein leiblicher, alter und äußerer Mensch 15 genannt.

[...] Nehmen wir uns vor den *inwendigen geistlichen Menschen*, um zu sehen, was dazu gehöre, daß er ein frommer, freier Christenmensch sei und heiße, so ist's offenbar, daß kein äußerlich Ding kann ihn frei noch fromm machen, wie 20 es mag immer genannt werden; denn sein Frommsein und seine Freiheit, wiedrum seine Bosheit und sein Gefängnis, sind nicht leiblich noch äußerlich. Was hilft es der Seelen, daß der Leib ungefangen, frisch und gesund ist, isset, trinkt, lebt, wie er will? Wiederum, was schadet es der Seelen, daß der 25 Leib gefangen, krank und matt ist, hungert, dürstet und leidet, wie er's nicht gern will? Dieser Dinge reichet keines bis an die Seelen, sie zu befreien oder zu fangen, fromm oder böse zu machen. [...]

(M. Luther, *An den Christlichen Adel deutscher Nation. Von der Freiheit eines Christenmenschen. Sendbrief vom Dolmetschen*, Reclam Nr. 1587/78a, p. 125f.)

Commentary:
The references to St. Paul are I. Corinthians 9,19 and Romans 13, 8 and Galatians 4,4. Luther refers here to Christians specifically, his references to *Innerlichkeit* and *Äußerlichkeit* must be seen in the context of the sinful old Adam and a new free man having been saved by the death of Christ. The apparently contradictory statements on freedom and servitude reflect rhetorical style in Luther's time. Man's twofold nature was particularly strongly emphasised by St. Augustine, himself at one time influenced by Jewish-Persian Manicheism, the doctrine of a constant battle between good and evil. The pamphlet was written by Luther in order to placate the Pope and to deflect any accusation of disobedience against the Church. One might wish to speculate, however, as to how Luther envisaged achieving spiritual freedom against all the odds of political oppression, given that he made the availability of the Scriptures in the vernacular such an important issue.

Vocabulary:
erworben = acquired; aufstellen = to make an assertion; untertan = subject; Knecht (m) = servant; widersprechend = contradictory; jeglicher = any; inwendig = inward; frei noch fromm = neither free nor pious; Bosheit (f) = wickedness; Gefängnis (n) = imprisonment; matt = exhausted.

2. M. Luther, *Wider die räuberischen und mörderischen Rotten der Bauern (1525)*

[...] Dreierlei gräuliche Sünden wider Gott und Menschen laden diese Bauern auf sich, daran sie den Tod verdienet haben an Leib und Seele mannigfaltiglich: Zum ersten, daß sie ihrer Obrigkeit treu und huldig geschworen haben, untertänig und
5 gehorsam zu sein, wie solches Gott gebietet, da er spricht: Gebt dem Kaiser, was des Kaisers ist [...] Weil sie aber diesen Gehorsam mutwillig und mit Frevel brechen und dazu sich ihren Herren widersetzen, haben sie damit verwirkt Leib und Seele, wie dies treulose, meineidige, lügenhafte,

10 ungehorsame Buben und Bösewichter zu tun pflegen. [...]
[...] Denn Aufruhr ist nicht ein schlichter Mord, sondern
wie ein großes Feuer, das ein Land anzündet und verwüstet.
Also bringt Aufruhr mit sich ein Land voll Mords,
Blutvergießen und macht Witwen und Waisen und zerstört
15 alles wie das allergrößte Unglück. Drum soll hier zuschlagen,
würgen und stechen, heimlich oder öffentlich, wer da kann
und bedenken, daß nichts Giftigeres, Schädlicheres,
Teuflischeres sein kann denn ein aufrührerischer Mensch,
gleich als wie man einen tollen Hund totschlagen muß.
(S. und C. Streller (eds), *Hutten, Müntzer, Luther, Werke
in zwei Bänden*, Vol. 2, Berlin/Weimar: Aufbau, 1989;
p. 259f [Passage slightly edited as far as spelling and
some wording is concerned.])

Commentary:
The three mortal sins referred to are: unfaithfulness to worldly
authority, rioting and rebellion with reference to the Gospel
in order to justify these deeds. Luther's attitude here is that
of a medieval man accustomed to a feudal system. He suggests that the authorities have been put in place by God and
that they therefore have the divine right to annihilate all rebellious peasants. Rebellion is compared with rabies (*Tollwut*),
its contagious symptoms have to be stopped through eradi-
cation of the infected element. Luther also vehemently opposes any suggestion that the Gospel recommends common
property, maintaining instead that baptism liberates only the
soul, but not body and property.

Vocabulary:
gräulich = ferocious; wider = against; mannigfaltiglich =
diverse; Obrigkeit (f) = authority; huldig = with allegiance;
gebietet = commands; mutwillig = wilful; Frevel (m) = wan-
tonness; widersetzen = to resist; verwirkt = forfeited; meineidig
= perjured; Bube (m) = rascal; Bösewicht (m) = villain; Aufruhr
(m) = uproar; verwüstet = ravaged; würgen = to throttle; toll
= rabid.

3. Die gründlichen und rechten Hauptartikel aller Bauernschaft und Hintersassesn der geistlichen und weltlichen Obrigkeiten, von denen sie sich beschwert glauben. (c. 1525)

[Translated into modern German for easier comprehension] [...] Zunächst einmal ist das Evangelium nicht die Ursache der Empörung und des Aufruhrs, weil es das Wort Christi, des verheißenen Messias ist, dessen Wort und Leben nichts lehret als Liebe, Friede, Geduld und Einigkeit, so daß alle, die
5 an Christus glauben, liebevoll, friedlich, geduldig und einig werden. Der Grund aller Artikel der Bauern [...] geht dahin, das Evangelium zu hören und auch danach zu leben. [...] Eine ganze Gemeinde soll den Pfarrer selbst erwählen und soll auch das Recht haben ihn wieder abzusetzen, wenn er
10 sich ungebührlich benimmt. Der erwählte Pfarrer soll uns das heilige Evangelium rein und klar predigen ohne jeden menschlichen Zusatz, Lehre oder Gebot. [...] Wir sind des Willens, daß von jetzt an dieser Kornzehnt, den die Gemeinde einsetzt, von unseren Kirchenpröbsten
15 eingesammelt und eingezogen werden soll, um damit dem von der ganzen Gemeinde erwählten Pfarrer einen angemessenen Lebensunterhalt zu ermöglichen. [...] Und was übrig bleibt, soll man den armen Bedürftigen geben (die im selben Dorf leben) [...]
20 Drittens ist es bisher Brauch gewesen, daß man uns als Leibeigene gehalten hat, wessen man sich erbarmen soll in Anbetracht der Tatsache, daß uns Christus alle mit seinem kostbaren Blutvergießen erlöst und erkauft hat, den Hirten wie auch den Höchsten, ohne Ausnahme. [...]

(S. und C. Streller (eds), *Hutten, Müntzer, Luther*, Vol. 1, Aufbau, 1989; pp. 275–8.)

Commentary:
Composed in Memmingen/Allgäu, possibly by the journeyman furrier Sebastian Lotzer with Pfarrer Christoph Schappeler as co-author. In essence much closer to Müntzer and Zwingli than to Luther. Written from a fundamentally

Christian point of view, but more modern than Luther in that the division between body and soul, heaven and earth has been overcome. The twelve articles contain basic human rights, amongst them the choice of clergyman, the use of taxation for a basic social welfare system and liberation from serfdom.

Vocabulary:
verheißen = to promise; Kornzehnt (m) = corn toll; Kirchenprobst (m) = provost; Lebensunterhalt (m) = livelihood; Bedürftige (m) = person in need; Leibeigene (m) = serf; sich in Anbetracht der Tatsache erbarmen = to have mercy with someone in view of the fact that.

4. Otto von Bismarck, Rede vom 10. März 1873 im Preußischen Herrenhaus über 'Königtum und Priestertum'

[...] es handelt sich nicht um den Kampf, wie unseren katholischen Mitbürgern eingeredet wird, einer evangelischen Dynastie gegen die katholische Kirche, es handelt sich nicht um den Kampf zwischen Glauben und Unglauben, es handelt
5 sich um den uralten Machtstreit, der so alt ist wie das Menschengeschlecht, um den Machtstreit zwischen Königtum und Priestertum, [...] den Machtstreit, der die deutsche Geschichte des Mittelalters bis zur Zersetzung des Deutschen Reiches erfüllt hat unter dem Namen der Kämpfe der Päpste
10 mit den Kaisern, der im Mittelalter seinen Abschluß damit fand, daß der letzte Vertreter des erlauchten schwäbischen Kaiserstammes unter dem Beile eines französischen Eroberers auf dem Schafott starb, und daß dieser französische Eroberer im Bündnis mit dem damaligen Papste stand. [...] Es ist
15 meines Erachtens eine Fälschung der Politik und der Geschichte, wenn man seine Heiligkeit den Papst ganz ausschließlich als den Hohenpriester einer Konfession oder die katholische Kirche als die Vertreterin des Kirchentums überhaupt betrachtet. Das Papsttum ist eine politische Macht
20 jederzeit gewesen, die mit der größten Entschiedenheit und

dem größten Erfolge in die Verhältnisse dieser Welt eingegriffen hat, die diese Eingriffe erstrebt und zu ihrem Programm gemacht hat. [...] Das Ziel, welches der päpstlichen Gewalt, wie den Franzosen die Rheingrenze,
25 ununterbrochen vorschwebte, das Programm, das zur Zeit der mittelalterlichen Kaiser seiner Verwirklichung nahe war, ist die Unterwerfung der weltlichen Gewalt unter die geistliche, ein eminent politischer Zweck, ein Streben, welches aber so alt ist wie die Menschheit; [...] Also dieser
30 Machtstreit unterliegt denselben Bedingungen, wie jeder andere politische Kampf, und es ist eine Verschiebung der Frage, die auf den Eindruck auf urteillose Leute berechnet ist, wenn man sie darstellt, als ob es sich um Bedrückung der Kirche handelte. Es handelt sich um Verteidigung des Staates,
35 es handelt sich um die Abgrenzung, wie weit die Priester-herrschaft und wie weit die Königsherrschaft gehen soll, und diese Abgrenzung muß so gefunden werden, daß der Staat seinerseits dabei bestehen kann. Denn in dem Reiche dieser Welt hat er das Regiment und den Vortritt. [...]
(Michael Freud (ed.), *Der Liberalismus*, K. F. Koehler, 1965; p. 197f.)

Commentary: (numbers in parentheses refer to line numbers in the text)
Given at the height of the *Kulturkampf* and shortly after the Franco–Prussian War, Bismarck carefully connects the Vatican with Germany's former enemy to suggest a 'Western', Latinate conspiracy against the German *Reich*, both in the days of the Middle Ages (7ff) and now under the Hohenzollern dynasty. The reference to Conradin's violent death in Salerno (12) suggests an artificial continuance from Hohenstaufen to Hohenzollern, thereby accentuating the anti-clerical stance. Bismarck's main argument: the Vatican does not restrict itself to theology, but is also an eminently political force. He implies, no doubt arguing from his Lu-theran background, that the Church should not get involved in politics, that there should be a clear division of power,

with the monarchic principle having precedence in the here
and now.

Vocabulary:
einreden = to make someone believe; Zersetzung (f) =
destruction; Entschiedenheit (f) = determination; Eingriff (m)
= interference; Unterwerfung (f) = submission; Verschiebung
(f) = false shift; Abgrenzung (f) = demarcation; Vortritt (m)
= precedence.

5. 'Positives Christentum' from the journal *Wille und Macht*, 15th April 1935

Der Nationalsozialismus bejaht aber das Christentum – gleich,
ob es als Kirche oder als Glaube, im politischen oder im
religiösen Bezirke in Erscheinung tritt – nicht schlechthin;
er bejaht es nur, wenn es positiv ist, wenn es die Grenzen in
5 sich und gegenüber der politischen Macht so wahrt, wie es
aufgezeigt worden ist. [The precise definition of the connection between Christianity and 'political power' is further
explained]
Was ist politisch? Politisch ist alles, was in den irdischen
10 Formen der *Organisation*, des Wortes und Bildes, der Schrift
und der Gebärde in Erscheinung tritt und *für die Gemeinschaft
des Volkes auch nur die geringste Bedeutung hat*.
Und was ist religiös? Religiös ist alles, was in irdisch nicht
faßbaren Formen als Glaube an Überirdisches, als Gefühl der
15 Unendlichkeit, als Sehnsucht nach Dingen jenseits der den
Menschen sichtbaren Welt fühlbar wird.
(Walter Hofer (ed.), *Der Nationalsozialismus, Dokumente
1933–1945*, Frankfurt a.M.: Fischer, 1957; p. 127.)

Commentary:
Note the strict division between the political and the religious realm, with the latter being restricted entirely to the transcendental. The first sentence is skilfully arranged so that its
negation is extremely vague (bejaht . . . nicht schlechthin).

Vocabulary:
bejahen = to affirm; gleich = regardless; Bezirk (m) = sphere; in sich und gegenüber der politischen Macht = within itself and *vis-à-vis* its political domain; wahren = to preserve; aufgezeigt = demonstrated; irdisch = earthly; Gebärde (f) = gesture; geringst = least; faßbar = tenable; Überirdisches (n) = spiritual.

Topics for further study

1. Which, in your opinion, are the main positive, and which the main negative features of 'German' Protestantism? Give reasons for your judgement.
2. Explain Luther's concept of 'calling' and of 'work' and compare these concepts with their Calvinist equivalents.
3. To what extent could Luther be described as a revolutionary?
4. Give a very brief description of Bismarck's *Kulturkampf* and explain to what extent Bismarck's policy can be interpreted as 'Lutheran'.
5. Has the *Stuttgarter Schulderklärung* resolved the Lutheran problem with regard to the churches' attitude towards politics?

3

The individual and the state in eighteenth and early nineteenth century Germany

The emergence of modern democracy in Western Europe, the one-sided reception of the Enlightenment by German men of letters and the emergence of civic values at the expense of liberalism but in accordance with newly emerging national energies within a European context. As a result, strong influence on cohesive values of state and Volk *at the expense of the individual's political involvement in public affairs.*

Introduction

We have already seen how the peculiar nature of the Holy Roman Empire delayed the development of a German national identity and how the Lutheran attitude to worldly issues served to create a division between cultural and political matters. The catastrophe of the Thirty Years War (1618–48) almost reversed the progress towards this national identity, while for most other European countries, this period coincided with the attainment of national greatness and various imperialist exploits in the case of Britain, France and Spain. At the end of the War, the Empire had suffered the loss of between 30–40 per cent of its population, experienced a most calamitous decline in commerce and agriculture and had been deprived of vast territories on all its frontiers. It took almost a century for population levels to recover. Even worse, however, was the decline in politics and culture. Politically, the Thirty Years War resulted in the virtual extinction of the supremacy of the *Reich* and a drastic increase in particularism: 'Germany' fragmented into more than 300 principalities, most of them with a population of less than 10,000, each with an outsize petty court and costly administration. Trade and personal mobility were severely restricted, Rhine shipping had to pass thirty-seven custom controls between Basel and the estuary.[1] With the individual territorial states maintaining their absolutist regimes in political, commercial and cultural matters, an element of complacency and provincialism crept in which offered little scope for the emerging political philosophy of the Enlightenment. There was, however, great opportunity for talent in the vast administrations which supported these courts and the number of civil servants in Germany to this day has its origin in German *Kleinstaaterei*. German men of genius served in their state's military academies (the young Schiller); in the many universities (Kant, Hegel, Fichte); as court officials (Bach, Goethe, Handel); in the service of the state churches (Herder). Unlike most of their European counterparts, they had little direct access to distant cultures in India, the Middle East or America, but often found an outlet for their intellectual energies in the realms of metaphysics or abstract speculative thought. There was no room for a Locke or a Montesquieu on German soil and the first great stages of the political philosophy of the Enlightenment virtually bypassed the German scene. Immanuel Kant's (1724–1804) famous essay 'Was ist Aufklärung?' (1784) gives a memorable definition, but keeps the subject matter general and abstract:

Aufklärung ist der Ausgang des Menschen aus seiner selbstverschuldeten Unmündigkeit. Unmündigkeit ist das Unvermögen, sich seines Verstandes ohne Leitung eines anderen zu bedienen. [. . .] Habe Mut, dich deines eigenen Verstandes zu bedienen ist also der Wahlspruch der Aufklärung.[2]
(Enlightenment is man's exit from his self-willed immaturity. Immaturity is the inability to make use of one's intellect without the guidance of another. [. . .] Have the courage to make use of your own intellect is therefore the motto of the Enlightenment.)

The individual and the state   57

Kant's definition has lost nothing of its precision and it can be applied to all human activities, including politics. However, the same essay distinguishes between two kinds of judgement and it is this distinction which reveals Kant's reluctance to adopt enlightened citizenship, despite his belief that the French Revolution (1789) demonstrates a moral regeneration of man:

> Ich verstehe aber unter dem öffentlichen Gebrauche seiner eigenen Vernunft denjenigen, den jemand als Gelehrter von ihr vor dem ganzen Publikum der Leserwelt macht. Den Privatgebrauch nenne ich denjenigen, den er in einem gewissen ihm anvertrauten bürgerlichen Posten, oder Amte, von seiner Vernunft machen darf.[3]
>
> (By the public use of our judgement, I understand the use which a person makes of it as a scholar before his entire audience of readers. The private use is that which he makes of his judgement in a particular civil post or office.)

The two types of judgement are specifically related to a person's freedom within the state and Kant was of the opinion that a restriction of our private freedom would not hinder the progress of the Enlightenment.

We recognise certain similarities between Kant's statement on the twofold nature of judgement and Luther's twofold definition of freedom. Both men see themselves as loyal subjects of their respective princes, but not as free citizens. The public domain of freedom is permitted within the province of learning and theoretical knowledge, but when it comes to civic matters, when one enters the social and political sphere, one's freedom is restricted. Heinrich Heine, commenting to his French readers on Kant's philosophy some 50 years later, is aware of the dichotomy between the public and private use of freedom. He believes that Kant's philosophy was more revolutionary than Robespierre's execution of the King, in that it freed man from the constraints of religion. Both, Kant and Robespierre, however, are seen as petit-bourgeois *Spießbürger*: 'die Natur hatte sie bestimmt, Kaffee und Zucker zu wiegen, aber das Schicksal wollte, daß sie andere Dinge abwögen, und legte dem Einen einen König und dem Anderen einen Gott auf die Waagschale . . .'⁴ (Nature had chosen them to weigh coffee and sugar, but fate determined that they should weigh other things and put a king on to the scales of the one and a God on to the scales of the other).

This German tradition of political culture has suffered from a bifurcation of private and public attitudes towards freedom, and as recently as 1965 Ralf Dahrendorf saw the domination of private over public virtues as a typical stumbling block in Germany's political development, symptomatic of her lack of liberal attitudes. Public virtues focus on 'the general intercourse between men', they rely on fairness and accentuate 'getting along with each other'.⁵ They are predominantly social values which lay the foundation for liberal democracy, in that they regulate the private worlds of the individual in accordance with social rules. Private virtues, on the other hand, 'provide the individual with standards for his own perfection, which is conceived as being devoid of society, [. .] intent on honesty and profoundness rather than ease and lack of friction'.⁶ Private virtues are not virtues of participation, the social and political process is of secondary importance. 'This is why the prevalence of private virtues may become an instrument of authoritarian rule.'⁷ Dahrendorf demonstrates how a society dominated by private virtues will consider a society ruled by public virtues as hypocritical. He also illustrates how such a society will develop an aversion to the contract-like concept of the state. Dahrendorf's speculative use of these two types of virtue still offers valuable insights into the different attitudes of British and German social life; his association of public virtues with modernity⁸ has become a principle for disciples of the Enlightenment. And yet, it would be misleading to condemn out of hand the 'German tradition' based on a predominance of romantic private virtues. As Dahrendorf himself noted, public virtues are not the prerogative of Anglo-American democracies, and recent developments have shown that the liberal conventions associated with these virtues can

all too easily degenerate into the egoism of the 'ME generation', leading to a loss of these same virtues.

Our discussion of Herder's concept of *Volk*, of Fichte's
notion of *Nation* and of Hegel's definition of *Staat* will demonstrate that there has, nevertheless, been a tradition of German political culture which tried to build on the achievements
of the French Revolution and the Enlightenment and, though
less 'liberal' than its Anglo-American counterpart, has contributed to the development of a civic culture. Given the fragmented nature of Germany during these years, it is not
surprising that the emerging political culture put great emphasis on social values, placing the individual firmly within
the community, and clearly giving less regard to his or her
personal contribution to society.

The second stage of the Enlightenment after 1750 saw the
rebirth of German philosophy and literature but, as a result
of the final decline of the Empire, political philosophy was
less prominent. Instead, it attempted to modify the existing
Franco-Latin rationalism, with its universalist, logocentric
claims, and sought to develop an organic world-view, based
on a rediscovery of nature and history, of humankind's need
for religion and of the existence of psychic and irrational
powers. Such was the political and cultural domination of
France, that it is not surprising that the intellectual movement in Germany strove to restrict any further French influence. Leading figures of the Enlightenment such as Leibniz,
Wolff, Thomasius, Johann Jakob and Friedrich Karl von
Moser, Justus Möser and many others, rallied to the defence
of German culture, often in direct contrast to their countries'
princes living in imitation of Louis XIV, and the nobility and
middle classes indulging themselves in a French *à la mode*
life-style and all but abandoning their native language. G. E.
Lessing (1729–81) refers to this 'Francomania' as a *locus
communis*[9] and experienced it personally since he not only
failed to get support for his National Theatre project, but
was also rejected in favour of a Frenchman for the position
of Librarian at the Berlin court of Frederick the Great. This

example not only bears witness to French hegemony over German culture, but also illustrates the emerging emancipation from France, an emancipation which also affected the German reception of Western European enlightened philosophies and in itself constituted part of the Enlightenment.

Herder's concept of *Volk*

Traditional research used to place J. G. Herder (1744–1803) in the vicinity of Hamann's religious understanding of language and therefore in the anti-rationalist *Sturm und Drang* movement. Contemporary research tends to focus more on Herder's relationship with Rousseau and the late Enlightenment[10] and, in particular, on his concern with the achievement of *Humanität*. It, therefore, emphasises Herder's attempted reconciliation of the Christian tradition with the rationalist systems of the Enlightenment. His humanist ideal led him to distance himself from Kant's abstract concept of freedom[11] and from any form of rationalist 'universalism', and to seek instead the achievement of a holistic system which would re-integrate reason into nature and the individual into the community of family and *Volk*. Herder viewed freedom not as an absolute transcendental value, differing sharply in this respect from Rousseau and Kant, but as part of our sensuous human condition. Humans function within organisations, they are 'constituted' [Vol. V, pp. 131–4] within a larger organisation for, unlike animals, they are not dominated by instincts and, therefore, need language and education. No one can live for themselves alone; each is knit into the texture of the whole [Vol. V, p. 134].

In his essay 'Über den Ursprung der Sprache' (1770), Herder argues that the acquisition of language symbolises the extent and limitation of our freedom: language not only provides us with a vehicle for self-expression, it also shapes and organises our thoughts. Similar arguments are employed to refute the notion that human reason exists as an absolute value. Humans must acquire reason through experience, and since no one lives long enough to gather a sufficiently large body of experience, our rationality as well as our experience are rooted in tradition, in history. Modern research has shown that Herder based these insights on the perception theory of his age, but reinforced them with theological arguments: 'Die Seele [...] erkennt nichts aus sich, sondern was ihr von innen und außen ihr Weltall zuströmt, und der Finger Gottes zuwinket.' [Vol. VIII, p. 194] (The soul has no knowledge from within itself, but only from what it gains from within and without the universe and from what God's finger indicates.) Whilst maintaining a critical distance from the absolutist ideas of the political philosophy of the early Enlightenment, Herder seems to follow Rousseau in the notion that humankind has to return to nature, to a more primitive state of society in order to find the precondition for human perfection. The further human societies stray from the state of the *Naturvölker*, the more extreme will society become, posing a severe threat to the integrity of the individual. Herder demands some kind of social *palingenesis*, a rebirth into the natural state of man in order to avoid the emergence of political despotism [Vol. XIII, p. 382]. Indeed, he initially welcomed the French Revolution as such a *palingenesis*, expecting it to rejuvenate society and to bring about freedom, brotherhood of man and equality, in short the aspired to *Humanität* [Vol. V, p. 575f]. It would not only transform mechanical dynastic states into organic nation states based on the principle of self-determination, but would also allow the individual complete self-fulfilment, the attainment of ultimate consciousness.[12] This can only be achieved within a community and the individual is embedded in such organic communities as family and *Volk*. In 'Über den Ursprung der Sprache', Herder demonstrates in great detail how the individual does not exist in his own right, 'er ist in das Ganze des Geschlechts eingeschoben, er ist nur eins für die fortgehende Folge' [Vol. V, p. 116]. (He is embedded in the generation as a whole, he is only one element of the continuing succession.) Individuals gain their personality through family ties and, in particular, through language which binds us into family and nation.

The most important common element in the formation of a *Volk* is its common language; 'each nation speaks the way it thinks and thinks the way it speaks' [Vol. V, p. 125]. Language links us with our past; the sharing of a particular historical tradition is grounded in language. Herder rejects the concept of the *Vielvölkerstaat* as existed in Austria and Prussia and defines *Volk* as a natural element of the human race, endowed with its own language which it must preserve as its most distinctive and sacred possession. Language is as much the embodiment of a *Volk*'s soul or character as it is the expression of an individual's unique personality. He attacks the notion that language is of divine origin and instead holds the view that it developed naturally. This natural development applies also to each *Volk*. Herder views the *Volk* in anthropomorphic terms, attributing to it a body, soul, language and culture, relating it to climate and submitting it to the changes of history, endowing it with different ages throughout its evolution [Vol. I, p. 151]. The preservation of a *Volk*'s language and culture is therefore of vital importance; in order to overcome the divisions in Germany he advocates the drawing together of different churches and the nurturing of a national spirit. He not only attacks the excessive influence of French culture, but also the imitation of antiquity. 'When will our public', he asks, 'cease to be this three-headed apocalyptic beast, poorly Greek, French and British?' [Vol. I, p. 217]. The establishment of a German culture based on foreign models could only lead to 'disease, flatulence, abnormal surfeit and approaching death' [Vol. V, p. 510]. Instead he advocates the observance of folklore and the emulation of other European cultures and languages which had achieved cultural autonomy. To this effect he planned the establishment of a 'Patriotic Institute to foster a common spirit in Germany' ('Idee zum ersten patriotischen Institut für den Allgemeingeist Deutschlands') [Vol. XVI, p. 600].

These cultural views found their counterpart in political opinions. Herder was opposed to a hereditary monarchy, favouring instead a republic based on written law. At the same time he contested Rousseau's concept of a *Contrat Social*[13] which, he felt, would create a barrier between nature and culture and would run counter to his belief that each nationality is a product of nature. Where Rousseau's *Contrat* was to make a people inter-dependent, Herder reserved this synthesising energy to culture, to history. The political transformation from a hereditary monarchy to democratic self-government should be aided by wise men, writers, artists, working from within the national soul, expressing the innermost feelings of the *Volk*'s collective experience and, at the same time, stimulating its cultural awareness. Herder calls these men 'aristo-democrats'; they 'emerge by virtue of their exceptional political wisdom and patriotic dedication to the nation'.[14]

We recognise in all these ideas the strong homogeneity of Herder's philosophy, which neither gives independence to the individual nor grants a cosmopolitan openness to the *Volk*. And yet, to condemn Herder's thought as a precursor of racism would be completely to misunderstand his intentions.[15] He was opposed to the development of the polygynous theory of different cultures, arguing instead that 'there is but one and the same species of man throughout the whole earth' [Vol. XIII, p. 252].

A comparison of Herder's opinions on the relationship of individual and community with that of Daniel Defoe (1659–1731) pondering on the importance of personal virtue, of individualism, albeit from the perspective of an English gentleman, will demonstrate a basic difference in political culture. Defoe considered the rich racial and cultural mix of England as an advantage:

> While ev'ry nation that her pow'rs reduced
> Their languages and manners introduced;
> From whose mixed relics our compounded breed,
> By spurious generation does succeed,
> Making a race uncertain and unev'n,
> Derived from all the nations under Heav'n.[16]

Describing England as 'Europe's sink', where 'she voids all her offal outcast progeny',[17] he spoke up for what in today's terminology would be described as a multi-cultural, or at least pluralist, society: 'Fate jumbled them together, God knows how; Whate'er they were, they're True-born English now.' The distinguishing element to emerge from this 'mixture of all kinds'[18] is 'personal virtue'; it gives nobility and has become the distinctive feature and common denominator of *The True-born Englishman* (1701). Defoe's 'Conclusion' stands in strong contrast to Herder:

Then let us boast of ancestors no more,
Or deeds of heroes done in days of yore,
In latent records of the ages past,
Behind the rear of time, in long oblivion placed. [...]
What is't to us, what ancestors we had?
If good, what better? or what worse, if bad? [...]
For fame of families is all a cheat,
'Tis personal virtue only makes us great.[19]

Defoe's 'personal virtue' is based on common sense and public-spiritedness. It is, to use Dahrendorf's terminology again, a public virtue, something everyone can aspire to. Defoe is a typical representative of the liberal middle-class tradition which defended its individualism even in times of nationalism. Society was based on constitutional law which was to protect the individual from any infringement of his personal freedom.

For Herder, and most German men of letters after him, this concept was difficult to grasp. What distinguished Herder's philosophy from those of the liberals in France and Britain was that he saw no need for a separation of legislative, executive, judicial or federal powers [Vol. V, p. 516]. His idealistic concept ruled out any possibility of the misuse of political power or a conflict of interests. Thinking in terms of organisms and totalities, he paid little attention to the rights of the individual, but emphasised organic, historically matured, natural units.

The individual and the state   65

Seen from a liberal democratic vantage point, Herder's philosophy neglects two important elements for the establishment of democracy: firstly, he underestimates the social factor by concentrating far too much on a middle-range of members of the *Volk* to the exclusion of both its lowest sector and the aristocracy (Text 1). The middle range is the culturally productive one [Vol. XXIV, p. 174]; it groups together farmers, fishermen, soldiers, craftsmen, in short the heroes of the *Volkslied*. As a consequence, he is oblivious to any tensions within society and dismissive of those aspects of the Enlightenment which emancipated individuals and afforded them the rights of 'life, liberty and the pursuit of Happiness'.[20] Secondly, Herder overemphasised the natural ties of the *Volk*, seeing the individual members as completely *naturverbunden*. Even the process of humanisation, achieved through education, will not primarily further the individual, but will lead towards a community of *Völker*, all wedded to the principles of *Humanität* and existing in a happy community of nations.

J. G. Fichte's notion of the Germans as *Urvolk* and Romantic nationalism

Fichte (1762–1814) bridges the rationalist stance of Kant and the nationalist and political concept of Herder, having been profoundly influenced by both. His philosophy is complex and apparently contradictory; it cannot be discussed in more than the most rudimentary way. Past decades have frequently blamed Fichte for the rise of nationalism, even to the extent of seeing him as a forerunner of fascism. Nothing could be further from the truth. Ten years after his death, under the reactionary regime of the Holy Alliance a *Promemoria* was published, accusing Fichte of destroying the Christian morals of his students. His educational writings were condemned for their populist nature and for advocating the abolition of class differences in Germany.[21] Already in his Jena lecture 'Über die Bestimmung der Gelehrten' (1794) Fichte demanded of those who through good fortune had acquired an excellent education, that they should contribute towards the education of humankind in order to place people at a higher level of civilisation.[22] His entire philosophy is even more the result of the dismal state of German politics than was the case with Herder; in order to understand their position, we may need to compare them, particularly Fichte, with today's intellectual leaders in Third World countries: they too need to rely on an exaggerated position of national pride to promote their country's cultural and political emancipation.

Fichte began his career as a Jacobin radical, so excited by the French Revolution that he even advocated the annexation of Germany by France.[23] The tenor of his philosophy is the principle of freedom and the limitless sovereignty of reason which makes man the unchallenged arbiter of reality. As his philosophy developed, the freedom of the individual became increasingly involved with the role of the state, with the state necessarily evolving from man's social nature. As each individual is essentially involved with the freedom of others, all individuals must desire a rational state where mutual relations are governed by the rule of law, law being based on the concept that the freedom of the one must not impinge upon the freedom of others. As individuals, we are all members of an organic totality in which each part supports the whole. Such totalitarian ideas are more akin to international socialism than to fascism, since they do not relate to a *Führer* principle. Indeed, Fichte's whole philosophy is directed against the German political leaders of his age, as emerges in his theory on education. His economic work, *Der geschlossene Handelsstaat* (1800), describes a socialist utopia in which the state controls all economic and political life and the individual is completely subject to its law. The Romantic poet Novalis (1772–1801), himself a disciple of Fichte's, comments on these ideas as follows: 'Der vollkommene Bürger lebt ganz im Staate – er hat kein Eigentum außer dem Staate. Jeder Bürger ist Staatsbeamter, seine Einkünfte hat er nur als solcher.'[24] (The perfect citizen lives entirely within the state – he has no property outside the state. Every citizen is a civil servant, he draws his income solely as such.) And elsewhere: 'Um Mensch zu werden und zu bleiben, bedarf er *eines Staates*. [. . .] Ein Mensch ohne Staat ist ein Wilder. Alle Kultur entspringt aus dem Verhältnisse eines Menschen mit dem Staate.'[25] (In order to become and to remain a human being you need *a state*. [. . .] A man outside the state is a savage. All culture originates from man's relationship with the state.) What matters therefore is the achievement of the state and not of the individual. Ultimately, the individual has no rights except as a citizen and all his endeavours must be aimed at ensuring the well-being of the state.

Fichte developed these ideas further in his famous *Reden an die deutsche Nation* (1808), held in Berlin at the time of Napoleon's victory over the Austrian and Prussian armies, when the possibility of forming a German nation state had receded even further following the dissolution of the Holy Roman Empire. The concept of patriotic education (*Nationalerziehung*) is a central part of Fichte's address: having been forsaken by its aristocracy and the upper middle classes, the country had to rely on the mass of its people, inspiring in them the awareness of patriotic citizenship. The new citizen would be the product of a state-controlled education which would foster the establishment of a German character.[26] Language plays a central part in Fichte's education programme; he believed that the German language, unlike French or English, had remained free of foreign influence. Other nations had adopted Greek and Roman concepts into their language and national heritage, without assimilating them into their own culture. To give an example: the idea and the word 'humanism' are derived from the Latin *homo*. While most people are unaware of this connection, the word becomes for them an abstract concept. The Germans, Fichte claims, have 'trans-lated', assimilated the Latin term and speak of *Menschenliebe* or *Menschlichkeit*,[27] which enables them to understand the word intellectually and emotionally and to integrate it into their own culture and their own mode of thinking. Holding such a high opinion of the purity of the

German language, Fichte defines the German people as an *Urvolk*[28] whose mission lies in a general regeneration of culture and morality, while still recognising that other nations have played similar roles in the past and believing that each such nation is part of a divine plan. Although the nationalistic tenor in Fichte's *Reden* cannot be overlooked, it is important to understand its character in context. Starting from an assumption of the purity and integrity of the German language, Fichte maintains that, by virtue of these qualities, it could preserve our human cultural tradition better than other languages. He refers in particular to Luther's translation of the Bible and the Reformation, and sets both events in the context of popular German culture, emphasising that in these instances it was the totality of the people who produced and perpetuated these cultural values. Of particular importance to Fichte is the leading role of scholarship and poetry in enlightening and educating, and thus in revitalising, a people.

Fichte's concept of *Urvolk* must, therefore, be seen as an entirely cultural one, with a major educational obligation, rather than as a racist or chauvinist notion. Minor philosophers of Fichte's time corrupted his ideas and voiced jingoistic attitudes, amongst them Ernst Moritz Arndt and *Turnvater* Jahn whom Heinrich Heine described as *Franzosenfresser*[29] on account of their fiercely anti-French sentiments. Romantics such as Jacob Grimm, on the other hand, defined the ideal of a *Volk* in more universal terms, but again with particular reference to *Sprache*. They ignored the political and territorial problems of the nation state by declaring, 'daß einem Volk, das über Berge und Ströme gedrungen ist, seine eigene Sprache allein die Grenze setzen kann'[30] (that the borders of those peoples, who have expanded beyond mountains and rivers, can be defined exclusively by virtue of their language). F. E. Schleiermacher (1768–1834) arrived at his concept of the state from his theological studies and was strongly influenced by German pietism. Like Fichte and Herder, he, too, believed in the generating power of *Volk* or *Staat*, and gave both priority over the individual, who develops fully only within the state. He is opposed to the eighteenth century constitutionalists who believed that the best state is the least obtrusive, and warns against seeing the state as a necessary evil (Text 2).

Hegel's concept of the State

Hegel's (1770–1831) position is somewhat different from that of Herder and Fichte in that he approaches the relationship of the individual and the state from a more classical tradition, attempting to reconcile Plato's concept of state as a system of justice, with the Christian concept of individual freedom. However, the influence of Herder and Kant is clearly felt in Hegel's early philosophy. Basing himself on Plato, but following his German contemporaries, Hegel sees morality not as a private and introspective matter, but as a force integral to the community. Troubled by the fragmented state of the modern world, Hegel seeks to renew the community of Plato. This he seeks firstly in his conception of *Volksreligion* which was to restore the homogeneity of culture, embedding the individual within it. He defined the Greek *polis* as a work of art, since it had achieved a harmonious totality between its individual members, overcoming any distinction between human beings as individuals and human beings as citizens, between private and public matters.[31] In religious rather than political terms Hegel favoured community over society. His friend, the poet Hölderlin (1770–1843), recognised the same dilemma but related it more specifically to German fragmentation (Text 3). Whilst for Hegel folk religion of the Greeks was integrated into the life of the community, modern religion created deep social divisions, contributing to the loss of community spirit. Where ancient *Volksreligion* is naturally allied to freedom, our Christian religion makes us into citizens of heaven and alienates us from our human sensations.[32] People in modern times, therefore, have to return to some kind of *Volksreligion*, embedded in the history and the traditions of its people and here Hegel finds himself in the company of philosophers such as Herder and Rousseau.[33]

Hegel later turned away from purely religious considerations in favour of history and economics. However, the fragmentation of modern man is still uppermost in his mind and it is this which persuades him to give priority to the state, to society over the individual. *Volksreligion* gives way to philosophy, whose task is to reconcile the various opposing aspects of human life in order to overcome modern man's estrangement from the environment. We recognise the philosophical discipline of dialectics in these ideas and for Hegel the dialectical process is set in motion by the *Weltgeist*, which advances in a direction which will ultimately allow people to achieve total self-awareness. With the *Weltgeist* as the highest level of activity, other spirits, from the *Völkergeister* down to the individual *Geist*, play a far less important role. Social and political life and personal self-development are inter-related, but because individuals are incapable of distinguishing between themselves and their environment, they can only achieve greater self-awareness, a better knowledge of themselves, through *Arbeit*. Arguing very much along traditional Protestant lines, Hegel conceives of work as the means by which an individual can achieve personal awareness. It is at this point that the economic argument takes over from the earlier religious and moral concepts. Through work, man achieves a higher degree of self-awareness which in turn leads to new patterns of integration with inter-dependence of individuals and social groups. Hegel repeatedly demonstrates how the individual must – for his or her own sake – be integrated into larger entities. Language is seen as one medium which can lead to new patterns of social integration, firstly by developing individual self-awareness and secondly by binding the individual to the community of his people.[34] The inter-relationship of individuals can only function within the state, which itself represents the highest embodiment of morality.[35] Developing out of the family via the modern notion of the *bürgerliche Gesellschaft* (civic society), the state also allows the individual the full development of self-realisation, to interact with the desires and needs of others, motivated by the mutual love which members of a family feel for one another.[36] This self-realisation can only be achieved by personal partici- pation in the political world as a whole. As the modern state becomes the realisation of the ethical idea,[37] the individual is furnished with higher, universal ends, the state acting as some form of *concrete universal*, linking 'universality with specificity and individuality'[38] and thus overcoming the social fragmen- tation which was the source of Hegel's major anxiety. The concluding paragraph of Hegel's *Grundlinien der Philosophie des Rechts* (1821) contemplates the end of a long hard battle, between the heavenly ideal and worldly reality, which culmin- ates in the reconciliation of both worlds, bringing about a synthesis of reason and reality.

This discussion of the rather complicated and difficult political philosophies of Herder, Fichte and Hegel will have demonstrated the extent to which these three have distanced themselves from the earlier notions of the Enlightenment, especially in so far as the role of the individual is concerned. Whilst British, French and American philosophers gave pride of place to the individual, their German counterparts felt the necessity of placing the individual in a wider context, be it *Volk*, nation or state. The satirical verse of Defoe serves as a clear example of the differences of approach not only be- tween earlier and later representatives of the Enlightenment, but also in Western and German attitudes. And yet, Defoe's insistence on 'personal virtue' as the hallmark of the true born Englishman is perhaps closer than at first realised to the trans-individualist ideas developed by our German philoso- phers, in that personal virtue acts as a restraining and civilis- ing influence on an otherwise rather barbaric and uninhibited group of individuals. Having noted the neglect of political individualism we must recognise that the German debate on *Volk* and 'state' was, nevertheless, deeply indebted to those principles of the Enlightenment that attempted to realise humanist ideas, universal peace and the establishment of a family of nations living together in harmony.

Neither should Dahrendorf's preference for public rather

than private virtues be seen in isolation. While expressing the post-1945 option for Anglo-American political culture, he yet acknowledges that one type of virtue does not exclude the other. A one-sided preference for public virtues can bring about an atrophy of human values and can even lead to 'democracy without liberty [...] to a totalitarianism that has to forbid the privacy of its citizens in order to uphold its power'.[39] Some German teachers of political culture have in recent years written in defence of traditional values in this area. Karl Rohe sees the cardinal difference between Anglo-American and continental democracies in the emergence of an Anglo-American *Gesellschaftskultur vis-à-vis* a continental *Staatskultur*.[40] The hallmark of the latter is the belief in the incorruptibility and competence of the state and its government, which has been translated in the Federal Republic of Germany into the forms of the *Rechtsstaat* and the *Wohlfahrtsstaat*, both guarantors of stability and pillars of the new democratic order. Far from criticising such an 'etatism', as was still the case in the 1960s,[41] Rohe sees its emergence in historical terms, as a defence against outside intervention and as a mechanism to overcome the fragmentation of the country. As a result, the *Staatskultur* strengthens legal structures rather than social conventions and may well offer a more efficient form of government.[42] What seems to be overlooked in Rohe's argument is the concurrent weakening of civic culture, the neglect of personal responsibility in the public sphere, in short the very virtues which we associate with Western liberal democracy. We shall return to this problem in Chapter 6.

Otto Dann's study *Nation und Nationalismus in Deutschland* analyses the specific form of German patriotism and nationalism and attempts to place its development in a European perspective. In an effort to overcome the traditional image of German nationalism as inspired by historians of Bismarck's era,[43] Dann focuses on the bifurcation of *Volksnation* and *Reichsnation*. The former has its origins in the Napoleonic wars, and was influenced by the cultural elite

The individual and the state   73

of Herder, Fichte and the Romantics. The latter harks back to the traditions of the Holy Roman Empire and finally becomes dominant in 1871 with the formation of a German nation state built with the support of all the major political factions.[44] Despite the various problems it encountered, in particular the continued uncertainty over its *völkische* or *Reichstradition*, Dann sees the Germany of the late nineteenth century emerging as a modern state in its own right, and opposes the notion of a *verspätete Nation*. He also seems to play down the German deficit as far as the involvement with the early traditions of the Enlightenment is concerned, and in particular the alleged absence of a tradition of civic culture.

The whole debate on the relationship between the individual and nation/state will be raised in later Chapters where we will investigate the role of the German cultural elite with reference to Western European forms of politics and culture, touch on the political deficit in the German education system and examine to what extent the theory of a German *Sonderweg*, a German political development in opposition to Western traditions of a political Enlightenment, can be justified.

Notes

1 H. Schmidt, 'Zerfall und Untergang des alten Reiches (1648–1806)', in Vogt, *Deutsche Geschichte*, p. 219.
2 I. Kant, *Werke in 12 Bänden*, Vol. XI, Wiesbaden: Wissenschaftliche Buchgesellschaft, 1960–64; p. 53.
3 *ibid.* p. 56
4 H. Heine, *Sämtliche Werke*, Vol. 8/1 [Düsseldorfer Ausgabe], M. Windfuhr (ed.), Hamburg: Hoffmann und Campe, 1979; p. 82.
5 R. Dahrendorf, *Society and Democracy in Germany*, New York: Anchor Garden City, 1969; p. 286f.
6 *ibid.* p. 286
7 *ibid.* p. 288
8 *ibid.* p. 294
9 G. E. Lessing, *Hamburgische Dramaturgie*, O. Mann (ed.), 2nd edn, Stuttgart: Kröner, 1963; p. 392. Frederick the Great (1712–86), though later acclaimed a German national hero, had a very low opinion of German literature and favoured French influence and culture.
10 W. Koepke (ed.), *Johann Gottfried Herder. Language, History and the Enlightenment*, Columbia: Camden House, 1990; p. 5.

11 J. G. Herder, *Sämtliche Werke*, Vol. VIII, B. Suphan (ed.), Berlin: Weidmannsche Buchhandlung, 1877–1913; p. 194. [Subsequently in this Chapter quoted in the text, in English translation, with Vol. and page numbers in square brackets.]

12 *ibid.* Vol. XIII, p. 154. cf. also R. E. Ergang, *Herder and the Foundations of German Nationalism*, New York: Columbia University Press, 1976; pp. 82ff; F. M. Barnard, *Herder's Social and Political Thought. From Enlightenment to Nationalism*, Oxford: Clarendon Press, 1965; chapter 5.

13 'Du contrat sociale ou principes du droit politique' (1755): A 'Social Contract' which binds all individuals, including kings to some general will and which lays the foundation for a constitutional state.

14 F. M. Barnard, '"*Aufklärung*" and "*Mündigkeit*": Thomasius, Kant and Herder', DVJs 57.2 (1983); p. 43.

15 *ibid.* p. 45

16 D. Defoe, *The True-born Englishman*, in G. Grigson (ed.), *The Oxford Book of Satirical Verse*, Oxford: Oxford University Press, 1980; p. 99.

17 *ibid.* p. 101

18 *ibid.* p. 104

19 *ibid.* p. 108f

20 cf. American Declaration of Independence, first two paragraphs.

21 *Promemoria* von Beckedorff, Eylert *et al.* über den gegenwärtigen Zustand des Erziehungswesens, in H. and W. Schuffenhauer (eds), *Pädagogisches Gedankengut bei Kant, Fichte, Schelling, Hegel, Feuerbach*, Berlin O.: Pädagogische Bibliothek, 1984; p. 37.

22 J. G. Fichte, 'Über die Bestimmung der Gelehrten', in *Jenaer Schriften und Reden*, Vol. 2, Jena, 1954; p. 27.

23 O. Dann, *Nation und Nationalismus in Deutschland, 1770–1990*, Munich: Beck, 1993; p. 54.

24 Novalis, *Schriften*, Vol. 3, R. Samuel (ed.), Stuttgart: Kohlhammer, 1968; Nr. 189, p. 273.

25 *ibid.* Nr. 394, p. 313

26 For a more thorough discussion cf. H. James, *A German Identity 1770–1990*, London: Weidenfeld and Nicolson, 1989; pp. 42ff.

27 R. Eucken (ed.), *Fichtes Reden an die deutsche Nation*, Leipzig: Insel, 1909; p. 67.

28 *ibid.* pp. 109ff

29 Heine, *Sämtliche Werke*, Vol. 15, p. 20. His attitude towards Fichte, despite severe criticism of his transcendental philosophy, is favourable in its praise of his democratic liberalism. (*Sämtliche Werke*, Vol. 8/1, p. 94.)

30 J. Grimm, lecture at *Frankfurter Germanistenversammlung* [1846], quoted from P. Kluckhohn, *Das Ideengut der deutschen Romantik*, 4th edn, Tübingen: Niemeyer, 1961; p. 113.

31 For further study cf. R. Plant, *Hegel*, London: Allen and Unwin, 1973; p. 24.

32 G. W. F. Hegel, *Frühe Schriften, Werke 1*, 2nd edn, Frankfurt a.M.: Suhrkamp, 1990; p. 41f.

The individual and the state   75

33 cf. Plant, *Hegel*, p. 36.
34 *ibid.* p. 108
35 Hegel, *Grundlinien der Philosophie des Rechts, Werke 7*, § 257.
36 *ibid.* § 182
37 *ibid.* § 257
38 Plant, *Hegel*, p. 171.
39 Dahrendorf, *Society and Democracy*, p. 294.
40 K. Rohe, 'Politisches System und politische Kultur in der
    Bundesrepublik Deutschland: Befunde, Probleme, Perspektiven', in W.
    Jacobmeyer (ed.), *Die Bundesrepublik Deutschland und die Vereinigten
    Staaten von Amerika. Aspekte der politischen Kultur, der Wirtschafts-
    beziehungen und der Sicherheitspolitik*, Braunschweig: Georg-Eckert-
    Institut für internationale Schulbuchforschung, 1984; pp. 25–55.
41 K. Sontheimer, *Grundzüge des politischen Systems der Bundesrepublik
    Deutschland*, 5th edn, Munich: Piper, 1976; p. 86f.
42 Rohe, 'Politisches System', p. 36.
43 Dann, *Nation und Nationalismus*, p. 66.
44 *ibid.* p. 311

Suggestions for further reading

Barnard, F. M., *Herder's Social and Political Thought. From Enlightenment
to Nationalism*, Oxford: Clarendon Press, 1965; in particular chapters
2–5.

Dahrendorf, R., *Society and Democracy in Germany*, New York: Anchor
Garden City, 1969; in particular chapter 19.

Dann, O., *Nation und Nationalismus in Deutschland, 1770–1990*, Munich:
Beck, 1993.

James, H., *A German Identity 1770–1990*, London: Weidenfeld and
Nicolson, 1989.

Plant, R., *Hegel*, London: Allen and Unwin, 1973.

Textual studies

1. Herder, Briefe zur Beförderung der Humanität

Was ist Publikum? Ein sehr unbestimmter Begriff, der, wenn
man alle Eigenheiten des einzelnen Gebrauchs und Mißbrauchs
seiner Benennung absondert, ein allgemeines Urteil, wenigstens
eine Mehrheit der Stimmen in dem Kreise, in welchem man
5 spricht, schreibt oder handelt, zu bezeichnen scheint. Es gibt
ein reales und ideales Publikum; jenes, das gegenwärtig um
uns ist, und uns seine Stimme wo nicht zukommen läßt, so
doch zukommen lassen kann; das ideale Publikum ist zuweilen

so zerstreut, so verbreitet, daß kein Lüftchen uns aus der
10 Entfernung oder aus der Nachwelt den Laut seiner Gedanken
zuführen mag.

VOM PUBLIKUM DER HEBRÄER: Das Hebräische Volk
ward von seinem Ursprunge an als ein *genetisches Individuum*,
als ein Volk betrachtet. Der sterbende Stammvater sprach zu
15 seinen Söhnen für die ganze Reihe zukünftiger Zeiten. [...]
Als es in vielen Tausenden um den Berg Sinai gelagert dastand,
sprach der Gesetzgeber im Namen seines Gottes zu ihm, als
zu *einer Person*, die dieses Gottes Knecht und gerettetes Kind
sei. Er forderte von ihm Achtung und Liebe des Gesetzes
20 als von einem moralischen Wesen. [...] Daher der hohe,
weitschallende Ton des Patriotismus in den hebräischen
Psalmen und Propheten. Wo und in welcher Sprache sein
Nachhall ertöne, er ergreift das Herz; ein Publikum wird
lebendig. Man findet sich in einer Versammlung, in der Einer
25 für Alle steht, Alle für einen. Die Last der Gebote, Segen und
Fluch trägt das ganze Volk auf seinen Schultern. Danklieder
tönen von Allen empor; auch über die kleinsten Begebnisse
des Individuum werden sie angenommen, weil dies Individuum zum ganzen Volk gehört. [...]
30 Haben wir dies Publikum der Hebräer? Mich dünkt, jedes
Volk habe es durch *seine Sprache*. Diese ist ein göttliches
Organ der Belehrung, Strafe und Unterweisung für Jeden,
der für sie Sinn und Ohr hat. [...] Wer in derselben Sprache
erzogen ward, wer sein Herz in sie schütten, seine Seele in
35 ihr ausdrücken lernte, der gehörte zum *Volk dieser Sprache*.
Ich vernehme noch Otfrieds Stimme, die Kern- und
Biedersprüche mancher alten Deutschen, die den Charakter
meines Volks in sich tragen, sprechen zu mir; Kaisersberg,
Luther predigt mir noch; und was auch von andern Nationen
40 in meine Mundart meisterhaft überging, ist die Stimme eines
Publikums geworden, zu dem auch ich gehöre. Mittelst der
Sprache wird eine Nation erzogen und gebildet; mittelst der
Sprache wird sie ordnung- und ehrliebend, folgsam, gesittet,
umgänglich, berühmt, fleißig und mächtig. [...] Daß unser

45 Deutschland durch seine Sprache sich dies Publikum in
solchem Umfange, mit solcher Festigkeit gegründet habe, wie
es hätte geschehen mögen, ist schwer zu zweifeln. Ganze
Länder sind davon abgerissen, Provinzen und Kreise verstehen
einander kaum, nicht nur nicht in Reden, sondern oft selbst
50 nicht in Schriften. Was in manchen Gegenden für Witz gilt,
wird in andern als niedriger Scherz verachtet; das Ganze hat
so wenig einen gemeinschaftlichen Schritt in der Kultur
gehalten, daß schwerlich eine Vorstellungsart zu finden wäre,
die auf alle Teile desselben, als auf *ein gemeinsames Publikum*,
55 mit gleicher Macht wirkte. Nicht aber nur Provinzen und
Kreise, selbst Stände haben sich voneinander gesondert, indem
seit einem Jahrhunderte die sogenannten obern Stände eine
völlig fremde Sprache angenommen, eine fremde Erziehungs-
und Lebensweise beliebt haben. [...] Ohne eine gemein-
60 schaftliche Landes- und Muttersprache, in der alle Stände als
Sprossen eines Baumes erzogen werden, gibt es kein wahres
Verständnis der *Gemüter, keine gemeinsame patriotische
Bildung, keine innige Mit- und Zusammenempfindung, kein
vaterländisches Publikum mehr.* Wenn die Stimme des Vater-
65 landes die Stimme Gottes ist, so kann diese zu gemeinschaftlichen, allumfassenden, und aufs tiefste greifenden
Zwecken nur in der *Sprache des Vaterlandes* tönen, sie muß
von Jugend auf, durch alle Klassen der Nation, an Herz und
Geist erklungen sein; so nur wird durch sie ein Publikum
70 verständig und verstanden, hörend und hörbar.
    (*Briefe zur Beförderung der Humanität*, Riga, 1795;
    the section bears the title 'Haben wir noch das Publikum
    und Vaterland der Alten?' Spelling has been modernised
    [XVII, 285–9].)

Commentary: (numbers in parentheses refer to line numbers
in the text)
(6f) The reference to an 'ideal public' introduces the historical dimension, so very important in Herder's concept of *Volk*.
(14) *Genesis 35*. Reference to Jacob and his twelve sons.

(16f) *Exodus 20*. Reference to Moses receiving the Ten Commandments.

(21) Patriotism here not in the nationalist sense, but closely related to *Publikum*.

(28f) Key message, subordinates the individual to the more important totality of the *Volk*.

(31) *Sprache* seen as a divine constituent which brings about the *Volk*.

(36) Otfried von Weißenburg, ninth century disciple of Hrabanus Maurus, rendered parts of the Gospels into Old-High-German poetry.

(38) Johann Geiler von Kaisersberg (1445–1510) popular preacher in Germany.

(44ff) A complicated negation: Germany did not develop the kind of language which could have produced a strong public.

(48f) Refers to the existence of strong dialects and a language which was still not standardised.

(56ff) The aristocracy and upper middle-classes spoke French.

(61) Typical of Herder's thinking in organic terms. The *Volk* is like a tree with individual tribes and families forming branches and twigs. Similarity to the 'family tree'.

(64f) From the Greek/Latin proverb: 'vox populi, vox Dei', originally attributed to Hesiod.

Vocabulary:

Eigenheit (f) = character; zukommen = make audible; zerstreut = dissipated; gelagert = gathered; weitschallend = resounding; Nachhall (m) = echo; Last (f) = burden; Begebnis (n) = event; Mich dünkt = me thinks; Belehrung (f) = tuition; Unterweisung (f) = instruction; vernehmen = to hear; Kern- und Biedersprüche (m) = pithy sayings; übergehen = devolve upon; mittelst = by means of; gesittet = mannered; umgänglich = civilised; niedriger Scherz = common joke; Vorstellungsart (f) = mode of thinking; Stand (m) = class; sondern = to separate; beliebt = favoured; Sproß (m) = offshoot; allumfassend = comprehensive.

2. F. E. D. Schleiermacher, 'Die Idee des Staates' (1802)

Wer so das schönste Kunstwerk des Menschen, wodurch er auf die höchste Stufe sein Wesen stellen soll, nur als ein notwendiges Übel betrachtet, als ein unentbehrliches Maschinenwerk, [...] der muß ja nur als Beschränkung fühlen, was ihm den höchsten Grad des Lebens zu gewähren bestimmt ist.

(*Monologen* [1802]. Quoted from P. Kluckhohn, *Ideengut*, p. 78.)

Commentary:
Sees the state as a work of art which gives human beings the opportunity to achieve the 'highest form of life'. Sees Rousseau's *Contrat Social* as too mechanistic, as soulless.

Vocabulary:
Stufe (f) = stage; Wesen (n) = essence; Maschinenwerk (n) = piece of machinery; Beschränkung (f) = limitation; gewähren = to guarantee.

3. Friedrich Hölderlin (1770–1843), *Hyperion* (1797)

Ich kann kein Volk mir denken, das zerrißner wäre, wie die Deutschen. Handwerker siehst du, aber keine Menschen, Denker, aber keine Menschen, Herren und Knechte, Jungen und gesetzte Leute, aber keine Menschen – ist das nicht, wie ein Schlachtfeld, wo Hände und Arme und alle Glieder zerstückelt untereinanderliegen, indessen das vergoßne Lebensblut im Sande zerrinnt?

(F. Hölderlin, *Sämtliche Werke*, Vol. 3, F. Beißner (ed.), (Stuttgarter Ausgabe), p. 153.)

Commentary: (numbers in parentheses refer to line numbers in the text)
A comment on the fragmentation of human beings, not directly in a political sense, but with reference to a lack of human identity in Germany. The reference to the battlefield

(5) and of torn limbs (5f) occurs repeatedly in German literature (Lenz, Büchner), it seems symptomatic for the view that Germany, in particular, is a fragmented country.

Vocabulary:
zerrissen = torn; Handwerker (m) = artisan; Knecht (m) = farmhand; gesetzt = mature; Schlachtfeld (n) = battlefield; zerstückelt = fragmented; zerrinnen = to soak away.

Topics for further study

1. Analyse the two types of *Vernunft* in Kant's essay '*Was ist Aufklärung?*' and discuss to what extent Kant is typical of the 'German tradition'.
2. Give a short definition of Herder's concept of *Volk* and compare his concept with your understanding of the nation state as it developed in eighteenth century France and Britain.
3. Examine the importance of *Sprache* in Herder's and Fichte's concept of *Volk*.
4. Examine the importance of the state for the individual as seen in Hegel's philosophy.

4

Weltliteratur and *Nationalliteratur* in their relationship to the Enlightenment

The reception of the Enlightenment in German literature; a continuation of Chapter 3: the cosmopolitan, eighteenth century tradition reflected in Goethe's thought; ancient Greece as a model for the perfection of the individual and the concept of an idealised humanity, based on aesthetic principles. Nationalliteratur *as a necessary complement to* Weltliteratur; *its increasingly anti-Western stance and final subversion in nationalist and racist politics. The problematic nature of a perceived* Kulturnation.

Introduction

This Chapter will define the terms *Weltliteratur* and *Nationalliteratur*, not in the strict sense as would be expected in a work of literary criticism, but more generally, in order to complement the observations made in the previous Chapter. In particular, we want to explore the extent to which literature had been receptive to the earlier stages of the Enlightenment and shall therefore focus on the attitudes of German writers towards other cultures and intellectual developments. Whilst some critics have attempted to trace the origins of a German national literature beyond the Reformation to the Middle Ages, we shall confine ourselves to the period from the second part of the eighteenth century onwards, in order to compare it with the development of the modern nation state in Europe. In this context, we shall also try to investigate the extent to which a strong emphasis on cultural union may have affected Germany's development into such a nation state.

Weltliteratur and its implications for the intellectual life of the early nineteenth century

Goethe (1749–1832) first mentions the term in 1827, towards the end of his life, at a time when the process of industrialisation was accelerating communication between European nations. In accordance with his view of the 'velocity' of literary intercourse,[1] Goethe was in search of vehicles for communication and comparison. Given his practical nature, Goethe was less interested in a methodological system of comparison than in seeing the whole project as a complement to the expansion in world trade, part of the growing cosmopolitanism of the eighteenth century. It is in a conversation with his friend and disciple, Johann P. Eckermann, recorded in the latter's diary, that he gives perhaps the best account of his literary reflections. Coming in from his garden, Goethe points to a novel by Manzoni which contains a dedication to Goethe. After a few complimentary remarks on Manzoni's work and an expression of regret that the Italian is so little known in Germany, he scans through the reviews and translations of some English journals, apparently ignoring Eckermann altogether. He leaves the room but later sends his servant to Eckermann with a cordial invitation to a literary chat. He converses with his friend about a translation of Sophocles which he wishes to compare with the work of another translator. Then the conversation turns to Carlyle, a great admirer of Goethe's and an important disseminator of German intellectual ideas in Britain. Next he mentions a review in the *Berliner Jahrbücher* by someone he had not yet come across, but who had attracted his interest. The review leads to a general discussion of French empiricism which he compares with German idealism, commenting on the advantages and disadvantages of both methods. From this topic the conversation meanders to the Indian caste system and from there to a general *bon mot* concerning the changing perceptions on democrats and aristocrats. Finally, he turns to aesthetics and the term *Weltliteratur*:

> Im ästhetischen Fach sieht es freilich bei uns am schwächsten aus, und wir können lange warten, bis wir auf einen Mann wie Carlyle stoßen. Es ist aber sehr artig, daß wir jetzt, bei dem engen Verkehr zwischen Franzosen, Engländern und Deutschen, in den Fall kommen, uns einander zu korrigieren. Das ist der große Nutzen, der bei einer Weltliteratur herauskommt, und der sich immer mehr zeigen wird.[2]
>
> (We are still rather weak in the field of aesthetics and it will take some time until we hit upon a man such as Carlyle. However, it is rather agreeable that now, with the closer traffic between the French, the English and the Germans we have the opportunity to correct one another. This is the great advantage that emerges from a world literature and which will become ever more obvious.)

The diary entry ends with a laudatory comment on Carlyle's *Life of Schiller* (1824) which focuses on aspects which might be overlooked by a German and compares this work with German studies on Byron and Shakespeare, which demonstrate greater insights than comparable English studies have so far produced.

This conversation has been reported in detail since it illustrates not only the superior perspective of a genius, well aware of his own fame in Europe, but also epitomises Goethe's late style, less passionate than in the days of his *Werther* (1774), and therefore more tolerant of other styles and opinions. The practical aspects of a world literature are clear to see: Goethe considers it mainly as a tool for comparison, in order to find models of 'best practice'. In contrast to later generations of critics, he was less interested in a canon of the greatest works of poetry, favouring instead the broader acquisition of literature from many different cultures currently of interest, which might in consequence be of benefit to his fellow countrymen.

Nor did he restrict the term to poetry, but included other works of more general interest.

An important part of the comparative nature of world literature is seen to be the translation of influential works. Goethe himself set an example with his rendering into German of Greek, Latin, Spanish, French and English literature, the work of the fourteenth century Persian poet Hafis, and his own adaptation of Persian literature in his *West-Östlicher Divan* (1814–19). This in turn encouraged Rückert, Platen and others to explore Persian styles in their own poetry, which helped to open up a German perspective on the East. The benefit of these translations, in Goethe's view, was not restricted to the recipient language and culture, but also affected the original, in that it helped towards a new interpretation and in turn stimulated further interest in the work's country of origin. A case in point was Coleridge's English translation of Schiller's *Wallenstein* (1800), which allowed for some kind of 'metempsychosis' into another period.[3] For the same reason Goethe enthusiastically supported Herder's translation of international folksongs in his *Stimmen der Völker in Liedern* (1807) and took a lively interest in translations of Shakespeare by German Romantics. Goethe's reaction to gaining new insights by reading works in translation is reminiscent of Keats' famous lines relating to Chapman's translations of Homer:

> Then felt I like some watcher of the skies
> When a new planet swims into his ken.[4]

Beyond the more direct art of translation, there was also the benefit of an international exchange of ideas, of themes and motifs: Goethe's own *Faust* reflects aspects of Byron's life and contains many references to ancient Greek mythology. French Romantic literature benefited from German influence and in particular Mme de Staël's *De l'Allemagne* (1813) contributed greatly towards a wider dissemination of German literature abroad. Some critics have expressed their concern over Goethe's 'Eurocentric' attitude towards

Weltliteratur. In *Studien zur Weltliteratur*, Goethe equates European with world literature,[5] but he might well have seen the exchange amongst European men of letters as a first stage towards a wider form of world literature.[6] A further reason might lie in Goethe's interest in the cosmopolitan concept of the Enlightenment, then largely restricted to Europe and America. The new world held a great fascination for Goethe and, though already 70 years old, he half playfully considered emigration to America.[7]

Some of the aspects of the Enlightenment which attracted Goethe were tolerance towards other cultures and nations; the notions of truthfulness and humanity; the international atmosphere of the great European cities. The latter in particular was a source of envy and admiration for Goethe. His highest praise was reserved for Paris, 'this metropolis of the world, where . . . men like Molière, Voltaire, Diderot and the like have kept up a current of intellectual life which cannot be found anywhere else on the whole earth'.[8] Aware of the lack of such a metropolis in Germany, he tried his best to remedy the situation by attracting promising men of intellect to Weimar, and in particular by creating literary salons and journals which were to facilitate a cosmopolitan urbanity:

> Diese Zeitschriften, wie sie nach und nach ein größeres Publikum gewinnen, werden zu einer gehofften allgemeinen Weltliteratur auf das Wirksamste beitragen; nur wiederholen wir, daß nicht die Rede sein könne, die Nationen sollen überein denken, sondern sie sollen nur einander gewahr werden, sich begreifen und, wenn sie sich wechselseitig nicht lieben mögen, sich einander wenigstens dulden lernen.[9] (These journals, as they gradually attract a wider public, will be very effective in contributing towards a general world literature; but, we must repeat, that it is out of the question that nations should think alike, they should only become aware of each other, understand each other and, if they cannot love each other, should at least tolerate each other.)

We recognise in this quotation Goethe's desire for the enlightened concept of tolerance and mutual understanding and he attempted to further these ideas as an avid reader and contributor to international as well as German periodicals: the French journal *Le Globe*, the *Edinburgh Review*, Schiller's *Horen* and Wieland's *Teutscher Merkur*. He founded *Kunst und Altertum*, largely dedicated to the dissemination of literary and cultural news and reviews.

Of particular importance to Goethe was the understanding of ancient Greek culture. From his conversations with Eckermann we read:

> Nationalliteratur will jetzt nicht viel sagen, die Epoche der Weltliteratur ist an der Zeit, und jeder muß jetzt dazu wirken, diese Epoche zu beschleunigen. [...] im Bedürfnis von etwas Musterhaftem müssen wir immer zu den alten Griechen zurückgehen, in deren Werken stets der schöne Mensch dargestellt ist.[10]
>
> (National literature is of little interest nowadays, this is the epoch of world literature, and everyone must work towards hastening its arrival. [...] given the need for something exemplary we shall always have to return to the ancient Greeks in whose works the beauty of man is portrayed.)

This sentence has often been misunderstood, Goethe as well as Schiller standing accused of succumbing to the *Tyranny of Greece* over Germany.[11] E. M. Butler's influential study, first published in 1935, maintains that eighteenth century Germans, while moved by the beauty of ancient Greece, ignored its political culture, adhering instead to a sterile purity of form which all too easily escaped into the world of utopia, as portrayed in such great works as Lessing's *Laocoon* (1766), Goethe's *Iphigenie* (1787) and Hölderlin's *Empedokles* (1797). There is some truth in this criticism, especially in so far as it was to affect the German education system and, earlier, Winckelmann's distilled aesthetic vision of Greece as 'edle Einfalt und stille Größe'[12] (1755) (noble simplicity and serene greatness) (Figure 5). An examination of the Greek heroes in

Figure 5: Humboldt University building in Berlin, originally built in 1766 as a palace for Prince Henry of Prussia. Observe its neo-classical design. Since the foundation of the Humboldt University, throughout the nineteenth and well into the twentieth century, university buildings and *Gymnasien* were built in this neo-classical style, symbolising the 'Greek renewal' in German classicism. (Printed with kind permission of *C. H. Beck Verlag*, Munich)

German classical literature would demonstrate that they achieve a splendid isolation: Iphigenia banished as priestess in a temple; Empedocles driven to sacrifice himself in order to save his idealist world; and Schiller's poem *Die Götter Griechenlands* (1788) celebrating an ideal pre-Christian harmony between gods and men. Schiller in particular hoped 'to reunite the politically divided world under the banner of truth and beauty' (Text 1). Later generations have all too often categorised German classical writers as entirely non-political and have banished them to an artistic ivory tower. However, a closer study of Goethe's enthusiasm for ancient Greece would reveal that nothing was further from his mind than an escape into an unreal world. The student of *Iphigenie* will know how much of Goethe's personal experience, in particular his friendship with Frau von Stein, has become part of the drama. What is at issue in Goethe's veneration of ancient Greece is the perfection of the human race,[13] itself a noble aim of the Enlightenment.

Two related key concepts, *Wechselwirkung* and *Spiegelung*, may help towards a better understanding of Goethe's attitude towards the Greek ideal. The former term was introduced by Kant, but Goethe's idea of a dynamism of polarities, expressed as the interplay between systole and diastole (contraction and expansion), may convey an even more accurate description. The idea is indebted to contemporary science, in particular to new discoveries in electricity. The term *Spiegelung*, too, is closely influenced by Goethe's thinking in polarities, but has its roots more in mysticism than in science.[14] Both concepts suggest that there is a lively interplay between subject and object, between the 'I' and the 'Other', that true *Selbsterkenntnis* will inevitably lead to *Welterkenntnis* and vice versa. The Goethean concept of *reine Menschlichkeit*, idealised in ancient Greece, thus becomes Goethe's personal aim of self-perfection, for a state of serenity and peace of mind. Broadly oversimplified, we can see Goethe's life-long striving for human perfection as a variation on the modern day formula of the Enlightenment as a continuous process ('unvollendetes Projekt der Moderne').[15] The modern tradition of hermeneutics[16] with its origins in German Romanticism is also firmly rooted in the exchange and interchange of 'Self' and 'World', with its whole process of learning, of understanding based on reflection and reception, on the process of translation in the widest sense. In our day, a new branch of German Studies, intent on trans-national understanding and the promotion of tolerance has again taken up the living relationship of the own and the other, 'das Eigene und das Fremde'.[17]

When Goethe dedicated a copy of his *Iphigenie* to the Berlin actor Wilhelm Krüger (1827) with the verse: 'Alle menschlichen Gebrechen sühnet reine Menschlichkeit' (all human failings are redeemed by pure humanity), he was referring indirectly to his own 'conversion' by Charlotte von Stein, to the viewpoint of subsuming one's own ego into the wider ethical concern with humankind. The somewhat utopian energy in Goethe's striving for perfection also found expression in his joining the Free Masons, that illustrious organisation of enlightened humanity. Other famous contemporary members were Lessing, Mozart and Herder. Goethe enthusiastically supported Herder's *Ideas towards the Philosophy of the History of Mankind* (1784–91) as yet another step towards the achievement of mutual understanding amongst nations. During its composition he conversed daily with Herder and the book could almost be described as a joint venture.[18] Herder, for his part, encouraged the study of ancient Greece as an important aspect of achieving humanism [J. G. Herder, *Sämtliche Werke*, Vol. IV, p. 401].

Although, as we have seen, Goethe created the term *Weltliteratur*, the concept itself was already well known and promoted in the works of Wieland, Lessing, Lichtenberg, Hölderlin and Schiller, and continued in the writings of the early generation of Romantics such as Novalis, the Schlegel brothers and Tieck. It survived Goethe and his age to enter literary tradition, documented even at times of great nationalist fervour, if only in opposition to the most aggressively chauvinistic trends. Even the authors of the *Communist Manifesto* of 1848 turned their attention to this literary term:

An die Stelle der alten lokalen und nationalen Selbstgenügsamkeit und Abgeschlossenheit tritt ein allseitiger Verkehr, eine allseitige Abhängigkeit der Nationen voneinander. [...] Die nationale Einseitigkeit und Beschränktheit wird mehr und mehr unmöglich, und aus den vielen nationalen und lokalen Literaturen bildet sich eine Weltliteratur.[19]
(The old local and national self-sufficiency and isolation has been replaced by a universal traffic, a universal dependence

of all nations on one another. [...] National one-sidedness and limitation is less and less possible and from amongst the many national and local forms of literature a world literature is emerging.)

Marx and Engels attribute this change from a local to a universal literature to the bourgeoisie, and it is not certain whether, given their general condemnation of the bourgeoisie, they see this development as beneficial. In the context in which the quotation appears it would seem, however, that the bourgeoisie is seen as the great moderniser, albeit a harsh and ruthless one. The authors of the *Communist Manifesto* certainly interpreted world literature in the spirit of Goethe, seeing 'intellectual production' develop alongside material change. Another great Communist and originator of the literary term Socialist Realism, Maxim Gorky, was in no doubt as to how to assess Goethe's term:

> The greater and more intensive man's interest in his neighbour, the sooner will come about the process of fusion of the good creative principles into one uniform energy, the sooner we complete our road to Calvary which will lead to the world-festival of mutual understanding, respect, brotherhood and the glorification of man through free labour.[20]

Thomas Mann might well have been aware of these pronouncements when, on the occasion of the centenary of Goethe's death (18th March 1932), a time of fanatical nationalism, he spoke of 'Goethe as representative of the bourgeois age', seeing him as someone who would transcend the limitations of bourgeois society and move towards a universal world order, even 'wenn man das Wort allgemein genug und undogmatisch verstehen will, ins Kommunistische'[21] (if we wish to understand the word sufficiently generally and undogmatically, into communism). Mann himself had completed a volte-face here, given his celebration of Goethe's *Volkhaftigkeit* and distancing him from Western influences, some 20 years earlier.[22] Fritz Strich's notable study, *Goethe und die Weltliteratur*, could not be published until 1946, as his attempt to interpret Goethe's concept had been misunderstood during the period of nationalism and fascism. Instead of seeing German literature as the pinnacle of all world literature, as was the tendency in the early twentieth century, Strich focused on its comparative aspect and pleaded for the foundation of 'Weltliteraturgeschichte' as a literary discipline,[23] a suggestion which was later to take shape in the field of Comparative Literary Studies. Whilst in our own 'One World' scenario, the debate no longer centres on a canon of the best of all literatures, there is still a tendency towards 'Eurocentrism'. On the other hand, today's standardisation, aided by the modern media, has done much to devalue the idea of world literature in favour of a renewed interest in regionalism and of a private preference for one's own individual taste.

Nationalliteratur and the concept of a German *Kulturstaat*

Though coined at about the same time as *Weltliteratur*, the term is less well defined and more difficult to place. The ideas of Herder and Fichte, discussed in the previous Chapter, have already demonstrated that the desire for a nationally independent literature was a legitimate one, given the hegemony of France over Germany in all cultural matters. Poets of the Baroque period, supported by the aristocracy, had already formed German *Sprachgesellschaften* with the aim of rendering the popular German language into a literary medium. Leading representatives of the Enlightenment and the *Sturm und Drang*, amongst them the philosophers Leibniz and Thomasius and the writers Möser, Klopstock and Wieland promoted a revival of German literature. Wieland advocated the cultivation of a national literature in order to kindle 'the sacred flame of patriotism in every German heart' and to inspire in the scattered population of 'Germania' that kind of community spirit which 'a great, noble, brave and enlightened people are worthy of'.[24] Scores of patriotic poems were written, but failed to achieve their political aim and prompted Goethe and Schiller to the ironic advice:

> Zur Nation euch zu bilden, ihr hofft es, Deutsche, vergebens;
> Bildet, ihr könnt es, dafür freier zu Menschen euch aus.[25]
> (To build up a nation, you hope in vain, you Germans; Form yourselves instead – you can do it – into freer people.)

The yearning for a national literature is, however, not restricted to Germany; similar movements emerged in Ireland and Scotland as a reaction to the dominance of English language and culture. This century has seen a continuation of these developments in many African and Asian countries and in the new literature of black America. It would also be misleading to see *Nationalliteratur* as the opposite of *Weltliteratur*; instead, the one was meant to complement the other and their mutual interchange was designed to benefit both. In the case of Goethe, his preference for *Weltliteratur* seems to have developed during his later period, as the young Goethe, in his nostalgic yearning for a bygone, better age, much more closely reflected the ideas of a *Nationalliteratur*. In his play *Götz von Berlichingen*, for instance, he displays more than a passing interest in national literature, deploring the fact that 'das Herz des Volcks ist in den Koth getreten'[26] [1771] (The heart of the people has been dragged in the mud).

Attempts to form a German national theatre were slightly more fruitful in their promotion of a literary and public language and a more united educated middle class. We can distinguish several phases in the development of a German national literature and shall restrict ourselves here to discussing the endeavour to found a national theatre during the Enlightenment and the *Sturm und Drang*, to the development of German studies during the Romantic period and to the nationalistic Wagnerian fervour of the second half of the nineteenth century.

In Goethe's *Theatralische Sendung* (1776) Serlo, one of the main characters, declares himself an advocate of a national German theatre and Wilhelm, the novel's hero, eventually reaches 'H***', a reference to Hamburg, Lessing's favoured location for a national theatre. At the same time, Wilhelm is intent on removing the theatre from the dominance of the aristocracy and of emancipating it in the new bourgeois world. This contrasts strangely with Goethe's own success with the Weimar Theatre which remained under the influence of the Sachsen-Weimar dynasty. In this fragmentary work Goethe follows the long tradition of German writers in search of such a theatre organised 'nach den besonderen Sitten und nach der Gemütsbeschaffenheit einer Nation'[27] (in accordance with the particular customs and the national disposition). Goethe's decision to abandon the novel is usually seen in the context of his first Italian Journey and his consequent espousal of classical antiquity and a set of more universal values.

Lessing, Dalberg, Iffland, the young Schiller and, a generation later, Richard Wagner were the main promoters of a national theatre. Lessing and his circle were successful in founding a first national theatre in Hamburg; its remit went beyond the merely literary: it sought to actively promote German plays instead of 'the eternal translations from foreign languages', a German *Lustspiel* which would portray the 'German character' and, most importantly, a stage financed by a wider, middle-class public audience.[28] Although the time proved not yet ripe for such an undertaking (Text 2), the search for a national theatre continued: Goethe's friend F. L. Schröder, the prototype for his literary figure Serlo, attempted to revive the idea of a national theatre in Vienna; he also cultivated a German opera and promoted Mozart's work. The national theatre established in Mannheim (1779) was of importance to the young Schiller: just as Hamburg had encouraged Lessing to write his *Dramaturgie*, the theoretical basis for a departure from the French theatre, so Mannheim was to inspire Schiller's *Die Schaubühne als moralische Anstalt betrachtet* (1784). Schiller goes so far as to suggest that a German national theatre could bring about a German nation state, with a civilising effect which would permeate every aspect of human activity (Text 3). Attempts at establishing a national theatre continued throughout the nineteenth century, amongst them Richard Wagner's concept of the *Festspiel* which found its realisation in Bayreuth in 1872.

These efforts remained firmly within the realms of culture; they can be linked with the endeavour to create a German cultural nation. Although the term *Kulturnation* emerged much later and can be seen as potentially dangerous, in that it does not define the nation in clear geo-political terms, thus paving the way for later territorial demands,[29] its genesis reaches back to the late Enlightenment and efforts at liberating German culture from French domination. Wieland (1733–1813), anything but a German nationalist, defended the particularist nature of eighteenth century Germany on the grounds that it produced a host of diverse cultural activities and energies and, as illustrated above, concentrated the national spirit on the domains of philosophy, literature and art. Wilhelm von Humboldt (1767–1835) went even further. He considered politics to be a hindrance in the development of a nation. Writing to his friend Jacobi, he states:

> Ich rede überhaupt nicht von der politischen Stimmung, ich beschränke mich bloß auf das, was eigentlich national ist, auf den Gang der Meinungen und des Geistes, die Bildung des Charakters, die Sitten usf.[30]
> (I do not refer to the political mood but limit myself to that which is actually national, the development of opinions and of the intellect, the formation of character, of morals etc.)

In coining the term *Kulturnation*, Friedrich Meinecke attempted to return to the loosely defined federal character of pre-1871 Germany, in direct opposition to Bismarck's nation state, with the aim of placing Germany once again within a wider community of nations, of retaining the earlier spirit of

Weltbürgertum (Text 4). Contemporaries of Meinecke shared similar views: the Germanist G. G. Gervinus rejected the Prussian-dominated Second Reich in favour of the *großdeutsch* solution which would have included Austria and Richard Wagner felt the Second Reich could never be the true heir to the Holy Roman Empire.[31]

The Romantics approached the theme of national literature from a different angle. They sought inspiration from the rather vaguely defined Middle Ages and concentrated on folklore and the rediscovery of Germanic myths and epic poems. Their efforts led to the establishment of *Germanistik*, German studies as opposed to the conventional classical studies. Central to these activities were the brothers Jacob and Wilhelm Grimm, compilers of the famous fairy-tales, and among their circle of friends, the Romantic poets Clemens Brentano and Achim von Arnim, the Schlegel brothers, Ludwig Uhland, Joseph Görres and the autodidactic nobleman Joseph von Lassberg. In contrast to the representatives of the all-embracing, cosmopolitan world literature, those of national literature worked in a more analytical manner, attempting to rediscover and preserve the old German character, a process justified by Görres in the sentence 'Das Volk, welches seine Vergangenheit von sich wirft, entblößt seine feinsten Lebensnerven allen Stürmen der wetterwendischen Zukunft'.[32] (The people who jettisons its past, exposes its vital nerve endings to all the storms of a tempestuous future.)

Jacob Grimm (1785–1863) was not only co-author of the *Kinder- und Hausmärchen*, he also edited a very comprehensive *Deutsche Grammatik*, a *Deutsche Mythologie* and, together with his brother, the *Deutsche Sagen* and the famous *Deutsche Wörterbuch*, finally completed in 1961. In addition, both brothers edited countless medieval poems, lectured on Germanic and medieval German literature and life, and copied and preserved ancient manuscripts. The brothers Grimm, Gervinus, Görres, Heinrich Hoffmann von Fallersleben and many others were politically liberal and subject to frequent harrassment at the hands of autocratic German princes. By the end of the nineteenth century, however, a more fiercely nationalistic generation was to reject them.

This interest in old Germanic and early medieval writing led to the establishment of a body of national literature which was to influence significantly the concept of German nationhood. The one document which more than any other became associated with German nationalism was the *Nibelungenlied*, an epic poem with antecedents in Germanic times, but which takes its present form from the early thirteenth century. Rediscovered by the *Sturm und Drang* Swiss scholar J. J. Bodmer (1748), it soon became associated with Germany's emerging patriotism: a *Feld- und Zeltausgabe*, printed in Berlin, was carried in the knapsack of young German soldiers during the Napoleonic Wars. It was thus to emerge as the national poem of Germany, associated with a pugnacious anti-Western attitude, advocating a return to Germanic barbarism and to pre-Christian traditions. These tendencies found expression in two ways, firstly through a rejection of Western and classical literature in favour of the Germanic world, in particular the Scandinavian myths and sagas, and secondly through German nationalist politics. By the mid-nineteenth century Jacob Grimm was suggesting that Scandinavia was for Germanic research what Italy had been for those involved in classical studies,[33] thereby unintentionally contributing to the emerging dichotomy between world and national literature. The North achieved a mystical utopian significance, further enhanced by the enthusiastic reception of the Icelandic *Edda*, a motley collection of heroic songs, anecdotes and myths. Links were seen between these mythological and heroic tales and the characters of the *Nibelungenlied*, and these links found spectacular expression in Richard Wagner's operas. They also surfaced in the military and political propaganda of the Wilhelminian period when, on the eve of the First World War, the Kaiser assured his Austrian allies of *Nibelungentreue*. The military term *tarnen* (to camouflage) is taken from the poem and the 'Siegfried Line' of Second World War fame also belongs to this register. A wider discussion of these excesses of national literature could include the rejection of French and Latin influences in general, the attacks on Catholicism and the Germano-purism of Kleist, Jahn, Arndt and countless minor writers.[34]

Richard Wagner (1813–83) epitomises the increasingly anti-Western, outrageously racist development of national literature in the second half of the nineteenth century. Initially a critic of the autocratic political order of his day and of middle-class mediocrity, he became involved in the Revolution of 1848 and espoused an ill-conceived, vague form of socialist anarchism, partly under the influence of Mikhail Bakunin.[35] These ideas were occasionally interwoven with an almost megalomaniac belief in the royal rank of the artist, no doubt reinforced by his own seeming arrogance and self-deception. It was during this time that Wagner turned his attention to the *Nibelungen* which became the inspiration for his creative work. His essay 'Art and Revolution' was a by-product of his studies on the *Nibelungen* legends, published under the title 'The Wibelungs, World History out of Legend'.[36] Out of these activities developed the tetralogy *Der Ring der Nibelungen* which he completed in his Bayreuth house 'Wahnfried' in 1874. In contrast to the thirteenth century poem and to renderings by his own contemporaries, Wagner concentrated in the main on the presentation of mythical gods and demons, on pre-Christian myths, celebrating primeval chaos and destruction in opposition to all civilisation. The mythical hero Siegfried took on the dimension of a sun-god, but was also mysteriously allied to Christ as well as to the Barbarossa myth and the Holy Grail.[37] As a consequence of such a mythical pot-pourri, a dangerously racist and anti-Western ideology developed which would later effortlessly merge into National Socialism. By 1869 Wagner had become fiercely anti-semitic, attracting into his circle Count Arthur de Gobineau and Houston Stewart Chamberlain, the two most important promoters of modern racism. Under the aegis of Wagner's children, Bayreuth was to become a cultural show-piece of National Socialism.

And yet, Wagner cannot be viewed from this angle alone. Many famous men of genius surrounded and admired him and many of his ideas, though in a far less radical form, were widespread beyond Germany. Wagner's attempt at establishing Bayreuth as a national cultural centre is a case in point. The idea of the *Festspiel* for the regeneration of national art was not uncommon, and Wagner's intention of modernising and replacing traditional opera with something more comprehensive resulted in many innovations in music and drama. What is of interest here, however, is the manner in which the German preoccupation with literature and art led to an increasingly distorted view of political reality. Whilst the advocates of world literature lost support and were increasingly misrepresented, as illustrated by the reception of *Wilhelm Tell* on the centenary of Schiller's birth,[38] the champions of national literature became ever more deeply embroiled in nationalist and imperialist policies. The early nineteenth century preoccupation with ancient German manuscripts and a sentimental admiration for the Christian Middle Ages, once detached from the reality of the day, turned into a nationalistic fever which gripped those reactionary politicians and professors who could not come to terms with the modernist age of social democracy, world-wide commerce and technology. Repelled by this contemporary world, these advocates of national literature sought their political inspiration in history, ignoring the dangers which spring from a confusion of history and poetry with politics. It is in this context that Grillparzer warned against the path from humanism via nationalism towards barbarism.[39]

Notes

1 J. W. Goethe, 'Briefe', Vol. 43, *Sämtliche Werke* (Weimarer Ausgabe). Letter to Streckfuß (27th Oct. 1827), Weimar: H. Böhlaus Nachfolger, 1908; p. 136.
2 Goethe, *Sämtliche Werke* (Münchener Ausgabe), Vol. 19, J. P. Eckermann, 'Gespräche mit Goethe in den letzten Jahren seines Lebens', in H. Schlaffer (ed.), Munich: Hanser, 1986; p. 236.

3   Goethe, 'Briefe', Vol. 44, in *Sämtliche Werke* (Weimarer Ausgabe), Letter to Carlyle (15th June 1828), Weimar, 1909; p. 139f.

4   *The Poetical Works of John Keats*, H. W. Garrod (ed.), 2nd edn, Oxford: Clarendon Press, 1958; p. 45.

5   Goethe, 'Aufsätze zur Literatur', Vol. 42 II, *Sämtliche Werke* (Weimarer Ausgabe), Weimar: H. Böhlaus Nachfolger, 1907; p. 500.

6   F. Strich, *Goethe und die Weltliteratur*, Bern: Franke, 1946; p. 26f.

7   Th. Mann, 'Reden und Aufsätze 1', *Gesammelte Werke*, Vol. 9, Frankfurt: Fischer, 1960; p. 59.

8   J. P. Eckermann, *Gespräche mit Goethe*, H. Steger (ed.), Munich: Deutsches Verlagshaus Bong, 1949; p. 207.

9   Goethe, *Sämtliche Werke* (Weimarer Ausgabe), 'Schriften zur Literatur', Vol. 41 II, *Edinburgh Review* 38, p. 170, Weimar: H. Böhlaus Nachfolger, 1903; p. 348.

10 Goethe, *Sämtliche Werke* (Münchener Ausgabe), Vol. 19, J. P. Eckermann, p. 207.

11 E. M. Butler, *The Tyranny of Greece over Germany*, 2nd edn, Boston: Beacon Press, 1958.

12 J. J. Winckelmann, *Gedanken über die Nachahmung griechischer Werke in der Malerei und Bildhauerkunst*, G. Klingenstein (ed.), Leipzig: Velhagen and Klasing, 1929; p. 22.

13 W. Jens, *Nationalliteratur und Weltliteratur – von Goethe aus gesehen*, Munich: Kindler, 1988; p. 28.

14 L. A. Willoughby, 'Literary relations in the light of Goethe's principle of "Wiederholte Spiegelungen"', in E. M. Wilkinson and L. A. Willoughby, *Goethe, Poet and Thinker*, London: Arnold, 1962; pp. 153–66.

15 J. Habermas, 'Die Moderne – ein unvollendetes Projekt', in *Die Zeit*, 19th September 1980.

16 From Greek, 'art of interpretation', the manner whereby we gain a deeper understanding of the world around us. For further detail cf. Chapter 5.

17 *Gesellschaft für Interkulturelle Germanistik e.V.*, Vorstand A. Wierlacher. cf. also A. Wierlacher (ed.), *Das Fremde und das Eigene. Prolegomena zu einer Interkulturellen Germanistik*, Munich: judicium, 1985.

18 Strich, *Goethe und die Weltliteratur*, p. 243.

19 K. Marx, *Die Frühschriften*, Stuttgart: Kröner, 1971; p. 529.

20 Quoted from Jens, *Nationalliteratur*, p. 42 [author's translation].

21 'Goethe als Repräsentant des bürgerlichen Zeitalters', in Th. Mann, *Gesammelte Werke in 12 Bänden*, Vol. 9, Oldenburg: S. Fischer, 1960; p. 331.

22 T. J. Reed, *Thomas Mann, The Uses of Tradition*, Oxford: Clarendon Press, 1974; p. 287, pp. 334ff.

23 W. Kohlschmidt und W. Mohr (eds), *Reallexikon der deutschen Literaturgeschichte*, 2nd edn, Vol. 4, Berlin: de Gruyter, 1984; p. 827.

24 C. M. Wieland, *Werke*, Vol. 23, Kleine Schriften III (Akademie Ausgabe), Vorrede zu Schillers *Historischem Calender für Damen für das Jahr 1792*, Berlin: 1969; pp. 384–94.

25 F. Schiller, *Sämtliche Werke* (Säkularausgabe), Vol. 2, Stuttgart: Cottasche Verlagsbuchhandlung, [1904]; p. 103.

26 Goethe, *Werke* (Akademieausgabe), Vol. 1, E. Grumbach (ed.), Berlin: Akademie, 1958; p. 2a [Geschichte Gottfriedens, Motto].

27 *Reallexikon der deutschen Literaturgeschichte*, Vol. 2, p. 598.

28 *ibid.* p. 598f

29 Dann, *Nation und Nationalismus*, p. 37f.

30 Quoted from F. Meinecke, *Weltbürgertum und Nationalstaat. Studien zur Genesis des deutschen Nationalstaates*, 6th edn, Munich Berlin: R. Oldenbourg, 1922; p. 56.

31 G. G. Gervinus, *Geschichte der Deutschen Dichtung*, Vol. 1, Leipzig: Engelmann, 1871; p. vii and R. Wagner, *Meistersinger*, finale.

32 J. Görres, *Die teutschen Volksbücher*, J. Prestel (ed.), Leipzig: [1926], p. 13.

33 *Reallexikon der deutschen Literaturgeschichte*, Vol. 4, p. 852.

34 cf. Kohn, *The Mind of Germany*, Chapters 3 and 4.

35 R. Wagner, *My Life* (transl. by A. Gray), M. Whittall (ed.), Cambridge: Cambridge University Press, 1983; p. 384ff.

36 *ibid.* p. 425f

37 Kohn, *The Mind of Germany*, p. 195.

38 Schiller centenary 1859. An example of the misinterpretations of *Tell* in a *völkisch* manner is H. Cysarz, *Schiller*, Halle/Saale: Niemeyer, 1934; Chapter 4.

39 F. Grillparzer, *Sämtliche Werke*, Historisch kritische Gesamtausgabe, A. Sauer und R. Bachmann (eds), 'Gedichte', 3. Teil, Sprüche und Epigramme Nr. 1182, Vienna: Gerlach and Wiedling, 1937; p. 213 [19 April 1848].

Suggestions for further reading

Jens, W., *Nationalliteratur und Weltliteratur – von Goethe aus gesehen*, Munich: Kindler, 1988.

Kohn, H., *The Mind of Germany, the Education of a Nation*, London: Macmillan, 1960; Chapters 2 and 3.

Mann, Th., 'Goethe als Repräsentant des bürgerlichen Zeitalters', in *Gesammelte Werke in 12 Bänden*, Vol. 9, Frankfurt a.M.: Fischer, 1960; pp. 297–332.

Textual studies

1. Friedrich Schiller, *Die Horen*, eine Monatsschrift, von einer Gesellschaft verfaßt und herausgegeben von Schiller [1794]: Öffentliche Ankündigung

Zu einer Zeit, wo das nahe Geräusch des Kriegs das Vaterland ängstigt, wo der Kampf politischer Meinungen und Interessen diesen Krieg beinahe in jedem Zirkel erneuert und nur all

zu oft Musen und Grazien daraus verscheucht, wo weder in
5 den Gesprächen noch in Schriften des Tages vor diesem
allverfolgenden Dämon von Staatskritik Rettung ist, möchte
es ebenso gewagt als verdienstlich sein, den so sehr zerstreuten
Leser zu einer Unterhaltung von ganz entgegengesetzter Art
einzuladen. [...] Aber je mehr das beschränkte Interesse der
10 Gegenwart die Gemüter in Spannung setzt, einengt und
unterjocht, desto dringender wird das Bedürfnis, durch ein
allgemeines und höheres Interesse an dem, was *rein menschlich*
und über allen Einfluß der Zeiten erhaben ist, sie wieder in
Freiheit zu setzten und die politisch geteilte Welt unter der
15 Fahne der Wahrheit und Schönheit wieder zu vereinigen.
   [...] Einer heitern und leidenschaftsfreien Unterhaltung
soll sie [die Zeitschrift] gewidmet sein und dem Geist und
Herzen des Lesers, den der Anblick der Zeitbegebenheiten
bald entrüstet, bald niederschlägt, eine fröhliche Zerstreuung
20 gewähren. Mitten in diesem politischen Tumult soll sie für
Musen und Charitinnen einen engen vertraulichen Zirkel
schließen, aus welchem alles verbannt sein wird, was mit einem
unreinen Parteigeist gestempelt ist. Aber indem sie sich alle
Beziehungen auf den *jetzigen* Weltlauf und auf die *nächsten*
25 Erwartungen der Menschen verbietet, wird sie über die
vergangene Welt die Geschichte und über die kommende die
Philosophie befragen, wird sie zu dem Ideale veredelter
Menschheit, welches durch die Vernunft aufgegeben, in der
Erfahrung aber so leicht aus den Augen gerückt wird, einzelne
30 Züge sammeln und an dem stillen Bau besserer Begriffe,
reinerer Grundsätze und edlerer Sitten, von dem zuletzt alle
wahre Verbesserung des gesellschaftlichen Zustandes abhängt,
nach Vermögen geschäftig sein.
   (*Säkularausgabe*, Bd. 16, Stuttgart und Berlin, p. 151f.)

Commentary: (numbers in parentheses refer to line numbers
in the text)
(1f) By May 1794 the French army of conscripts had re-
occupied all French territory and had repelled the British at

sea and forced the Austrian and Prussian armies back over the Rhine. In June and July alone the guillotine had claimed 1285 victims.

(9f) Schiller's intention: the readers should concentrate their minds on higher matters, on 'humanity' (12).

(16–19) Serenity is here synonymous with freedom from passion. 'Zerstreuung' is used in contrast to (9) as diversion, not distraction.

(21) In a similar vein to Goethe Schiller advocates the creation of a literary circle, dedicated to literature, history and philosophy.

(25f) Schiller's preoccupation with the past (history) and the future (philosophy) indicates a weakness of his project and reminds us of the statements by Karl Marx and Friedrich Nietzsche, referred to in the Introduction.

(29–31) These intentions are firmly rooted in the Enlightenment, as is his desire to improve mankind.

Vocabulary:
verscheuchen = to scare away; ebenso gewagt als verdienstlich = at once audacious and meritorious; Gemüt (n) = mind; unterjochen = to enslave; über allen Einfluß . . . erhaben = superior to all the influence of time; widmen = to dedicate; gewähren = to grant; Charitinnen (pl) = Greek goddesses of grace; durch die Vernunft aufgegeben = charged by reason; an dem stillen Bau . . . geschäftig sein = to work at the peaceful artifice of.

2. G. E. Lessing, *Hamburgische Dramaturgie* (1767/69)

Über den gutherzigen Einfall, den Deutschen ein Nationaltheater zu verschaffen, da wir Deutsche noch keine Nation sind! Ich rede nicht von der politischen Verfassung, sondern bloß von dem sittlichen Charakter. Fast sollte
5 man sagen, dieser sei: keinen eigenen haben zu wollen. Wir sind noch immer die geschworenen Nachahmer alles

Ausländischen, besonders noch immer die untertänigen Be-
wunderer der nie genug bewunderten Franzosen.

(Hamburgische Dramaturgie, O. Mann (ed.), Stuttgart,
2nd edn, 1963; p. 392.)

Commentary: (number in parentheses refers to line number
in the text)
The quotation not only bears witness to French hegemony
over German culture, but also illustrates an emerging emancipation from France.
(3f) Lessing emphasises the moral function of a national
theatre (cf. also Schiller, Text 3), he does not believe in its
political influence.

Vocabulary:
gutherziger Einfall (m) = good-natured inspiration; keinen
eigenen haben zu wollen = not wishing to have a character;
untertänig = humble.

3. F. Schiller, 'Die Schaubühne als moralische Anstalt betrachtet' (1784)

[. .] Unmöglich kann ich hier den großen Einfluß übergehen,
den eine gute stehende Bühne auf den Geist der Nation haben
würde. Nationalgeist eines Volks nenne ich die Ähnlichkeit
und Übereinstimmung seiner Meinungen und Neigungen
5 bei Gegenständen, worüber eine andere Nation anders meint
und empfindet. Nur der Schaubühne ist es möglich, diese
Übereinstimmung in einem hohen Grad zu bewirken, weil
sie das ganze Gebiet des menschlichen Wissens durchwandert,
alle Situationen des Lebens erschöpft und in alle Winkel des
10 Herzens hinunter leuchtet; weil sie alle Stände und Klassen in
sich vereinigt und den gebahntesten Weg zum Verstand und
zum Herzen hat. Wenn in allen unsern Stücken *ein* Hauptzug
herrschte, wenn unsre Dichter unter sich einig werden und
einen festen Bund zu diesem Endzweck errichten wollten
15 – wenn strenge Auswahl ihre Arbeiten leitete, ihr Pinsel
nur Volksgegenständen sich weihte – mit einem Wort, wenn

wir es erlebten, eine Nationalbühne zu haben, so würden
wir auch eine Nation. Was kettete Griechenland so fest
aneinander? Was zog das Volk so unwiderstehlich nach seiner
20 Bühne? – Nichts anderes als der vaterländische Inhalt der
Stücke, der griechische Geist, das große überwältigende
Interesse des Staats, der besseren Menschheit, das in denselbigen atmete.
(*Sämtliche Werke* (Säkularausgabe), Vol. 11, p. 98.)

Commentary: (numbers in parentheses refer to line numbers
in the text)
Compare this passage with Herder's definition of *Volk*, Chapter 3, pp. 61–6: emphasis on the cohesive aspect, importance
of literature and language. Consider also the references to
ancient Greece and via classicism to *Weltliteratur*. Place the
passage also in our discussion on a *Kulturnation*. Schiller begins with the stage and comes from there to the nation (17f).
(16) reference to *Volk* (*Volksgegenständen*) as opposed to
individuals, gains in importance with the Romantics and
German Studies.

Vocabulary:
stehende Bühne (f) = established stage; Übereinstimmung
(f) = harmony, accord; Schaubühne (f) = stage; durchwandern
= to traverse; erschöpfen = to exhaust; gebahntest = most
direct; Pinsel (m) = brush; Volksgegenstand = popular object;
weihen = to dedicate to; aneinander ketten = to chain together; das in denselbigen atmete = which breathed in [the
Greek plays].

4. Friedrich Meinecke, *Weltbürgertum und Nationalstaat*

[...] Höchste geistige und sittliche Werte schafft man, indem
man sich zunächst über das Wirkliche erhebt. So hat hier der
Gedanke der Nation in Deutschland einen neuen und tieferen
Inhalt bekommen dadurch, daß man alles Politische [...]
5 zunächst einmal aus ihm ausfegte und dafür alle die geistigen

Güter, die man gewonnen hatte, in ihn hineintat. Dadurch erhob man ihn in die Sphäre des Ewigen und der Religion. Dadurch nationalisierte man die bisherige universale Bildung, und so, daß man nicht sagen konnte und wollte, wo das
10 Universale aufhöre und das Nationale begönne.

> (*Studien zur Genesis des deutschen Nationalstaates,*
> 6th edn, Munich/Berlin, 1922; p. 59f.)

Commentary:
A dangerous statement in as far as it elevates the nation to an absolute value. Positive in as far as it speaks out against chauvinism at a time of extreme nationalism (1907), attempting to bridge the cosmopoliticism of world literature with the specific values of nationhood.

Vocabulary:
sich erheben = to rise; ausfegen = to sweep out; wo das Universale ... begönne = where the universal aspects cease and the national ones begin.

Topics for further study

1. Draw up a list of some 10–15 points, listing the major characteristics of *Weltliteratur* and of *Nationalliteratur*.
2. How far is the relationship between *Weltliteratur* and *Nationalliteratur* characteristic of nineteenth century German society?
3. Describe Goethe's attitude to foreign authors, which authors was he particularly interested in? Give reasons.
4. Give a very short definition of the term 'reine Menschlichkeit' (two or three sentences).
5. Give a very short definition of the term *Volksseele*.

5

Germany's 'pedagogical province'

The following points are discussed in this Chapter: state education and its lack of involvement in socio-political developments. The 'modernisation' of the Prussian education system after the defeat by Napoleon and its implications for the whole of Germany: the attempt to create a Kulturstaat. The departure from Western European concepts and their replacement by a utopian classical ideal. The erosion of this ideal by the perceived needs of industry and commerce, by an artificial, state-induced nationalism and by the emergence of a new 'mandarin' elite. The lack of democracy and the failure to promote individual character development in the twentieth century German education system.

Neo-classicism and the emergence of patriotic education

The origins of the modern day German education system reach back to 1809, when, following Napoleon's victory over Austria and Prussia, Wilhelm von Humboldt (1767–1835) was entrusted with the reorganisation of Prussia's schools. Although in office for only 16 months, Humboldt's reforms influenced the whole of Germany and shaped educational developments up to the present day. What Goethe was to literature, Humboldt was to education and the relationship between the two men was amicable and fruitful.

However, the beginnings of the modern education system must be seen as part of a wider reform programme: with the defeat of Prussia a new social order was necessary to rejuvenate the country. A programme of modernisation involved the abolition of serfdom and the introduction of agrarian reform, the liberalisation of trade regulations and the re-organisation of the army. Such reforms sought to achieve in part what the 1789 Revolution had attempted in France: an emancipation of the middle and lower classes at the expense of the nobility (Text 1).

In Humboldt's philosophy, the education of man played an important role, being part of the neo-classical idealist concept which had emerged with Winckelmann's rediscovery of ancient Greece and found its expression in the works of those champions of *Weltliteratur*, Lessing, Goethe and Schiller. The French hegemony over German culture, perhaps not surprisingly, led reformers to turn away from Western rationalism, seeking instead to revitalise their country by a return to the values of ancient Greece, the cradle of Western civilisation. Central to these ideas was the harmonious unfolding of all human activity, an unfolding which was based on man's interaction with the universe. Chapter 4 has illustrated how the polarity of *Welterkenntnis* and *Selbsterkenntnis* developed a concept of beauty, founded on the triad of universality, totality and individuality. As part of this concept, the process of education was based on the unfolding of all human faculties, in strong contrast to the intellectual and vocational, skill-orientated pedagogy of the Enlightenment. Such a comprehensive character formation was seen as an organic evolution, cultivated in a spirit of 'Einsamkeit und Freiheit',[1] outside the confines of state authority and free from social or economic considerations (Text 2).

Humboldt's friendship with Goethe and their similar approach to human development allows us to illustrate the neo-classical concept of education with reference to Goethe's famous soliloquy in *Faust*: Faust's desire for knowledge is free of any utilitarian or political motive; in an almost mystical desire to become 'Ebenbild der Gottheit', God's equal, he feels the urge to fathom 'was die Welt im Innersten zusammenhält'[2] (the innermost secret of the universe). This cannot be achieved by conventional studies, nor can it be confined to the intellect alone. An entirely new approach is needed; a fusion of the forces of the intellect to make them accessible to human comprehension. The means for such a colossal undertaking is, once again, *Sprache*, though perhaps less in the modern sense of 'communication' and more in the Greek meaning of *logos*. Translating the opening verses of St. John's Gospel, Faust struggles to give the Greek term a meaning which transcends *Wort*, *Sinn* and *Kraft*, finally arriving at *Tat*, action.[3] Rendered in contemporary terms, language becomes the means whereby we appropriate the outside world in order to make it our own and to find our true self in the resulting harmony of one with the other. The whole process is of an aesthetic rather than a practical nature: its aim is the achievement of a synthesis between truth and beauty, of the harmonious interaction between man and universe.

A closer analysis might reveal here some of the tenets of the Enlightenment: the broad demands of a general, universal education found expression in the education formula of Pestalozzi (1746–1827), in an equal development of 'Kopf, Herz und Hand'[4] (head, heart and hand), and the Faustian interpretation of *logos* as *action* can be related to Rousseau's emphasis on *Arbeit*. The latter saw the need to bridge the void between *citoyen* and *homme naturel*,[5] and the former aimed to give a broad education to the underprivileged classes. The educational ideals of Humboldt and German neo-classicism, however, remain abstract, isolated from the concerns of citizenship within the state and remote from any practical considerations of social life. Humboldt is frequently described as having no interest in political matters and his letter to Goethe, written in France during the Revolution, is usually quoted as evidence: 'Um das Politische, wissen Sie, bekümmere ich mich nicht.'[6] (As you know, I am not concerned with politics.) However, Humboldt's philosophy of self-centred individuality was neither completely egocentric, nor totally void of political calculation. It attempted instead to liberate the individual from restrictive state intervention, reflecting the broader humanist aspirations of the age. Humboldt's essay 'Ideen zu einem Versuch, die Grenzen der Wirksamkeit des Staates zu bestimmen' (1792) (Ideas towards an attempt to define the limits of the effectiveness of the state) attributes a *Nachtwächterfunktion* (Nightwatchman's function) to the state: while the state should give material support to education, providing well-educated teachers and optimum teaching conditions, it should not interfere in education policy and should avoid becoming a *Zuchtmeister der Gesellschaft*[7] (disciplinarian of society). An education leading to human emancipation was the only means of fulfilling those aims attributed by Humboldt to the Prussian king, namely to compensate for the territorial losses of the war by intellectual and cultural achievements.[8]

Humboldt's practical results were considerable, given his short period in office. He influenced the development of the *Gymnasium*, the German grammar school, well into the twentieth century and became the founder of the modern German university. His impact on elementary education was less visible, although his initiative introduced special colleges for elementary school teachers in close proximity to Pestalozzi's theories. The *Gymnasium* became an institution for the dissemination of knowledge (*Wissenschaft*) rather than facts; it replaced the *Lateinschule* with its vocational regimentation and introduced a new breed of teacher, the *Philologe*, the 'friend of language and reason'. As a result, the *Gymnasium*'s main impetus was towards language learning, particularly the classics. Learning was a student-centred, individualistic, organic unfolding of the personality; the teacher's role was that of a helper in the gentle acquisition of knowledge. Much of the curriculum was of an aesthetic and philosophical nature with symmetry and harmony as important goals.[9] By 1810 teachers were required to have a scholarly qualification and students needed the *Abitur*[10] to enter higher education. In short, the *Gymnasium* was entirely geared towards a subsequent university career, shunning specialist education in favour of involvement with the broadest kind of knowledge.

The newly founded university in Berlin (1810), soon followed by others in Breslau, Bonn and Munich, would continue this general education. It was designed as an alternative to the existing academies which chiefly offered a vocational qualification in a single subject. In addition to academic self-government and freedom of teaching, also enjoyed by universities in other countries, Humboldt's university also gained *Lernfreiheit*, freedom for students to choose their own subjects, their own teachers and even the possibility of moving between universities. Such flexibility was possible only at the expense of a rigid curriculum and course structure; learning had become a form of quest, not unlike that in the contemporary *Bildungsroman*,[11] its goal was *Wissenschaft*, knowledge in general and self-knowledge in particular, with the ultimate aim of character development.[12] Furthermore, learning and research went hand in hand and both the traditional German *Vorlesung* (lecture) as well as the *Seminar* introduced the student into a community of academics who saw it as their continuous aim to pursue knowledge and to share the excitement of their research with their students. Humboldt's university was elitist in the sense that it strove to nurture the best minds of the country, free of any restrictive course or examination structure; it was certainly not a model for today's mass education.

Humboldt's apparent scepticism towards state interference can be explained by the nature of the contemporary state: it was illiberal, intent on defending its corporate society and incapable of perceiving the wider national trends which a liberal education programme sought to foster. The age of Fichte and Hegel saw a change in the nature of the state and such scepticism seemed no longer merited: Prussia had become the German standard bearer, firstly of political liberalisation during the 'War of Liberation' (1812–15) and later, after the 1848 Revolution, of the national vision. A comprehensive national plan for education could thus be entrusted to the state, with the ultimate aim of achieving nationhood through education. At the same time, educational policy moved away from the Humboldtian desire to integrate man into nature and turned more towards a synthesis of man with history and culture, in short with social and public issues.[13]

Fichte's own development may illustrate this. Uppermost

in his philosophy was the concept of freedom, a freedom achieved by action, in that it liberated the individual from the constraints of nature and enabled it to become truly emancipated from external pressure. At the same time, however, the individual must emerge from the eighteenth century 'Reich der Selbstsucht'[14] (age of egoism) and spur on the intellect to nobler, freer aims, thus achieving *Selbständigkeit*, Fichte's term for emancipation (Text 3). Fichte sought to achieve this by educational reform, based on the French revolutionary concept of patriotism. These ideas, particularly in his vision of a *Nationalerziehungsplan* (national concept of education), were developed in his *Reden an die deutsche Nation* (1807/8). Like Humboldt, Fichte was chiefly concerned with the development of humanism, but in contrast to Humboldt, he also emphasised the common social factor and the importance of physical work as a means of overcoming divisive class differences, 'daß dieselbe nicht Bildung eines besonderen Standes, sondern daß sie Bildung der Nation schlechthin werde'[15] (so that it does not become education of a particular class, but education of the whole nation) (Text 4). Fichte was greatly motivated by Pestalozzi's love for the common people; a love whose binding force would overcome the remnants of the corrupting influence of an egoistical society.[16] Fichte followed Pestalozzi and Rousseau in promoting the organisation of *Erziehungskolonien* (educational colonies), emphasising their comprehensive intellectual and physical vigour, but Pestalozzi's emphasis on the role of the family was replaced by that of the state. This public political element was thus strengthened and further underlined by Fichte's call for all pupils to attend the same school, irrespective of social background.

Access to university education, too, should be decided by talent and achievement, and not according to social status. Whilst universities, as far as possible, should be physically and ideologically separated from a still corrupt society, students, nevertheless, should be educated in a sense of responsibility towards the community which sponsored their education. When Fichte became *Rektor* of the newly founded Berlin University (1810), he strove to attract the best minds to Berlin, aiming to create a centre for national education for all the German-speaking countries. Berlin became a focus for young patriotic Germans, other thinkers contributing to its development with Romantic and patriotic ideas. Friedrich Ludwig Jahn, known as *Turnvater*, introduced para-military exercises and open-air gymnastics together with folk dancing and tuition in ancient German folklore. The aim of this movement was the cultivation of 'vaterländisches Gefühl'[17] (a patriotic feeling), perseverence and self-denial, ideas steeped in Romantic philosophy and epitomised in the works of the Romantic painter Caspar David Friedrich who also promoted old German traditions in opposition to a Western life-style (Figure 6).

Some of these ideas were soon to degenerate into unbridled nationalism and anti-French, even anti-Western, hyperbole which in time destroyed the new roots of German liberalism. However, we must attempt to consider the issue from various angles. Many German literary figures such as Goethe, Hegel and Jean Paul admired Napoleon as 'prince of peace'[18] and moderniser, most German rulers welcomed Napoleon and acknowledged his authority in return for territorial gains and privileges. In contrast to these admirers of Napoleon, other factions, particularly within Prussia, were able to draw on the newly generated patriotic climate: the War of Liberation, though in the first instance a struggle against Napoleon, was also an attempt to liberate the German population from the internal despotism of its own princes and to aspire to constitutional government and – ultimately – a German nation state. Students from the new university of Berlin, which became the centre for 'national-liberal' activities, played a leading part in this development. They formed *Landsmannschaften*, with individual houses accommodating students from the various German states. Under the influence of patriots such as Jahn and Fichte, the *Landsmannschaften* began to form into an all German *Deutsche Burschenschaft*:

Figure 6: Caspar David Friedrich, *Zwei Männer in Betrachtung des Mondes*, 1819; the two men wear *altdeutsche Tracht*, the Romantics' portrayal of medieval dress. The painting was executed in the year of the *Karlsbader Beschlüsse* and Friedrich is alleged to have commented: 'Die machen demagogische Umtriebe' (They are up to demagogic activities). The subject-matter and the comment suggest that the picture is dedicated to the re-awakening of German national feeling; the partially uprooted oak tree symbolises an ailing Germany and the fir trees to the right represent the greening of a new Christian spirit. (Printed with the kind permission of *Bruckmann Verlag*, Munich; book by G. Unverfehrt, *Caspar David Friedrich*, Munich, 1984)

its aim was not only the formation of a democratic German nation state, but also to oppose the class system, particularly the duelling activities of the aristocratic corps at the universities.[19] Many of these patriotic sentiments were ill-defined and romantic; black, red and gold, allegedly the colours of the Holy Roman Empire, were chosen as the national emblem. In 1817 a vast gathering met at the Wartburg castle to celebrate the three hundredth anniversary of the Reformation and the recent defeat of Napoleon. The patriotic liberal movement was soon to be suppressed by the newly established

'German Confederation' (*Deutscher Bund*), but would re-emerge during the 1848 Revolution, discussed in the next Chapter.

The impact of industrialisation on the German education system

We have seen how the neo-classical education system managed to engender a spirit of patriotism and democracy amongst students and teachers. This development was not entirely devoid of romantic and chauvinistic trends and the process of industrialisation was to prove a severe test of its adaptability. The reasons for the emerging problems were in part to be found within the idealistic concepts of German neo-classicism, but were also the result of the German Confederation's policy of repression and reaction which stifled patriotic aspirations and prevented the development of Fichte's proclaimed *Selbständigkeit*. Three weaknesses in particular characterised education at the beginning of the industrial age: the old preference given to private over public virtues,[20] rooted in Humboldt's extreme individualism, the priority of the arts, particularly the classical languages, over sciences and pragmatic learning and finally the failure to bring about a reconciliation between a still rather elitist education system and nineteenth century social developments.

A brief resumé of major political and social changes since the inception of the Humboldtian system will illustrate its shortcomings in the new industrial age. The demise of the Holy Roman Empire of the German Nation in 1806 and the defeat of Napoleon in 1813/14 ushered in a new political order. The Vienna Congress (1815), far from rewarding those sections of society – amongst them the university circles – which had contributed to the defeat of Napoleon, resorted instead to an extremely reactionary strategy, hoping to reverse the advances in freedom and democracy achieved since the French Revolution. The concepts of *fraternité*, *liberté* and *egalité* were perverted into the fraternity of the three rulers of Austria, Prussia and Russia who together formed the Holy

Alliance. Liberal principles were suppressed in favour of censorship and political persecution, particularly in evidence at the universities; and with the promise of democratic constitutions rescinded, a system based on a loose confederation of some forty 'souveräne Fürsten und freie Städte'[21] (sovereign princes and free cities), known as the *Deutsche Bund*, took its place.

Article I of the Holy Alliance defined fraternity in a particularly reactionary manner:

> Entsprechend den Worten der Heiligen Schrift, welche allen Menschen heißt sich als Brüder zu betrachten, werden die drei Monarchen vereinigt bleiben durch die Bande einer wahren und unauflöslichen Brüderlichkeit, [...] indem sie sich ihren Untertanen und Heeren gegenüber als Familienväter betrachten [...], um Religion, Frieden und Gerechtigkeit zu schützen.[22]

(In accordance with the words of Holy Scripture, which instructs all men to consider themselves as brothers, the three monarchs will remain united through the bonds of a true and inseparable fraternity ... in that they consider themselves *vis-à-vis* their subjects and armies as fathers of a family ... in order to protect religion, peace and justice.)

Though fairly low key until the mid 1830s, when Nuremberg and Erlangen became the first cities to be linked by rail and the economist Friedrich List instituted the formation of a customs union, *Deutscher Zollverein* (1834), with Prussia as the dominant state, social and economic changes now began to develop at a very rapid pace. During the last two thirds of the nineteenth century the German population more than doubled and the ratio of rural population to townspeople changed from 1:3 to 5:4.[23] Cities expanded rapidly, Berlin growing more than fivefold during this time. Productivity too increased at breathtaking speed: iron production rose nearly thirtyfold between 1834 and 1900. Considering these changes, it is little wonder that we also witness a new public consciousness. The values of humanism, of metaphysical

abstract philosophy and of individualism gave way to a preoccupation with science and technology, with positivism and
to the emergence of mass movements such as socialism and
nationalism. Compared with Britain and France, Germany
still lagged behind in these developments, but the emerging
changes were sufficiently forceful to affect its education system. However, the growing bifurcation between the reactionary policy of the *Deutsche Bund* and the economic and
social process of modernisation ensured that a consistent
education policy failed to develop, in contrast to other Western European countries.

Elementary school education This was least affected by neo-
classical ideas and had been strongly influenced by Pestalozzi's
Volksbildung. His idea was to educate the poorer elements of
society and the rural population as a means of moulding them
in the cause of an ethical rejuvenation of the *Volk*, based on
the Christian values of family life. We have seen how Fichte,
influenced by Pestalozzi, attempted to politicise these ideas
towards a greater autonomy for the common people. As a
result of such efforts, elementary school teachers became more
aware of social change and were eager to play a full part in
the emancipation both of their pupils and their local, usually
rural communities. These new teachers, themselves often from
the lower social strata, showed missionary zeal in their
attempt to eradicate illiteracy, educating their children in the
new spirit of national liberalism through a wide-ranging,
generally useful curriculum.

Adolf Diesterweg, director of several influential seminaries
for teachers in Prussia (1820–47), played a particularly important role in disseminating a progressive *Volksbildung*. He
ceaselessly promoted a philosophy reflecting the spirit of the
Enlightenment, encouraging a modern attitude towards religion and combatting orthodoxy and mechanical learning (Text
5). He also encouraged the formation of teachers' associations and an ethos of professionalism. His democratic liberalism influenced the political role played by elementary school
teachers during the 1848 Revolution: an *Allgemeiner Deutscher*

Lehrerverein was founded, which demanded the abolition of the existing tripartite school system in favour of comprehensive education, the replacement of church control by secular authorities and an improved social status for elementary school teachers.[24] After the Revolution had been suppressed, this type of school suffered the severest restriction. The Prussian king blamed the teachers and the directors of seminaries in particular:

All das Elend, das im verflossenen Jahr über Preußen hereingebrochen ist, ist Ihre, einzig Ihre Schuld, die Schuld der Afterbildung, der irreligiösen Massenweisheit, die Sie als echte Weisheit verbreiten, mit der Sie den Glauben und die Treue in dem Gemüt meiner Untertanen ausgerottet und deren Herzen von mir abgewandt haben.[25]

(All the misery, which in the bygone year has befallen Prussia, is your, and only your fault, the fault of pseudo-education, of irreligious mass-wisdom, which you spread about as genuine wisdom and with which you have eradicated faith and loyalty in the minds of my subjects and with which you have turned their hearts away from me.)

The clock was turned back a generation by the *Stiehlsche Regulative* (1854), whose author, Ferdinand Stiehl, served as co-ordinator of elementary schools and teacher seminaries until 1872. His decree insisted on strict orthodox adherence to religion in all educational matters, on the indoctrination of love for the monarchy and on an exclusively practical and vocational attitude towards learning (Text 6). Teaching was to be restricted to the 'three Rs', folk singing and religious education were given a new prominence, the mechanical learning by heart of the catechism became the rule. Teachers were no longer instructed in pedagogy and the reading of classical German literature, of Goethe and Schiller, was forbidden, even in their own time. Whilst this decree was not universally observed, it undoubtedly hindered the preparation of young people for the industrial age. By 1870 the old-fashioned restrictive education which had become a handicap to Germany's industrial development was under attack by the industrialist and liberal politician Friedrich Wilhelm Harkort:

> Gleich wie der Hindu durch Kasten, so drücken wir durch Mangel an Unterricht den unteren Ständen den Stempel der Dienstbarkeit fürs Leben auf. In Beziehung auf das Volk kann von unseren gelehrten Schulen nicht die Rede sein. Nur die Bemittelten können der bedeutenden Kosten wegen die höheren Lehranstalten und Privatinstitute besuchen.[26]
> (Like the Hindu caste system, we too impress on to the lower social classes the seal of life-long servitude through lack of education. Our learned schools do not relate to the people. Only the well-off can attend the more advanced schools and private institutes on account of their considerable costs.)

By 1870 the term *Volksbildung* had completely changed its meaning. No longer a national education programme with the aim of democratic self-government, as understood by Fichte, it had become instead the education of the common people in a spirit of submission to the authority of the state.

Following a further advance in industrialisation after German unification in 1871, the needs of industry demanded a much greater emphasis on industrial training and vocational education, particularly as the erosion of the old guilds and the introduction of total free trade had seen a virtual collapse of the system of apprenticeship and training. Georg Kerschensteiner (1854–1932), an education reformer from Bavaria, brought about a fundamental change which still dominates today's vocational training and further education in Germany. By achieving the synthesis of Pestalozzi's *Volksbildung* with some of the neo-classical concepts of general education and humanism, he devised an educational programme which gave respectability to manual and vocational work. He also liberated the humanist ideals from their restriction to intellectual and cultural matters, opening the whole system of education to twentieth century social and political imperatives. Kerschensteiner was interested in character formation, in the education of a work-force which would take an active part in social and political developments in the public sphere. This would lend dignity to the workplace and engender a sense of public responsibility in ordinary workers by educating them in the realisation of citizenship. His principle is encapsulated in the words: 'In allen Schulen müssen wie die geistigen und moralischen, so auch die manuellen Fähigkeiten entfaltet werden.'[27] (All schools must develop intellectual and ethical, as well as practical abilities.)

Kerschensteiner's concept of *Arbeitsschule* and *Berufsschule* laid the foundation of Germany's dual system of vocational training. Practical skills obtained at the workplace were complemented by a general and moral education given in state schools. These schools educated young people in a spirit of discipline and obedience towards the state, a very characteristic aspect of Germany's political culture, designed to protect young people from the 'Irrlehren der Sozialdemokratie'[28] (heresy of social democracy). At the same time, they also taught business German, accountancy and general science, thus providing their pupils with specific skills which would contribute towards their craftsmanship (Text 7).

The *Gymnasium* Although seen to prosper during this period of industrialisation, it was to prove less able to adjust to the demands of a modern industrial society. A very brief analysis of the *Gymnasium* curriculum will demonstrate its shortcomings: whereas the *Gymnasium* in Prussia in 1816 gave pride of place to languages at the expense of mathematics and sciences in a ratio of 19:6, this ratio had changed by 1859 to one of 15:11, but widened again by 1901 to a ratio of nearly 3:1.[29] The battle for the curriculum alone demonstrates an obvious reluctance on the part of the *Gymnasium* to embrace the new tendencies inherent in industrialisation. Geared towards university education and having abandoned its original aim of becoming a school for a wide section of society, in favour of providing an elitist education, it was less preoccupied with the concerns of industrialisation. In particular its *Berechtigungswesen*, the 'right to certain positions', gradually became a bastion of conservatism. Whilst the *Gymnasium* had at first managed to break down barriers between the bourgeoisie and the nobility, by the middle of the century it had itself erected new barriers to produce an 'educational nobility', which served in higher positions in the civil service and the army, their education based almost exclusively on neo-classical ideas and an upper middle-class culture. The *Einjährige*, introduced in 1818 and enforced until 1914, meant that the *Abitur*, the *Gymnasium* leaving certificate, entitled a young man to 1 year's military service as opposed to 3 years for other school leavers. It also bestowed on its holder officer status and other important social privileges.[30]

This reactionary social tendency of self selection and its rejection of technological progress, brought the Gymnasium under increasing suspicion from political circles. In an age of burgeoning nationalism, its cosmopolitan outlook and emphasis on classical languages became increasingly suspect. Whilst Latin was tolerated as the language of church and state administration, Greek came to be seen as the language of insurrection.[31] The place of Greek, mathematics and the natural sciences was reduced in the syllabus and the *Gymnasium* became even further removed from the needs of an industrialised society. As a consequence, the new *Realschulen*, concentrating on natural sciences and modern languages, gained in importance. Finally, a third type of higher school, the *Oberrealschule* came to prominence on the grounds of its nationalist, 'German' outlook. At the 1890 *Schulkonferenz* the young German Kaiser expressed his preference for these newer schools, since they seemed more effective in fighting the upsurge of socialism and had taken the lead in a German national education system showing strong para-military aspects. His speech illustrates the new nationalist tone:

Wenn die Schule das getan hätte, was von ihr zu verlangen ist, ... so hätte sie von vornherein von selber das Gefecht

gegen die Sozialdemokratie aufnehmen müssen. ... Wir müssen als Grundlage für das Gymnasium das Deutsche nehmen; wir sollen nationale junge Deutsche erziehen und nicht junge Griechen und Römer.[32]
(If the school had done what was expected of it, ... then it would have from the beginning and of its own accord taken up the fight against social democracy. ... German must become the basis for the Gymnasium; we must educate young Germans and not young Greeks and Romans.)

By the end of the nineteenth century the *Realgymnasium* and even the *Oberrealschule* were given the right to award the *Abitur*, even though their students were somewhat restricted in the choice of subject which could be studied at university. **University education** This followed similar trends. The Humboldtian university increasingly saw itself in competition with the new polytechnics and technical high schools (*Technische Hochschulen*). Their development had begun in the larger cities during the 1820s and 1830s, but it was only at the turn of the century that they were empowered to award doctorates in specific subjects such as engineering. High unemployment amongst graduates from the arts and humanities increased the pressure felt by traditional universities and by the end of the century, the feeling of a cultural crisis was widespread. The existing culture was seen as under threat, from the masses and from French socialism on the one hand, and on the other from the Manchester school of *laissez-faire* economics and in particular from positivism.[33] As a result, there emerged at one extreme a youth culture which sought a radical break with the Wilhelminian tradition and attempted to escape into pre-industrial life-styles and a utopian world of natural, free education. At the other extreme, we witness the emergence of the mandarin type. The term *mandarin* was adapted from the Chinese to denote 'a social and cultural elite owing its status primarily to educational qualifications, rather than to hereditary rights or wealth'.[34] The term related specifically to those university teachers who – increasingly threatened by the new tendencies, not least in their material position – attempted to counter this threat by an exaggerated self-esteem in regard to their specialist education and with recourse to a fiercely nationalist and ultimately racist position. This German academic intelligentsia featured frequently as a pressure group which sought to become politically involved in the education of the young nation and to play the role of a German *Kulturträger* (guardian of culture). Social mobility within their own ranks was almost halted, more than ninety per cent of all university professors came themselves from an academic background.[35]

The new discipline of *Geisteswissenschaften* accelerated this development. The term, though derived from John Stuart Mill's concept of 'moral science', developed in opposition to the natural sciences, with the study of man as its central object. Although harking back in many respects to the neo-classical relationship of self and world, its defensive attitude towards positivist studies, together with a subjective, value-orientated outlook often gave it a conservative, even reactionary nature. This was seen particularly clearly in the promotion of a *Weltanschauung*, a world view, determined by time, place, ethnic origin and religion and directed against empirical research, in that it was associated with the human faculties of thought, will and feeling.[36] Its advocates turned away from Western cognitive traditions to adopt an attitude described by Max Weber as *Gesinnungsethik*, an idealised ethical standpoint, separated from any political responsibility.[37]

Fritz K. Ringer saw the traditional German concept of the *Kulturstaat* as the root of such a non-political attitude, which would in time assume an increasingly right-wing position:

> With few exceptions, all the German academics dreamed of a state or of a political party which would create social harmony out of conflict, which would be guided by cultural and ethical objectives and by the ideal of German greatness in world affairs.[38]

Such a vision was of course dangerous and led eventually to the subversion of intellectual aspirations by political power and reason, manifested in an anti-democratic, anti-semitic and fiercely nationalistic stance. The anti-democratic notion, though by no means limited to the German scene,[39] began its influential re-emergence in late nineteenth century Germany where it joined other conservative elements in a denunciation of social democracy. Science and French positivism were held responsible for 'die leeren Ideale eines Staates, der nach den Grundsätzen der Gleichheit geregelt ist.'[40] (the empty ideals of a state which is regulated by the principles of equality.) Before 1928 no Social Democrats were to be found in the ranks of German professors,[41] and whilst a number of modernists amongst them spoke up for liberal principles, even their attitude towards democracy was somewhat strange.

The development of a nationalist *Weltanschauung* led many German intellectuals into the 'pseudo-idealistic world of anti-semitism and aggressive nationalism'.[42] Anti-semitism in university circles was of a largely indirect and subtle nature. Indeed, the percentage of orthodox Jews amongst German university teachers was high, but few of them managed to attain the position of fully salaried professor. The explanation for this lies mainly in the strong representation of the *Alldeutsche Verband* (Pan-Germanic League) among German professors who supported its aggressive nationalist cultural policy and spoke up for the expansion of a German navy. These so-called *Flottenprofessoren* preached the cultural and moral supremacy of the new Germany, directed in particular against imperialist British policies.[43]

The situation reached its climax with the outbreak of the First World War (1914). Celebrated by many mandarins as the victory of idealism over politics, as the resurgence of those moral and irrational *völkisch* forces that had been suppressed by the materialism of technological modernity,[44] the War was seen as a *Kulturkrieg*, in which German culture had to assert itself against Western civilisation. A surprisingly large number of German university professors felt obliged to make public speeches in favour of the war effort, emphasising that there was no divide between the 'Prussian' military leadership and the representatives of German culture.[45] One of the most vehement condemnations of the British 'trader spirit' issued from the economist Werner Sombart, who saw the War as the confrontation between two world views, the (British) trader and the (German) hero:

> Trader and hero: they constitute the two great opposites, the two poles, as it were, of all human orientation . . . The trader approaches life with the question: what can you give me . . . The hero approaches life with the question: what can I give you [. . .] The trader speaks only of 'rights', the hero only of his 'duties'.
>
> [The trader] regards the whole existence of man on earth as a sum of commercial transactions which everyone makes as favourably as possible for himself [. . .] Within this conception of life, material values will thus be given an important place. [. . .] Consequently, economic interests will . . . gradually subordinate other aspects of life.[46]

Sombart's outpourings are, however, not isolated. Thomas Mann's infamous quarrel with his brother Heinrich epitomised the confrontation between German 'Kultur' and French civilisation, the latter standing for the decadent Western values of the Enlightenment, the former for 'Natur, Geschlossenheit, Stil, Form, Haltung, Geschmack, [. . .] geistige Organisation der Welt, und sei das alles auch noch so skurril, wild, blutig und furchtbar.'[47] (nature, wholeness, style, form, attitude, taste [. . .] intellectual organisation of the world, however scurrilous, wild, bloody and terrible this might be.) . . .

Heinrich Mann is himself an example of the existence of another school of German mandarins, amongst them famous names such as Max and Alfred Weber, Friedrich Meinecke, Ernst Troeltsch, Ferdinand Tönnies, Georg Simmel and many others. Following Germany's defeat, they gave their support to the newly established Weimar Republic, pledging to work constructively 'within the framework of the existing democratic-republican political order'.[48] Some former critics of democracy, such as Thomas Mann, later demonstrated a change of mind, speaking up openly and courageously for the new democratic order, even during the advent of fascism. A majority of German intellectuals and writers, however, returned to pre-modern concepts, rejecting the rationalist and liberal principles of the Enlightenment in favour of a nationalist *Bindung* (involvement). The *Konservative Revolution*, an ideological counter-movement, opposed to socialism and Western values, was determined to restore the monarchy and some form of corporate state. Its chief protagonists were the writer Arthur Moeller van den Bruck, the Austrian sociologist Othmar Spann, the publicist Ernst Niekisch, and also such eminent poets as Stefan George, Gottfried Benn, Ernst Jünger and Hugo von Hofmannsthal. There is little doubt that their fiercely anti-democratic stance did much to formulate an anti-Western view which bridged the gap between nationalism and socialism to pave the way for a 'Third Reich'[49] and help Hitler to power. Most university professors and an even larger percentage of students had expressed their contempt for Western democratic 'Positionen und Begriffe im Kampf mit Weimar, Genf, Versailles',[50] condemning the integration of the new Republic into the international spirit of the League of Nations and interpreting the peace of Versailles as *Schandfrieden* (peace of shame).

The position after the Second World War was different, in that a policy of re-education was imposed by the allied forces, aided by a general desire amongst Germans to put the dark chapter of National Socialism behind them. However, a closer study of the education policy in the Western zones in the first phase of post-war Germany (until 1965) would demonstrate that the reactionary forces still attempted a comeback. A notable study, *Education and Society in Modern Germany*, came to the conclusion in 1949 that 'conservative and nationalistic professors block the path of progress'[51] and the radical critic Luc Joachimsen published a devastating critique of the

German education system at the height of the education reform movement (1971). Discussing the relationship between state and school she declares:

Ich meine die Zusammenhänge zwischen den in Reih und Glied lernenden 'ABC-Schützen' und den in Reih und Glied marschierenden Todesschützen. Ich meine die Zusammenhänge zwischen 'braven' Befehlsempfängern vor der Schultafel und niemals auch nur eine Frage gedacht habenden Befehlsempfängern in Auschwitz. [...] Ich meine die Zusammenhänge zwischen dem Aussortieren und Auslesen von Eliteschülern mit Herrenbewußtsein und Durchschnittsschülern mit Sklavenbewußtsein und der Verteilung von Herrenvölkern und Sklavenvölkern über die Erde.[52]

(I mean the connection between the ABC learners who learn in rank and file formation and the sharpshooters marching in battle formation.

I mean the connection between honest obedience in front of the blackboard and the obedience in Auschwitz of those who had never thought of questioning a command. [...]

I mean the connection between the selection of elite students with a master attitude and average students with the attitude of slaves and the distribution of a master race and a slave population across the globe.)

Our final Chapter will attempt to answer what at the moment must remain the anxious question as to how far the German education system has managed to adapt to the demands of a modern Western, democratic industrial society and where shortcomings and pitfalls still exist within it.

Notes

1 W. von Humboldt, *Werke*, Vol. 4, A. Flitner und K. Giel (eds), Darmstadt: Wissenschaftliche Buchgesellschaft, 1964; p. 191.
2 J. W. Goethe, *Faust, Der Tragödie erster und zweiter Teil* (Hamburger Ausgabe), E. Trunz (ed.), Verses 382f.

3   *ibid.* verses 1224–1237
4   J. H. Pestalozzi, 'Wie Gertrud ihre Kinder lehrt', in A. Reble (ed.), *Geschichte der Pädagogik, Dokumentationsband*, 2nd edn, Stuttgart: Klett-Cotta, 1992; in particular pp. 362–77.
5   J. J. Rousseau, *Emile ou de l'éducation*, F. and P. Richard (eds), Paris, 1964; p. 225f.
6   W. von Humboldt, 'Letter to Goethe', in F. Meinecke, *Weltbürgertum und Nationalstaat*, Munich/Berlin: R. Oldenbourg, 1915; p. 12.
7   E. Spranger, *Wilhelm von Humboldt und die Reform des Bildungswesens*, Tübingen: Niemeyer, 1960; pp. 56f, 204f.
8   M. Behnen, 'Deutschland unter Napoleon. Retauration und Vormärz (1806–1847)', in Vogt (ed.), *Deutsche Geschichte*, p. 362.
9   For a good example see Goethe, *Wilhelm Meisters Wanderjahre*, 2. Buch, 1. Kapitel.
10 Edict of 1810: 'Prüfung der Kandidaten des höheren Schulamts', and Edict of 1812: 'Prüfung der zu den Universitäten übergehenden Schüler', in Reble, *Dokumentationsband*, pp. 407, 409.
11 Chief type of German novel. Main character acquires his education as character formation in close exchange and interchange with his environment. Of particular importance are the experience of love, nature, friendship, art and culture.
12 '... und dem Staat ist es ebensowenig als der Menschheit um Wissen und Reden, sondern um Charakter und Handeln zu tun'. W. von Humboldt, 'Über die innere und äußere Organisation der höheren wissenschaftlichen Anstalten in Berlin', *Schriften zur Anthologie und Bildungslehre*, A. Flitner (ed.), Frankfurt a.M.: Klett-Cotta, 1984; p. 84.
13 Reble, *Geschichte der Pädagogik*, Vol. 1, 17th edn, Stuttgart: Klett-Cotta, 1993; p. 203.
14 Fichte, *Reden an die deutsche Nation*, p. 3.
15 *ibid.* p. 16
16 *ibid.* p. 32
17 H. Ueberhorst (ed.), *Friedrich Ludwig Jahn 1778/1978*, Bonn–Bad Godesberg: Inter Nationes, 1978; p. 51ff.
18 Kohn, *The Mind of Germany*, p. 73.
19 U. Schlicht, *Vom Burschenschaftler bis zum Sponti*, Berlin: Colloquium, 1980; pp. 15–21.
20 cf. Dahrendorf, *Society and Democracy in Germany*, chapter 3.
21 Behnen, 'Deutschland unter Napoleon', p. 365.
22 Quoted from W. Mönch, *Deutsche Kultur, Von der Aufklärung bis zur Gegenwart*, 2nd edn, Munich: Hübner, 1971; p. 258.
23 Reble, *Geschichte der Pädagogik*, Vol. 1, p. 251f.
24 For the text of the proclamation cf. Reble, *Dokumentationsband*, p. 471.
25 Quoted from B. Michael and H. H. Schepp (eds), *Politik und Schule von der Französischen Revolution bis zur Gegenwart*, Vol. 1, Frankfurt a.M.: Athenäum, 1973; p. 313f.

26 F. Harkort, 'Bemerkungen über die preußische Volksschule und ihre Lehrer', in Harkort, *Schriften und Reden zu Volksschule und Volksbildung*, K. E. Jeismann (ed.), Paderborn: Schöningh, 1969; p. 12.

27 G. Kerschensteiner, *Wesen und Wert des naturwissenschaftlichen Unterrichts*, Leipzig: Teubner, 1914; p. 38.

28 Quoted from H. Blankertz, *Die Geschichte der Pädagogik von der Aufklärung bis zur Gegenwart*, Wetzlar: Büchse der Pandorra, 1982; p. 208.

29 Reble, *Dokumentationsband*, pp. 412, 459, 464.

30 cf. K. E. Jeismann, *Das preußische Gymnasium in Staat und Gesellschaft*, Stuttgart: Klett-Cotta, 1974; p. 360.

31 Blankertz, p. 168.

32 'Eröffnungsansprache zur Schulkonferenz 1890', in Blankertz, p. 170.

33 F. K. Ringer, *The Decline of the German Mandarins. The German Academic Community, 1890–1933*, Cambridge, MA: Harvard University Press, 1969; pp. 146–8.

34 *ibid.* p. 5

35 For a more detailed breakdown of figures cf. Ringer, *The Decline of the German Mandarins*, pp. 39–42.

36 *ibid.* pp. 315–20

37 cf. M. Weber, 'Politik als Beruf' [1919], in *Gesammelte politische Schriften*, J. Winckelmann (ed.), Tübingen: Mohr, 1988; p. 551ff.

38 Ringer, *The Decline of the German Mandarins*, p. 134.

39 cf. J. Carey, *The Intellectuals and the Masses*, London: Faber and Faber, 1992, and J. Ortega Y Gasset, *The Revolt of the Masses*, London: Allen and Unwin, 1932.

40 W. Dilthey, *Über die Möglichkeit einer allgemeingültigen pädagogischen Wissenschaft*, H. Nohl (ed.), Weinheim (n.d.), p. 85.

41 Ringer, *The Decline of the German Mandarins*, p. 141.

42 *ibid.* p. 135

43 *ibid.* p. 139f

44 *ibid.* p. 180

45 *ibid.* p. 182f

46 *ibid.* p. 183f [translation by Ringer, German version in Ringer, *Die Gelehrten*, Munich: Klett-Cotta, 1987; p. 171f.

47 Th. Mann, 'Gedanken im Kriege', *Neue Rundschau*, Vol. 2 (1914), p. 1471.

48 Ringer, *The Decline of the German Mandarins*, p. 202.

49 For a closer study cf. K. Sontheimer, *Deutschland zwischen Demokratie und Antidemokratie*, Munich: Nymphenburger Verlagsbuchhandlung, 1971; pp. 38–114; P. D. Stachura, *The German Youth Movement 1900–1945*, London: MacMillan, 1981, Chapter I,4; W. Laqueur, *Young Germany: a History of the German Youth Movement*, London: Transaction Books, 1962; F. K. Ringer, *The Decline of the German Mandarins*, in particular the Conclusion; G. K. Kaltenbrunner, 'Von Dostojewski zum Dritten Reich', in *Politische Studien* 20 (1969), 184–200.

50 C. Schmitt, *Positionen und Begriffe im Kampf mit Weimar, Genf, Versailles*, Hamburg: Duncker und Humbold, 1940.
51 R. H. Samuel and R. Hinton-Thomas, *Education and Society in Modern Germany*, London: Routledge and Kegan, 1949; p. 179.
52 L. Jochimsen, *Hinterhöfe der Nation. Die deutsche Grundschulmisere*, Reinbek bei Hamburg: Rowohlt, 1971; p. 66.

Suggestions for further reading

Blankertz, H., *Die Geschichte der Pädagogik von der Aufklärung bis zur Gegenwart*, Wetzlar: Büchse der Pandorra, 1982.
Laqueur, W., *Young Germany: a History of the German Youth Movement*, London: Transaction Books, 1962.
Reble, A., *Geschichte der Pädagogik*, 17th edn, Stuttgart: Klett-Cotta, 1993.
Ringer, F. K., *The Decline of the German Mandarins. The German Academic Community 1890–1933*, Cambridge, MA: Harvard University Press, 1969.
Samuel, R. H. and Hinton-Thomas, R., *Education and Society in Modern Germany*, London: Routledge and Kegan, 1949.

Textual studies

1. Wilhelm von Humboldt, 'Antrag auf Errichtung der Universität Berlin', Juli 1809 [Letter to the Prussian King, excerpts]

Weit entfernt, daß das Vertrauen, welches ganz Deutschland ehemals zu dem Einfluß Preußens auf wahre Aufklärung und höhere Geistesbildung hegte, durch die letzten unglücklichen Ereignisse gesunken sei, so ist es vielmehr gestiegen. Man hat
5 gesehen, welcher Geist in allen neueren Staatseinrichtungen Ew. Königl. Majestät herrscht, und mit welcher Bereitwilligkeit, auch in großen Bedrängnissen, wissenschaftliche Institute unterstützt und verbessert worden sind. [...] Nur solche höhere Institute können ihren Einfluß auch über die
10 Grenzen des Staates hinaus erstrecken. Wenn Ew. Königl. Majestät nunmehr diese Einrichtung feierlich bestätigten und die Ausführung sicherten; so würden Sie sich aufs neue alles, was sich in Deutschland für Bildung und Aufklärung interessiert, auf das Festeste verbinden: einen neuen Eifer und
15 neue Wärme für das Wiederaufblühen Ihres Staates erregen, und in einem Zeitpunkte, wo ein Teil Deutschlands vom Kriege verheert, ein anderer in fremder Sprache von fremden

Gebietern beherrscht wird, der deutschen Wissenschaft eine vielleicht kaum jetzt noch gehoffte Freistatt eröffnen.
(Wilhelm von Humboldt, *Werke*, A. Flitner and K. Giel (eds), Vol. IV, Klett-Cotta: 1964; p. 113f.)

Commentary: (numbers in parentheses refer to line numbers in the text)
The letter emphasises the importance of university education for political ends, for the development of a national German consciousness. It also demonstrates its indebtedness to the Enlightenment and to the rebuilding of Prussia and ultimately Germany in a modern, enlightened fashion.
(16) Refers to French domination over Germany. The whole of Southern Germany, the Rhineland and the kingdom of Westphalia were under French influence.

Vocabulary:
ehemals = in former times; Geistesbildung (f) = cultivation of the mind; hegen = to cultivate; Ew. Königl Majestät (f) = Your Royal Majesty; Bereitwilligkeit (f) = readiness; Bedrängnis (f) = affliction; bestätigten und sicherten (11–12) = subjunctive; Eifer (m) = fervour; Freistatt (f) = sanctuary.

2. Über die innere und äußere Organisation der höheren wissenschaftlichen Anstalten in Berlin [1810]

[...] Da diese Anstalten ihren Zweck indes nur erreichen können, wenn jede, soviel als immer möglich, der reinen Idee der Wissenschaft gegenübersteht, so sind Einsamkeit und Freiheit die in ihrem Kreise vorwaltenden Prinzipien. Da
5 aber auch das geistige Wirken in der Menschheit nur als Zusammenwirken gedeiht, und zwar nicht bloß, damit einer ersetze, was dem anderen mangelt, sondern damit die gelingende Tätigkeit des einen den anderen begeistere und allen die allgemeine, ursprüngliche, in den einzelnen nur
10 einzeln oder abgeleitet hervorstrahlende Kraft sichtbar werde, so muß die innere Organisation dieser Anstalten ein ununterbrochenes, sich immer selbst wieder belebendes, aber unge-

zwungenes und absichtsloses Zusammenwirken hervorbringen
und unterhalten.

15 [...] daß bei der inneren Organisation der höheren
wissenschaftlichen Anstalten alles darauf beruht, das Prinzip
zu erhalten, die Wissenschaft als etwas noch nicht ganz
Gefundenes und nie ganz Aufzufindendes zu betrachten und
unablässig als solches zu suchen.

20 Sobald man aufhört, eigentlich Wissenschaft zu suchen, oder
sich einbildet, sie brauche nicht aus der Tiefe des Geistes
heraus geschaffen, sondern könne durch Sammeln extensiv
aneinandergereiht werden, so ist alles unwiederbringlich und
auf ewig verloren; verloren für die Wissenschaft [...] und
25 verloren für den Staat. Denn nur die Wissenschaft, die aus
dem Innern stammt und ins Innere gepflanzt werden kann,
bildet auch den Charakter um, und dem Staat ist es ebenso
wenig als der Menschheit um Wissen und Reden, sondern um
Charakter und Handeln zu tun.

(Wilhelm von Humboldt, *Schriften zur Anthropologie und
Bildungslehre*, A. Flitner (ed.), Ullstein, 1984; pp. 82–4.)

Commentary: (numbers in parentheses refer to line numbers
in the text)
The passage contains three major ideas: (a) 'Einsamkeit und
Freiheit' are essential for the pure perception and acquisition
of knowledge. Knowledge must therefore not be related to a
political or other end (1–4); (b) the pursuit of knowledge
must happen within a community of like-minded people, but
in such a way that they stimulate each other without domination or personal interference (5–14); (c) the acquisition of
knowledge is a neverending, life-long process, it cannot be
taught within a course structure. Its pursuit will lead to character formation, to true emancipation and will thereby lead
to political consciousness (15–29).

Vocabulary:
vorwaltend = prevailing; gedeihen = to prosper; hervorstrahlen
= to radiate; Aufzufindendes (n) = that which can be traced
or discovered; unablässig = incessant; Sammeln (n) =

accumulation; aneinanderreihen = to string together; unwiederbringlich = irrevocably.

3. Johann Gottlieb Fichte, *Reden an die deutsche Nation* (1807/8)

Was seine Selbständigkeit verloren hat, hat zugleich verloren
das Vermögen, einzugreifen in den Zeitfluß und den Inhalt
desselben frei zu bestimmen; es wird ihm, wenn es in diesem
Zustande verharrt, seine Zeit, und es selber mit dieser seiner
5 Zeit, abgewickelt durch die fremde Gewalt, die über sein
Schicksal gebietet, es hat von nun an gar keine eigene Zeit
mehr, sondern zählt seine Jahre nach den Begebenheiten und
Abschnitten fremder Völkerschaften und Reiche. [. . .] In
dieser Weise demnach werden diese Reden eine Fortsetzung
10 der ehemals gehaltenen Vorlesungen über die damals
gegenwärtige Zeit sein, indem sie enthüllen werden das neue
Zeitalter, das der Zerstörung des Reichs der Selbstsucht durch
fremde Gewalt unmittelbar folgen kann und soll.

(Reden an die deutsche Nation, R. Eucken (ed.)
1. Rede, Insel, 1909; p. 2f.)

Commentary: (numbers in parentheses refer to line numbers
in the text)
Fichte describes the relationship between *Selbständigkeit* as
independence and freedom of thought, and political emancipation. 'Was' (1) refers to the subject in general, to 'das Ich'
in particular. 'Fremde Gewalt' (5) refers primarily to foreign
rule, but can also be seen as any other form of outside domination. The loss of one's own time (6) is equivalent to the
loss of independence. The *Reden* are seen as a continuation
(cf. 9f) of *Die Grundzüge des gegenwärtigen Zeitalters* (1804),
in which Fichte describes the Romantic time-scale as moving
from original innocence via an age of sinfulness and egoism
into a new age of *Vernunftkunst* where man has found his
intellect in order to achieve complete reconciliation with the
world and society.

Vocabulary:
Vermögen (n) = ability; eingreifen = to intervene; Zeitfluß
(m) = flow of time; verharren = to remain; abwickeln = to
liquidate; Selbstsucht (f) = egoism.

4. Johann Gottlieb Fichte, *Reden an die deutsche Nation*

Ein Haupterfordernis dieser neuen Nationalerziehung ist es,
daß in ihr Lernen und Arbeiten vereinigt sei, daß die Anstalt
durch sich selbst sich zu erhalten den Zöglingen wenigstens
scheine und daß jeder in dem Bewußtsein erhalten werde, zu
5 diesem Zwecke nach aller seiner Kraft beizutragen. [Dies wird
vor allem darum gefordert,] [. . .] weil das gegründete Vertrauen,
daß man sich stets durch eigene Kraft werde durch die Welt
bringen können und für seinen Unterhalt keiner fremden
Wohltätigkeit bedürfe, zur persönlichen Selbständigkeit des
10 Menschen gehört und die sittliche, weit mehr als man bis
jetzt zu glauben scheint, bedingt. [. . .] Auch in den neuesten
Zeiten und bis auf diesen Tag ist die Bildung der vermögenden
Stände betrachtet worden als eine Privatangelegenheit der
Eltern, die sich nach eignem Gefallen einrichten möchten,
15 und die Kinder dieser wurden in der Regel nur dazu angeführt,
daß sie sich selbst einst nützlich würden; die einzige öffentliche
Erziehung aber, die des Volkes, war lediglich Erziehung zur
Seligkeit im Himmel; die Hauptsache war ein wenig Christentum und Lesen und, falls es zu erschwingen war, Schreiben,
20 alles um des Christentums willen. Alle andere Entwicklung
der Menschen wurde dem ohngefähren und blind wirkenden
Einflusse der Gesellschaft, in welcher sie aufwuchsen, und
dem wirklichen Leben selbst überlassen.

(*Reden*, 10. Rede, Insel, 1909; pp. 182, 188f.)

Commentary: (numbers in parentheses refer to line numbers
in the text)
Fichte's insistence on the combination of learning and manual
work is primarily intended to give the student the kind of
self-realisation through work which Rousseau and – later –

Pestalozzi demanded. He recognises the need to combine the purely didactic with the material component as part of his national education plan. He thereby endeavours to emancipate education from domination by social class and by the church.

(3f) Read: wenigstens [möglich] erscheine.

(10f) Fichte recognises the relationship between material and moral independence, hence his revolutionary demand for emancipation from capital and church (13 and 17f) and the freeing from parental influence, a demand which was repeatedly made until the 1960s.

Vocabulary:
Haupterfordernis (n) = main demand; Anstalt (f) = institution; Zögling = pupil; Unterhalt (m) = subsistence; nach eigenem Gefallen = as it pleases them; anführen = to instruct; Seligkeit (f) = salvation; erschwingen = to afford; ohngefähr = ungefähr = rough.

5. Adolf Diesterweg, 'Prinzipien zur Gestaltung der Zukunftsschule' (1866)

Befreiung des Lehrerstandes von der Unterordnung unter einen anderen Interessen und Tätigkeiten zugewandten Stand – dagegen Anerkennung der Rechte der Lehrer, als Bürger eine eigene Meinung zu haben und dieselbe in den gesetzlichen
5 Schranken aller zu äußern und zu betätigen – kurz: gesetzliche Regelung aller ihrer Verhältnisse – und dadurch die Schöpfung der Möglichkeit der Charakterbildung des Standes, dem die große Aufgabe der Grundlegung der Erziehung einer großen Nation anvertraut ist, und dessen Stellung der Würde dieser
10 hohen Mission entspricht. – ein [sic] Ziel, welches, solange die Welt steht, noch von keiner Nation weder erkannt, noch weniger erreicht ist.

(A. Diesterweg, in *Rheinische Blätter* (1866), quoted from H. Blankertz, *Die Geschichte der Pädagogik*, Büchse der Pandora, 1982; p. 161.)

Commentary:
The passage is written in telegram style; it contains the programme for a new type of elementary education and is directed against the *Stiehlsche Regulative* (cf. Text 6). It demands
a liberal, democratic education, associated in the 'German
tradition' with national character education.

Vocabulary:
Lehrerstand (m) = teaching profession; Schranke (f) = limit;
Grundlegung (f) = foundation; anvertrauen = to entrust.

6. Ferdinand Stiehl, *Preußische Regulative* (1854)

Dagegen muß es als eine wichtige Aufgabe der Schullehrer
angesehen werden, bei dem heranwachsenden Geschlecht und
in ihrer Umgebung Kenntnis der vaterländischen Erinner-
ungen, Einrichtungen und Personen aus der Vergangenheit
5 und Gegenwart, und damit Achtung und Liebe zu der
Herrscherfamilie vermitteln zu helfen.... Mit Zuversicht
kann erwartet werden, daß unter Anwendung der obigen
Grundsätze die Seminarien ihren wahren Beruf immer
bestimmter und erfolgreicher erfüllen werden. Unpraktische
10 Reflexion, subjektives, für die Zwecke einfacher und gesunder
Volksbildung erfolgloses Experimentieren wird ihnen
fernbleiben. Unter Festhalten christlichen Grundes in Leben
und Disziplin werden sie immer vollständiger zu dem sich
ausbilden, was sie sein müssen, Pflanzstätten für fromme,
15 treue, verständige, dem Leben des Volkes nahestehende Lehrer,
die sich in Selbstverleugnung und um Gottes willen der
heranwachsenden Jugend in Liebe anzunehmen Lust, Beruf
und Befähigung haben.

(Quoted from A. Reble, *Geschichte der Pädagogik,
Dokumentationsband*, 2nd edn, Klett-Cotta, 1992; p. 475.)

Commentary: (numbers in parentheses refer to line numbers
in the text)
(3–6) The 'patriotic education' is now limited to the Hohenzollern dynasty.

(9–13) Intellectual activities of any kind are rejected as un-
healthy, restricting education to pure functionalism.
(12–18) The new type of teacher must be disciplined and
brought up in a narrowly defined Christian manner, the virtues of self-denial, piety and faithfulness are contrary to the
political virtues of a liberal democracy.

Vocabulary:
Herrscherfamilie (f) = dynastic family; vermitteln = to convey; Zuversicht (f) = confidence; Seminarium (n) = academy
for teachers; fernbleiben = to be absent from; Festhalten
(n) = retention; Pflanzstätte = nursery; Selbstverleugnung
(f) = self-denial.

7. Georg Kerschensteiner, 'Der Begriff der Arbeitsschule' (1911)

Vor allem ist klar, daß niemand ein in unserem Sinne brauch-
barer Bürger eines Staates sein kann, der nicht eine Funktion
in diesem Organismus erfüllt, der also nicht irgendeine Arbeit
leistet, die direkt oder indirekt den Zwecken des Staats-
5 verbandes zugute kommt. [. . .]
Die selbständige geistige Arbeit ist noch mehr ein Kennzeichen
der Arbeitsschule als die selbständige manuelle Arbeit. Nur
hat sie in der Volksschule die allerbescheidensten Grenzen,
und selbst innerhalb dieser können noch viele nicht genügend
10 gefördert werden. Sie ist trotzdem das *wesentliche* Merkmal
der Arbeitsschule, da ja auch die manuelle Arbeit zu
selbständiger geistiger Tätigkeit schon im Rahmen der
Volksschule anregen soll. Die selbständige geistige Arbeit
verlangt aber möglichstes Zurückdrängen der alten Formen
15 der *Überlieferung* von Wissen zugunsten aktiver *Erarbeitung*
des Wissensstoffes überall da, wo und soweit es möglich
ist.
        (Quoted after Reble, *Geschichte der Pädagogik*,
        Dokumentationsband, pp. 524–30.)

Commentary: (numbers in parentheses refer to line numbers in the text)
(1–5) Kerschensteiner emphasises the importance of *Arbeit* for citizenship, very much in Rousseau's sense. The unabridged text emphasises this relationship even more.
(6ff) Intellectual work must be encouraged, but manual work can lead to independent thought.
(15) *Überlieferung* is seen as passive, inappropriate for education into citizenship, whereas the active appropriation of knowledge will lead to logical thought and *Charakterbildung*.

Vocabulary:
brauchbar = useful; Staatsverband (m) = state association; zugute kommen = to be of use; zurückdrängen = to force back; erarbeiten = to acquire.

Topics for further study

1. Discuss Humboldt's reform of the University and analyse to what extent its emphasis on scholarship and character education influenced the German education system.
2. In how far did Fichte's education concept, as developed in *Reden*, constitute a continuation of Humboldt? Focus in particular on his ideas of comprehensive education and on his emphasis on national education.
3. Examine the involvement of the German elementary school teacher in the development of a German national spirit and compare this with the reactionary response by the Prussian state after 1848.
4. Attempt to define Ringer's concept of the German 'mandarin' and discuss to what extent this type has influenced the anti-modernist, anti-democratic German political culture of the late nineteenth and early twentieth century?

6

The rise of the *Bürger* and the establishment of a nation state

An introduction to the concept of a German Sonderweg *(special development) with particular reference to its socio-historical implications. The following points are discussed: the cultural emancipation of the German 'middle class' during the first half of the nineteenth century; its search for family values and its reluctant participation in liberal politics. A brief analysis of the Revolution of 1848 and of its failure is given. Bismarck's alternative of 'Blood and Iron', the establishment of the Second Reich and its semi-feudalist social order are considered and voices of criticism both from within and beyond the* Reich *are presented.*

Introduction

Read in conjunction with the three previous Chapters, this Chapter will attempt to trace the development of Germany from the decline of the Holy Roman Empire (1806) to the development of the Second Reich (1871), witnessing a change in the socio-political chemistry of Germany. From being known as 'Volk der Dichter und Denker',[1] a somewhat introspective people, yet to achieve national unity while playing a leading role in culture and philosophy, Germany was to emerge as Europe's premier nation in economic and military terms. Given that this transformation occurred within the space of some fifty years and was accompanied by half a dozen wars or major conflicts, it is not surprising that the new Germany began to acquire an increasingly negative image, reinforced by its provocative demands for a leading part in the imperialist struggle for worldwide domination, for Germany's 'Platz an der Sonne'[2] (place in the sun).

It is in this historical context that the term *Sonderweg*[3] gained its significance. Its origins can be traced back to at least the beginning of the nineteenth century, and a closer examination of the concept will reveal important differences in its interpretation in different periods. Philosophers such as Herder and Fichte, and writers from J. Möser to Arndt recognised Germany's uniquely weak and backward political and social state and sought to offer solutions to its dilemma – frequently based on cultural criteria. Advocates of Germany's 'special development' after 1871, however, also exalted the country's success in the fields of industry, education and military affairs whilst viewing with contempt its neighbour's perceived degenerate nature. The humiliating defeat of the First World War and – even more – the collapse of National Socialism with its much proclaimed *Stunde Null* (Hour Zero) seemed to spell an end to such dreams of German superiority, but not to the claim of a German *Sonderweg*. The 1950s and 1960s saw its re-emergence as a mirror image: formerly positive German characteristics were blamed for the rise of fascism. 'The glorification of martial virtues, the abject obedience of the subject (*Untertan*), inwardness, and contempt for supposedly mechanical western values, were variously seen as characteristic German aberrations from enlightened western ways of thinking.'[4] During the following decades this reverse image of a German *Sonderweg* was questioned, in an attempt to explain the 'peculiarities of German history', by challenging the Western norms against which the alleged German aberration was measured. In the wake of this debate, but certainly not in the same ideological track, the *Historikerstreit* was to take up the theme again, making it an issue of political correctness and relating it to the whole problem of national identity.[5] Not surprisingly, the matter has refused to die and has gained renewed importance with Germany's reunification.

Unable to enter into a debate of this magnitude we can attempt only to map out the differing views and arguments. Furthermore, rather than take issue with the various schools of historians, we shall attempt to observe the whole subject matter from the viewpoint of culture studies, as *Kulturwissenschaftler*. For this reason, we are less interested in the question of whether there is in fact a German *Sonderweg*, but will rather pursue an analysis of those opinions which hold to this view, be it myth or reality. Our discussion of the rise of the *Bürger* and the simultaneous decline of German idealism can at best map out major stages and important directions in this development; our comments on the Revolution of 1848 will be restricted to those aspects which help explain the demise of liberal in favour of nationalist issues and the account of the establishment of a second German *Reich* will be restricted to those features which explain its downfall some fifty years later.

The Rise of the *Bürger* (1800–48)

The literature, philosophy and music of the early nineteenth century was to a large extent still based on the various German courts with Duke Karl August creating a centre of German neo-classical culture in Weimar. Much of the literary production of Goethe and Schiller, Wieland and Herder was produced at this court, developed as a result of the literary discourse between a small circle of like-minded, civilised men and women and often performed at the Weimar Court Theatre. The Romantic movement began to turn away from this court culture and flourished in the slightly more open university climate of Jena or Berlin, Bonn, Heidelberg, Tübingen or Vienna, though still largely confined to a narrow social stratification.

The 1830s saw a marked change in direction: the French July Revolution, the deaths of Hegel (1831) and Goethe (1832), were seen as the end of an era, either bemoaned as 'a crisis in which everything that was formerly valid seems to have become problematical'[6] or celebrated as the advent of a new age where art would converge with the political, social and technological advance of man:

Indessen, die neue Zeit wird auch eine neue Kunst gebären, die mit ihr selbst in begeistertem Einklang sein wird, die nicht aus der verblichenen Vergangenheit ihre Symbolik zu borgen braucht und die sogar eine neue Technik, die von der seitherigen verschieden, hervorbringen wird.[7] (Meanwhile, the new age will give birth to a new form of art, which will be in enthusiastic harmony with its own time, which will not have to borrow its symbols from a faded past and which will even bring forth a new technology, quite different from traditional ones.)

A closer examination would elicit that preparations for the new age were already in place: the Stein–Hardenberg reform programme (1807–09) and the new spirit at the universities had created a national consciousness, awakening an element of public awareness and beginning to make inroads into the middle and upper echelons of the administration. 'In most of German Europe [...] the balance of political power after 1815 had clearly shifted from the ruler to the professional civil service'.[8] The contemporary historian B. G. Niebuhr recognised this as early as 1815 when he observed that 'freedom depends much more on the administration [Verwaltung] than on the constitution [Verfassung]'[9] and German civil servants, educated in the new liberal climate, were soon to play a leading part in the modernisation of Prussia and other German states. They recognised that a more liberal regime, free of petty limitations and foolish privileges would afford them an enhanced influence over the nobility or incompetent rulers; their own advancement was consequently linked to the advance of reason, to increasing public awareness and – ultimately – to democracy. However, by the mid 1840s, the growing number of academics seeking posts in the public administration and the competition for employment led to political quietism amongst them. After the 1848 Revolution a new generation of civil servants developed into the disciplined, authoritarian administrators whom we nowadays associate with the Prussian *Beamte*.[10]

In the meantime, however, the political reverberations of the French July Revolution (1830) were felt in German cities as far apart as Aachen, Frankfurt, Munich and Leipzig, despite the 'lack of social direction' caused by the fragmented political system.[11] Most of the participants in political unrest were students, journeymen, craftsmen and merchants, with those liberals from the middle strata of society few and far between. The torchbearers of political opposition were to be found amongst university professors such as Hoffmann von Fallersleben, the author of the German national anthem, the Göttingen Seven, seven professors, including the brothers Grimm, Gervinus and the historian Dahlmann, sacked from Göttingen University on account of their political activities. The more left-wing radical intellectuals were usually not attached to any public office; some, like the young Marx, existed as journalists, other writers (Herwegh, Heine, Büchner, Börne) went into early exile, thus finding themselves even more marginalised from their public. This uneven and disjointed state of affairs is hardly surprising at a time when we cannot yet speak of a German middle class.

The late emergence of a German middle-class has several causes. The particularist nature of the country, with its several hundred individual states, the lack of a natural capital or cultural centre, the backward nature of German industry and trade and the dominant position of an administrative or clerical elite all played their part. Even where there was some distinct sign of political activity, as during the Revolution of 1848/49, 'the problem was not passivity but fragmentation'.[12] To the foreign observer, such as Germaine de Staël, Germany was a culturally and philosophically fertile country, but otherwise rather backward, gaining its charm precisely from such backwardness (Text 1). Indeed, until the 1870s we have to distinguish between *Bürgertum* and *Bourgeoisie*, the former associated with the life of small towns and cities, traditional crafts and trades and various salaried posts at the many courts or universities and the latter emerging rapidly, after 1850, allied to the big cities, to industry and developing capitalism.

The period of the *Bürger* is known as the *Biedermeier* (1830–48), based on traditional life-styles and marked by political abstention. The idyll was the preferred style in art and literature, as in life, concentrating on genre, the intimate family scene of a small town or village, depicting these domestic settings either with affection or with irony, in the latter instance frequently containing a tiny grain of melancholy. The paintings and wood cuttings of Richter or Spitzweg in Germany serve as good examples of this type of art (Figure 7). In Austria it flourished even more in the works of Daffinger, Waldmüller, von Amerling, von Saar, von Paumgarten, von Schwind and a host of other artists. These painters attempted to bridge the divide between art and life by turning towards *Gebrauchskunst* (applied art) and by focusing on rural settings as well as bourgeois life-styles. The outside world, framed through a window, or viewed from a safe vantage point, can tease the imagination without any risk of the measured life-style being threatened by such uncontrollable external forces as politics, for 'the overwhelming majority of Germans had nothing to do with the liberal movement'.[13] Contemporary narratives of Eichendorff and Hoffmann offer a similar picture: the latter's *Der goldene Topf* describes a group of tobacco-smoking, punch-imbibing titled gentlemen. The bourgeois heroine fervently aspires to nothing more than the position of 'Frau Hofrätin', in a stylish hat and Turkish wrap, with a fashionable address near the palace, where in her elegant négligé at the bay window, she takes breakfast served by her house maid.[14] The more seriously portrayed protagonist in Adalbert Stifter's *Nachsommer* is an ardent collector of minerals, a keen observer and explorer of his Alpine homeland, a faithful restorer of local works, arts and crafts and a solicitous preserver of the environment. The world of politics is alluded to, but never allowed to intrude. Biedermeier society thus succeeded in creating the first independently bourgeois life-style, based on the relatively secure world of domesticity, making a virtue

Figure 7: Ludwig Richter, *Die gute Einkehr*. The scene depicts a family idyll of complete domesticity, down to the dogs and ducks in the foreground and the turtle doves over the gateway. Observe also the prominence of children, a new feature of the German *Biedermeier*. The scene is protected from the outside world by the gateway and garden wall; this separation of homelife from 'wild' nature is typical of the *Biedermeier*. (Printed with the kind permission of *Verlag Karl Robert Langewiesche/Nf. Hans Köster KG*, Königstein)

out of its somewhat circumscribed milieu and distancing itself from the dangerous and alien world of politics.

The real focus of political activity lay beyond these confines, amongst craftsmen and apprentices, amongst students, professors and the wider intellectual circles. Literary clubs and coffee houses became important centres for the development of political discourse, though the Carlsbad Decrees[15] (1819) restrained public debate, keeping it within the club house or the salon. Subversive activity was suspected everywhere; censors, often in the guise of the local police, operated in every avenue of public life, universities, newspapers, local clubs or societies. Lack of resources and plain stupidity on the part of the censors made them an issue of public debate and sharpened people's sensitivities and responses, a situation not unlike the situation found more recently in Eastern Europe. Mocking the censor became a favourite pastime; Heine reduced a whole passage to blank spaces, allegedly as a result of censorship, apart from the words – spaced out over the page – 'die deutschen Censoren Dummköpfe'[16] (German censors blockheads).

The newly acquired bourgeois values lay outside this public sphere and became epitomised in the figure of the 'deutsche Michel', a rather sleepy, *petit bourgeois* man with no ideals or public ambition, sitting by his stove all day long, smoking his long pipe and wearing his night-cap. This figure was scorned by left wing writers such as Heine, Herwegh and Hoffmann von Fallersleben who parodied in lullaby style Michel's lack of political activity (Text 2). The name itself derived from the archangel Michael, Lucifer's chief antagonist and patron saint of the Holy Roman Empire.[17] This heroic emblem was transformed into its opposite and mocked as a figure of fun who had lost all social cohesion and merely deferred to authority, incapable of aspiring to political power himself. The 'deutsche Michel' would rather cultivate his own family values within the *Wohnzimmer* or the *gute Stube* (front room), his haven of domesticity and *Gemütlichkeit*. A largely false, facile harmony was being created with loving mothers and children, dutiful fathers, wise and benign grandparents. So strong was this newly created idyll of family life that even its most ardent critics could not escape it: Heine submerged his own origins in a strange myth in order to disguise his illegitimate birth and even Karl Marx disowned his illegitimate son.[18] The emphasis of Christmas shifted from the church to the home, where the *Biedermeier* family indulged in singing and games, celebrated with gifts, especially toys for the children who were at the centre of the festivities; a symbol of 'verinnerlichter Harmonie, mit der sie [die Familie] alle Konflikte beschwichtigen und für einige Stunden die Utopie einer heilen Welt hervorzaubern möchten'[19] (... spiritualised harmony with which the family resolved all conflicts and attempted to conjure up for a few hours the utopia of a safe and sound world).

Women who had previously enjoyed a small measure of domestic emancipation lost some of their independence, becoming less involved in family enterprises and devoting themselves entirely to the three 'Ks', Kirche–Küche–Kinder.[20] However, by concentrating entirely on domestic duties, they developed a new kind of authority, which may explain the relatively strong position of women's associations, influenced in particular by Louise Otto–Peters' (1819–1895) *Frauenzeitung*. A relationship has been observed between this domesticated position of women and men's conservatism:

Nicht bloß durch die Sorge um die Familie selbst, sondern auch durch die stetig ausgesprochene und stumme Mahnung der Frau wird der Gatte dem Bestehenden verhaftet, und die Kinder erleben in der mütterlichen Erziehung unmittelbar die Einwirkung eines der herrschenden Ordnung ergebenen Geistes.[21]

(Not only because of his concern for the family as such, but also as a result of both a constantly articulated and silent reproach by his wife, the husband becomes rooted in tradition, and the children experience through their maternal upbringing the immediate influence of a spirit which is obedient to the existing order.)

Heinrich Hoffmann's popular children's book *Der Struwelpeter* (1845) exhibits the domestic values of the time: disobedience leads to disaster and is punished in the most cruel manner, meticulously described and memorably illustrated. Whilst the popularity of *Struwelpeter* extended to Britain and became symptomatic for Victorian values, the dominance of its bourgeois morality was more inescapable in Germany, where the development of a middle-class political culture was further inhibited by the country's fragmented state and by the profoundly German impact of state regulation:

> In contrast to England, where the administration was small and semi-autonomous corporations regulated the professions, most German governments assumed increasing power over the training for, admission to and regulation of careers in law, medicine, education and the church.[22]

The gulf between personal freedom, based on private virtues, and political freedom, the enfranchisement of public affairs, is characteristic for the spirit of the German *Biedermeier*. Liberals spared no effort in defending their basic freedoms from censorship, economic and social disabilities, yet failed to pursue their political and constitutional rights with equal vigour: 'the capstone of the free society – the right to self-government [. . .] was blunted by the prevalent depreciation of political life'.[23] It is with this cleavage in mind that we shall look at some aspects of the 1848 Revolution.

The 1848 Revolution and its failure

Rather than an historical account of the Revolution, this section will offer some general observations which may throw light on the reasons for the ultimate failure of a movement which has been described as one of the greatest examples of political upheaval in the history of Germany.[24] Although it is customary to speak of **the** Revolution, in fact a cluster of revolutions erupted in 1848 – in Vienna, Berlin and most other German states, producing conflicting opinions as to their political ends and objectives. Whilst the middle classes favoured demands for a national constitution and freedom of the press, the rural masses demanded freedom from oppressive living conditions, from absentee landlords and from material poverty. The urban working population, on the other hand, sought their salvation in social freedom, a decent education and the kind of socialism proclaimed by Wilhelm Weitling in his *Die Menschheit, wie sie ist und wie sie sein soll* (1839) and in the *Communist Manifesto* (1848) of Marx and Engels.

The different objectives were further complicated by national issues: even as the Frankfurt Assembly attempted to formulate a new federal constitution for Germany based on liberal principles, public interest was being diverted by the Schleswig-Holstein issue in the North, problems with the Dutch province of Limburg in the West and with Posen in the East, as well as with the destiny of the Tirol, all threatening the involvement of foreign countries. The resolution of the Schleswig-Holstein issue and the skirmishes between Poles and Germans in Posen allowed national aspirations to hinder the progress of liberal reform; in both cases Prussia gained in public esteem as champion of the national cause. A related matter involved rivalry between Austria and Prussia: should the new Germany be *großdeutsch*, to include Austria, or should it content itself with the *kleindeutsch* solution, leaving the German parts of Austria to their own devices? The issue itself invoked religious fears in many Southern German states, fearful of a dominant Prussian Protestant hegemony. And yet, the events of March 1848 were initially very successful. The Prussian and Austrian governments were rendered ineffective, both dynasties ready to surrender political control to the revolutionaries, and the smaller German states either prepared to conform to the constitutional demands of the revolutionaries (Baden) or were so riddled by corruption and intrigue (Bavaria) that they did not count politically.

The members of the 'Paulskirche Assembly' in Frankfurt saw it as their function to give the German fatherland a new order. They were, in the majority, administrative officials and lawyers, teachers and other academics; virtually none of them were craftsmen or peasants.[25] The elected President of the Assembly was the prime minister of Hesse, Heinrich von Gagern, a moderate of great integrity, whose proclaimed aim was the creation of a German constitution, based on national sovereignty.[26] The Assembly, operating during a period of unprecedented political turmoil, was nevertheless successful in formulating a set of democratic *Grundrechte* (basic rights) which, closely modelled on the Constitution of the United States, was to form the nucleus of the future constitutions of Weimar (1919) and Bonn (1949). They included freedom of movement, equality before the law, the inviability of the individual and his/her abode, access to public office, the abolition of the death penalty[27] and virtually all the individual rights associated with modern constitutions. Although frequently accused of political inertia and lengthy debate – Herwegh called the Assembly the 'Parla- Parla- Parlament'[28] – it nevertheless drew up a progressive liberal programme, even if this was far removed from the more radical demands of the craftsmen's federations and 'democrats'. The famous liberal scholar of German, Gervinus, felt compelled to comment negatively on the March events:

Ein solches Überstürzen der Dinge ist nie in der Geschichte erlebt worden. Unsere schönen Hoffnungen einer ruhigen Reform unserer Zustände sind erschüttert. Wir sind unserem 1792, fürchten wir, näher als unserem 1789.[29]

(Such a precipitate rush of events has never before been experienced in history. Our finest hopes for a quiet reform of our circumstances have been dashed. We are closer, we fear, to our 1792 [September massacres in Paris, execution of king Louis XVI] than to our 1789.)

There can be little doubt that – had the Revolution been successful – a liberal German nation state would have emerged, anchoring Germany into the Western system of political culture. A week after the passage of the *Grundrechte*, the President of the Assembly led a delegation to Berlin to offer the imperial crown to Frederick William IV. The king's rejection, though not unexpected, demonstrated the unbridgeable divide between the liberal parliamentarians and the old conservative order. Emphasising his divine rights, the king refused to accept this 'dog collar with which they [the Assembly] want to leash me to the revolution of 1848'.[30] His letter to an old friend and delegate to the Paulskirche was even more explicit:

> Man nimmt nur an und schlägt nur aus eine Sache, die geboten werden kann, – und Ihr da habt gar nichts zu bieten; das mach ich mit meines Gleichen ab; jedoch zum Abschied die Wahrheit: Gegen Demokraten helfen nur Soldaten; Adieu![31]
>
> (One only accepts or rejects that which can be offered, – and you have nothing to offer me; I deal only with my equals in this matter; but in farewell, the truth: Only soldiers can help against democrats; Adieu!)

The king's reaction spelt the end of the Assembly; Austrian and Prussian delegates were withdrawn; a rump parliament of radical democrats moved to Stuttgart. When expelled by Württemberg soldiers, they attempted to re-form in Baden, where, with the capitulation of the fortress of Rastatt (23rd July 1849) the Revolution came to a brave, but ignominious ending.

Without entering into a further discussion of the reasons for the Revolution's failure, a brief resumé seems necessary. While there is no doubt that the Frankfurt Assembly took a long time to come up with a constitution and proposal for a national government, its efficiency in undertaking parliamentary business and arriving at a workable modern constitution deserves recognition.[32] Whether the Assembly constituted a fair representation of the revolutionary forces is more difficult to assess. We have seen how academic circles were over-represented and an examination of the various 'extra-parliamentary' opposition groups would indicate that the more radical factions consequently often felt out of step with the

Assembly. This, however, may well be in line with the revolutionary process as such, the French Revolution experiencing similar problems. Theories which relate the failure of 1848 to a weak and under-developed liberal bourgeoisie are nowadays refuted as reductionist, since they imply that there is only one model – usually that of the 1789 Revolution – with which all others must be compared.[33] A more recent study maintains that the Revolution failed not because of German society's political and economic backwardness, but because of its modernity, because of the complexity of its revolutionary constituents.[34] Our own analysis of Germany's *petit bourgeois* society can hardly give credit to such an interpretation, nor can we accept that the German princes count amongst the leading 'national-political' groups.

In conclusion, let us return to the public perception of the time. The competing national and liberal factions saw themselves confronted with an insoluble dilemma: Prussian troops had to be called upon to defend the national issue (Schleswig-Holstein) and when this conflict overtook the debate in Frankfurt, these same troops were called to the very heart of the Revolution to defend the liberal Assembly from radical and nationalist elements. The military resurgence, both in Austria and Prussia, was the result of perceived outside threats, Hungary, Bohemia or Italy, in the former case, or Denmark in the case of Prussia. The Counter-Revolution, enforced more vigorously by Prussia than by Austria, left bitter memories among many revolutionaries and contributed to the antagonism between Prussia and the southern German states which was to continue even after the unification of 1871. In the Palatinate and in Baden, the part played by Prince William of Prussia, after 1871 the Kaiser of the new German Reich, in defeating revolutionary troops was not forgotten, and lived on in folklore (Text 3).

The Establishment of the new German Reich (1871)
The failure of the Revolution also spelt the failure of liberal democracy: liberal energies were sacrificed in favour of

national aspirations which were artificially created and had little in common with the earlier national movement (1812–49). Developments since 1849 have been considered under different headings: Hans Ulrich Wehler views the process of modernisation in Germany as a double-revolution, a political and industrial revolution with the latter providing the more forward-looking impetus.[35] Many critics of Wehler point out that his formula is not far-reaching enough, that many additional factors outside and within Germany contributed to the emergence and subsequent development of the new *Reich*.

Events immediately following the failed Revolution indicated the strength of the counter-revolutionary movement with the re-constitution of the reactionary *Deutsche Bund* (1850), the abolition of the democratic *Grundrechte* (1851) and a return to an anti-liberal, repressive system. But whilst the repression led to a certain depoliticisation of the population, it could not stop the process of modernisation in industrial and social terms, nor could it halt the national momentum. The Schleswig-Holstein issue and in particular the Italian unification struggle against Austria (1858) contributed towards the foundation of the *Deutsche Nationalverein* (1860). The various Schiller celebrations (cf. Chapter 4) as well as other events such as the *Sängerfest* in Nuremberg (1861) and the congress of the *Turner* in Leipzig (1863) all fuelled the national debate. Political events gave Prussia the advantage over Austria, seen to act half-heartedly in Schleswig-Holstein while vigorously defending her own interests against the Italian nationalists. Prussia began to emerge as the leading force in the German national struggle. The historian Johann Gustav Droysen proclaimed Prussia's 'German vocation';[36] Bismarck, Prussia's prime minister and later German chancellor, stated that Germany did not look towards Prussia for its liberalism but for power[37] and his famous dictum that the important issues are resolved through 'blood and iron' and not by speeches and majority decisions all suggest that we are looking at a 'Revolution from above'.[38] Bismarck's own formula indicates that this revolution was by no means a peaceful or a natural one, but that its emphasis on a military solution was accompanied by the atrophy of liberal and cultural accomplishments.[39]

Taking the period from 1849–1918 as a whole, we can distinguish three major elements in the development of a German national consciousness, the role of the (Prussian) army, the effects of industrialisation and a general feudalisation of the bourgeoisie. Though coinciding in time and overlapping in some social and political respects, the three agents could not bring about the kind of national identity associated with many other European countries.

The establishment of the army as a state within a state: During the crisis of 1848, when the Prussian king had effectively given in to the revolutionaries, the military saw themselves as sole guardians of the old regime. The Prussian War Minister, Count Albrecht von Roon, declared the army to be the true 'fatherland'[40] and the new administration saw it as a school by which to discipline the nation. Whilst the 'sailor-suit' and other military style dress became a favourite children's fashion in other European nations, the general militarism in Germany was without equal. Even small children were indoctrinated with military songs and poems, illustrations in their story books reflecting this bellicose environment.[41] The constitutional conflict of 1862 which brought Bismarck to power, centred on the army and the Prussian government's insistence on three years' military service for civilians in order to instil into them 'das soldatische Wesen in seiner Totalität'[42] (totally soldier-like conduct). Bismarck's attitude further separated the military from constitutional government and liberal democracy.

The birth of the German *Reich* itself was the result of several wars (1806 and 1813 against Napoleon, 1848 against the revolutionaries, 1859 against Denmark, 1866 against Austria, 1870 against France), with the overall effect of a decrease in personal freedom and individual responsibility and an acceptance that 'might is right'. The proclamation of the *Reich* took place in Versailles, during a state of war, in the presence of

Figure 8: Anton von Werner, *Kaiserproklamation im Spiegelsaal von Versailles*; for a good commentary on the scene cf. W. Zank, 'Die Welle trug', *Die Zeit*, 18th January 1991; p. 33. The painting depicts the proclamation of the King of Prussia as *Deutscher Kaiser* by 36 German princes, surrounded by high-ranking officers, regimental standards and raised swords. Not one delegate from the *Reichstag* was present, the whole event was completely undemocratic. The new 'national' colours of black, red and white, were preferred by the Kaiser to black, red and gold, which had come 'from the gutter', i.e. from the people. (Printed with kind permission of *Archiv für Kunst und Geschichte*, Berlin)

princes and generals and where the delegation of parliamentarians was hardly noticeable.[43] The painting by Anton von Werner (Figure 8), though perhaps not historically correct in every detail, was, nevertheless, symptomatic of the new nation's image, as were its other symbols: the national anthem was dedicated to the emperor, not the empire or its people; the national colours of black, red and gold, the colours of democratic liberalism, were replaced by black, white and red, based on the black and white of Prussia.[44] The Kaiser had

Bürger *and nation state*   155

strong executive powers, amongst them supreme control over all military forces, over his chancellor and over the declaration of war. The elite within the *Reich* – in particular the officers and civil servants – was still dominated by the Prussian *Junker* (country gentleman) and life assumed a military tone, as illustrated in the novels of Fontane and Heinrich Mann. The lower orders of society, too, experienced their military service as an exercise in 'character building'; a popular cartoon bore the caption: 'und dann müßt ihr bedenken, als Zivilisten seid ihr hergekommen und als Menschen geht ihr fort'[45] (and then you should bear in mind, that although you came here as civilians, you are leaving as human beings).

By the end of the century, new ambitions boosted naval considerations at the expense of the army. This was not only a result of new colonial interests, but an attempt to reconcile the various internal conflicts and create an alliance of national and anti-parliamentary forces. The Chief of the Admiralty, Alfred von Tirpitz, considered the navy the 'battering ram' which was to bring about a new coalition of conservative forces or, failing that, to usher in an 'era of conflict' leading to war.[46] The *Flottenverein* and other national associations sought support from landowners, industrialists and a commercial middle class in their fight against socialism. More recent research has demonstrated that the inevitable drive to war was not caused primarily by a bellicose *Kaiser* or government, but by a militant population which occasionally even criticised the government for its policy of appeasement.[47] The language of politicians and the populace as a whole made abundant use of military jargon, reinforced by a general philosophy which suggested that growth was the only alternative to strangulation.[48] Offensive strategies had to be found to counter the policy of encirclement by the *Ausland*, a term for which no English equivalent exists and which to this day dominates German public consciousness, suggesting a polarity between Germany and the rest of the world. The idea of a 'wholesome war' as panacea against internal strife gained the upper hand and a general enthusiasm for war, though not limited to Germany, was the result. The course of the war was critically influenced by the primacy of military over political considerations; the policy of a total U-Boat war brought the USA into the conflict (1916) and the inflated hopes for military gain prolonged the struggle and made peace virtually impossible.

Effects of industrial growth: We have already discussed the relative lateness of Germany's industrialisation and need only a brief reminder of the incredible speed with which it finally developed. More important than both these phenomena was the fact that Germany's industrialisation coincided with the foundation of the *Reich*, with the development of the nation state. Modern historians have attempted to demonstrate that the 'German Couplet' of backward state and modern economy need not necessarily have led to a complete absence of liberalism;[49] public awareness at the time seems to qualify these findings.

The impact of the European industrial revolution in its national variations has been compared to that of the Copernican Revolution. It drew man into a new circuit of producer and consumer, often at the expense of liberal and humanist values.[50] As we have seen, Germany's industrialisation began in the 1840s with an enormous growth in population, concentrating particularly on large towns in industrial regions and leading to a complicated system of migration from rural areas into towns, from the Eastern regions to the North-West.[51] By mid-century, heavy industry had begun to establish itself, together with toolmaking, engineering and chemicals. Trade within the *Zollverein* doubled within ten years, stock companies sprang up and new banks were founded.[52] Alongside such developments, but often overshadowed by them, agriculture, too, underwent a process of modernisation, particularly on the larger Prussian estates. By 1900 German agriculture was one of the most advanced industries in Europe, taking full advantage of artificial fertilisers, stock breeding and modern machinery,[53] in strange contrast to an otherwise conservative rural population. Nevertheless, the emphasis continued to move steadily in the direction of industry and by 1866 the *Zollverein* states had become an industrialised society. Friedrich List, founder of the *Zollverein*, adjusted his liberal philosophy to German conditions and espoused the cause of active state intervention to help achieve international free trade. Although this customs union could not bring about a German national economy, it succeeded in creating 'the basis for a common German market'.[54]

The effects of industrialisation on the work-force are well documented: industrialisation became the cradle of the working classes. This development was in its infancy in 1848, as differences in the revolutionary activity of the bourgeoisie and the manual workers seem to indicate. It is not surprising that this divergence emanated from within the ranks of the newly emerging bourgeoisie who, wary of their radically democratic outlook, did not wish to make common cause with the workers. Early working-class organisations such as the *Allgemeine Deutsche Arbeiterverein* (1863) under its leader Ferdinand Lasalle remained faithful to the democratic aims of 1848. August Bebel and Wilhelm Liebknecht of the *Sozialdemokratische Arbeiterpartei* (1869) tried to forge a bond between the aspirations of a free and united Germany and those of an emancipated working-class.[55] They, nevertheless, remained in opposition to Bismarck's nation state and gave priority to the international and humanist ideals of the labour movement. Furthermore, they bitterly attacked a policy which had failed to produce a genuine *Volksstaat* and they thus opposed the annexation of Alsace-Lorraine, spoke up for ethnic minorities inside the *Reich* and opposed the armaments policy. Their aims were strengthened by opposition to Bismarck's anti-socialist laws (1878) and the two parties merged in 1875 as *Sozialdemokratische Partei Deutschlands* (SPD) to become the most numerous political force by 1890, with over one million members by 1914.[56] However, even before the

Kaiser's famous statement at the outbreak of war, that he no longer recognised any political parties, only Germans,[57] the SPD had become enmeshed in the general spirit of chauvinism and war fever, even if some of its leaders had been prepared to pay this price only in return for national recognition and an improvement in labour relations.

A feudalisation of the bourgeoisie: In his famous inaugural lecture (1895), Max Weber suggested that Germany's economic system should come under state supervision since it formed an essential element in the international struggle for supremacy.[58] As a consequence, Germany's leading industrialists should become part of the country's political elite. It was of great concern to Weber that the bourgeoisie had only reluctantly entered into this responsibility and that it had done so by imitating an outmoded *Junkertum*, a class of country squires, established to the east of the river Elbe. We can now see how right Weber was in his analysis of the bourgeois elite: 'the last decades of the nineteenth century in Germany did not see the nobility becoming bourgeois, but the bourgeoisie becoming "feudalised" '.[59] The defeat of France, resulting in the payment of indemnities of some five billion francs, ushered in the *Gründerzeit* (Promoters Boom Time), bringing an entrepreneurial class to power. They basked in their new glory, exhibited their wealth in ostentatious city palaces, sought ennoblement or grandiose titles (*Kommerzienrat*) and married into the impoverished nobility, thus gaining entry to the privileged classes.

The 'feudalisation' of the bourgeoisie was also enhanced by the *Dreiklassenwahlrecht*, an electoral system based on income, which further bound together these *nouveaux riches* and the old property owning classes. The vast expansion of the army and the civil service led to a stronger alignment of the aristocracy of wealth with that of heredity and, in the case of the civil service, of education. 'By 1910, 75 per cent of leading Prussian officials were sons of officials, army officers or landowners'.[60] Heinrich Hoffmann von Fallersleben satirised this emerging class in his *Gründerlieder*:

Was gehet *das* Verdienst mich an?
Nur *der* Verdienst ist noch mein Mann:
Ich will mir flechten selbst zum Lohne
Aus Aktien eine Bürgerkrone.[61]
(Why care about merit?/ My earnings are my master:/ For
my own reward I will weave/ A bourgeois crown of shares
for myself.)

The merger of political power with wealth is, of course,
typical of all modern capitalist societies. However, the situation in Germany seemed more extreme, thus 'violating deeper
prejudices and offering greater opportunities' to a nation
whose bourgeoisie 'had lost a revolution and whose Junkers
still dominated politics and the public ethos'.[62] The Junkers,
indeed, had survived industrialisation reasonably well, despite
earlier gloomy prophecies that 'the railroad locomotive is the
hearse in which feudalism will be carted off to the cemetery'.[63]
Whilst such a development would have brought Germany
more into line with its European neighbours, what actually
happened was almost the opposite: a predominantly Protestant bourgeoisie, brought up in the Lutheran rejection of
material wealth, sought an alliance with the old aristocracy
and the mandarin classes. In common hostility to the newly
emerging working-class and in fear of encirclement by neighbouring powers, the focal point of their aspirations was
the Berlin Court with its military splendour and imperial
ambitions.

Criticism of this newly emerging social order was slow to
surface, but gathered pace during the last decade of the century. One of the first to recognise the moral and cultural
decline which set in with the establishment of the *Reich* was
Friedrich Nietzsche who predicted the 'extirpation of the
German mind in favour of the German Reich' (Text 4).
Fontane's criticism of Bismarck and the monarchy is more
moderate: he saw the former as a 'mixture of superman and
sly-boots',[64] while the latter displayed an incongruous desire
for modern statesmanship based on an outdated concept of

state and society.[65] The dramatists and critics of the 1890s were far more vituperous in their analysis of the *Reich*: their outlet was the *Freie Volksbühne*, established in 1889 in the style of the Parisian *Théâtre libre*, proclaiming, in the service of truth, a 'social criticism' independent of socialist politics.[66] By 1890 a general sense of a cultural and political crisis was widespread. The conservative Maximilian Harden, co-founder of the *Volksbühne*, analysed the mood of despair and related it to the rapid economic growth of the previous decades. He singled out the *Fassadenkultur*, a pompous predilection for superficial glamour, not backed by any substance, together with the political megalomania of Germany's aspiring imperialism. His sure eye saw the advent of a world war which would destroy Germany:

Seit zehn Jahren wird das Lied geblasen, wird mit mühsamem Aufwand vielstelliger Ziffern bewiesen, daß wir morgen England beerben werden und übermorgen den Wettkampf mit den Vereinigten Staaten von Nordamerika wagen dürfen. [...] Die Rechnung hatte eben ein Loch. Für einen friedlichen Imperialismus [...] ist das Deutsche Reich zu arm, zu jung, zu hart vom Mißtrauen der Nachbarn bedrängt. Es mußte sich bescheiden, das Kolonialgebiet in den eigenen Grenzen suchen und auf die gefährliche Glanzrolle eines *arbiter mundi* verzichten oder sich [...] in das Abenteuer einer kriegerisch-expansiven Politik stürzen.[67]

(For ten years we have been hearing the same old song, demonstrated laboriously by impressive statistics that tomorrow we will take Britain's inheritance and the following day enter into competition with the USA. [...] The calculations were wrong. For peaceful imperialism, the German Reich is too poor, too young, too much beset by the mistrust of her neighbours. She should be modest, searching for colonialism within her own borders and renouncing the dangerous role of world arbitrator or she will plunge herself into the adventure of an expansionist war policy.)

Perhaps the most memorable image of impending doom comes at the end of Heinrich Mann's satirical novel *Der Untertan*: at the unveiling of a statue of Kaiser William I, patriotic speeches resound to celebrate the new alliance of Hohenzollern and Protestant, of military and economic might, only to have the ceremony interrupted at the crucial moment by an almighty thunderstorm which reduces proceedings to complete chaos and scatters the pompous participants in all directions.

Notes

1 The concept of Germany as 'Volk der Dichter und Denker' goes back to K. Musäus, Preface to *Volksmärchen der Deutschen* [1782]: 'Was wäre das enthusiastische Volk unserer Denker, Dichter, Schweber, Seher ohne die glücklichen Einflüsse der Phantasie.' G. Büchmann, *Geflügelte Worte. Der Zitatenschatz des deutschen Volkes*, Berlin: Droemer-Knaur, 1961; p. 162.

2 Bernhard von Bülow, 6th December 1897 with reference to Germany's claim to colonial possessions. Büchmann, *Geflügelte Worte*, p. 739.

3 For further comments cf. D. Blackbourn and G. Eley, *The Peculiarities of German History*, Oxford: Oxford University Press, 1991; p. 3.

4 *ibid.* p. 5

5 For a discussion of the 'Historikerstreit' cf. chapter 6 in R. J. Evans, *In Hitler's Shadow. West German Historians and the Attempt to Escape from the Nazi Past*, London: I. B. Tauris, 1989. For a further discussion of this term cf. Chapter 8.

6 J. J. Sheehan, *German History 1770–1866*, Oxford: Clarendon Press, 1898; p. 604.

7 H. Heine, *Sämtliche Werke* [Düsseldorfer Ausgabe], Vol. 12/1 [Gemäldeausstellung in Paris, 1831], p. 47.

8 Sheehan, *German History 1770–1866*, p. 430.

9 B. G. Niebuhr [1815], quoted from Sheehan, *German History 1770–1866*, p. 425.

10 E. Sagarra, *A Social History of Germany 1648–1914*, London: Methuen, 1977; p. 267f.

11 Sheehan, *German History 1770–1866*, p. 606.

12 *ibid.* p. 695

13 *ibid.* p. 448

14 E. T. A. Hoffmann, *Sämtliche Werke*, Vol. 2/1, H. Steinecke *et al.* (eds), Frankfurt: Deutscher Klassiker Verlag, 1993; p. 259.

15 A set of repressive laws, directed against liberal 'demagogues' and instigated by the governments of Austria and Prussia.

16 H. Heine, *Historisch-kritische Gesamtausgabe der Werke* [Säkularausgabe], Vol. 5, M. Windfuhr (ed.), Hamburg: Hoffmann and Campe, 1980; p. 116. (Düsseldorfer Ausgabe has the quotation in French.)

17 For a good explanation of the term cf. L. Röhrich, *Lexikon der sprichwörtlichen Redensarten*, Vol. 2, Freiburg, 1973; pp. 642–5. cf. also F. Stern, *The Failure of Illiberalism. Essays on the Political Culture of Modern Germany*, New York: Columbia University Press, 1992; p. 11, note 4; and *Brockhaus, Enzyklopädie in 20 Bänden*, Vol. IV, 17th edn, Wiesbaden: Herder, 1968; p. 567.

18 I. Weber-Kellermann, *Die deutsche Familie. Versuch einer Sozialgeschichte*, 3rd edn, Frankfurt: Suhrkamp, 1977; p. 115.

19 *ibid.* p. 226

20 *ibid.* p. 102

21 M. Horkheimer, E. Fromm, H. Marcuse (eds), *Studien über Autorität und Familie. Forschungsberichte aus dem Institut für Sozialforschung*, Paris, 1936; p. 69.

22 Sheehan, *German History 1770–1866*, p. 513f.

23 Stern, *The Failure of Illiberalism*, p. 11f.

24 Sheehan, *German History 1770–1866*, p. 658.

25 H. Jessen (ed.), *Die deutsche Revolution 1848/49 in Augenzeugenberichten*, Munich: dtv, 1973; p. 132.

26 *ibid.* p. 135

27 'Die Grundrechte der Reichsverfassung von 1849', in M. Freund (ed.), *Der Liberalismus in ausgewählten Texten*, Stuttgart: K. F. Koehler, 1965; pp. 40–8.

28 Sheehan, *German History 1770–1866*, p. 678.

29 Quoted from W. Bussmann, 'Zur Geschichte des deutschen Liberalismus im 19. Jahrhundert', in H. Böhme (ed.), *Probleme der Reichsgründungszeit*, Cologne/Berlin: Kiepenheuer und Witsch, 1973; p. 89.

30 Sheehan, *German History 1770–1866*, p. 691.

31 L. von Ranke, *Preußische Geschichte IV 1815–1871*, in H. J. Schoeps (ed.), Munich: Goldmann, 1966; p. 86.

32 M. Behnen, 'Bürgerliche Revolution und Reichsgründung', in M. Vogt (ed.), *Deutsche Geschichte*, p. 419.

33 This criticism is levied against Dahrendorf, *Democracy and Society in Germany*, in particular chapter 3, by G. Eley in Blackbourn and Eley, *The Peculiarities*, p. 57f.

34 Dann, *Nation und Nationalismus*, p. 126.

35 H. U. Wehler, *Geschichte als Historische Sozialwissenschaft*, Frankfurt: Suhrkamp, 1973; pp. 45–84; for a wider discussion of theories on modernisation cf. H. U. Wehler, *Modernisierungstheorie und Geschichte*, Göttingen: Vandenhoeck and Ruprecht, 1975.

36 cf. Behnen, 'Bürgerliche Revolution', p. 441.

37 Quoted from Dann, *Nation und Nationalismus*, p. 141.

38 W. Sauer, 'Das Problem des deutschen Nationalstaates', Böhme (ed.), *Probleme der Reichsgründungszeit*, p. 455.

39 D. Blackbourn speaks of a silent revolution (Blackbourn and Eley, *The Peculiarities*, p. 288), whereas G. Mann emphasises the problems associated with German unification, particularly the suppression of the liberal and democratic tradition (G. Mann, *Deutsche Geschichte des 19. und 20. Jahrhunderts*, Frankfurt a.M.: S. Fischer, 1958; p. 346f).

40 F. Meinecke, 'Boyen und Roon', *Historische Zeitschrift 77* (1896), p. 223.

41 cf. E. Humperdinck, *Sang und Klang fürs Kinderherz*, Berlin, 1900. Both songs and illustrations are rich in soldiers, national flags and military sentiments.

42 Behnen, 'Bürgerliche Revolution', p. 448.

43 cf. the painting by Anton von Werner. The issue came to prominence again with the unification of Germany in 1990, cf. also W. Zank, 'Die Welle trug. Zum Reichsgründungstag: Morose Emotionen in Versailles – Die deutsche Einheit war lange vor der Kaiserproklamation praktisch fertig', *Die Zeit*, 18th January 1991, p. 33f.

44 Dann, *Nation und Nationalismus*, p. 158f.

45 Behnen, 'Bürgerliche Revolution', p. 518.

46 V. R. Berghahn, *Germany and the Approach of War in 1914*, London: Macmillan, 1973; p. 57.

47 Behnen, 'Bürgerliche Revolution', pp. 546, 549.

48 One surprising example is the 'liberal' M. Weber, 'Der Nationalstaat und die Volkswirtschaftspolitik', in *Gesammelte politische Schriften*, 2nd edn, J. Winckelmann (ed.), Tübingen: Mohr, 1958; pp. 1–25, in particular p. 23.

49 cf. G. Eley in Blackbourn and Eley, *The Peculiarities*, p. 91.

50 H. Plessner, *Die verspätete Nation*, Stuttgart: Kohlhammer, 1962; p. 78.

51 Sheehan, *German History 1770–1866*, p. 455ff.

52 *ibid.* p. 375

53 *ibid.* p. 751

54 *ibid.* p. 504

55 Dann, *Nation und Nationalismus*, p. 178.

56 J. Dülffer, 'Deutschland als Kaiserreich (1871–1918)', in *Deutsche Geschichte*, M. Vogt (ed.), pp. 509–11.

57 Kaiser Wilhelm II on 1st August 1914: 'Ich kenne in meinem Volke keine Parteien mehr; es gibt unter uns nur noch Deutsche', in Dann, *Nation und Nationalismus*, p. 209.

58 Weber, 'Der Nationalstaat', p. 11f.

59 Sagarra, *A Social History*, p. 261.

60 *ibid.* p. 271

61 H. Hoffmann von Fallersleben, *Gründers Mittagslied*, in *Ausgewählte Werke in 4 Teilen*, H. Benzmann (ed.), Leipzig: Hesse [1905], Vol. 2; p. 222f.

62 Stern, *The Failure of Illiberalism*, p. 31.

63 F. Harkort (1842), *ibid.*, p. 34.

64 Th. Fontane, Letter to his daughter, 1st April 1859, *Gesammelte Werke*, 2nd Series, Vol. 7 [1908], p. 309.

65   K. Schreinert (ed.), *Theodor Fontane, Briefe an Georg Friedländer*,
     Heidelberg: Quelle and Meyer, 1954; pp. 309–11.
66   O. Brahm, 'Die freie Volksbühne', J. Schutte und P. Sprengel (eds),
     Die Berliner Moderne 1885–1914, Stuttgart: Reclam, 1987; pp. 408–13.
67   M. Harden, 'Die Krisis', in *Die Berliner Moderne*, p. 122.

Suggestions for further reading

Blackbourn, D. and Eley, G., *The Peculiarities of German History*, Ox-
    ford: Oxford University Press, 1984.
Sagarra, E., *A Social History of Germany 1648–1914*, London: Methuen,
    1977.
Sheehan, J., *German History 1770–1866 (The Oxford History of Modern
    Europe)*, Oxford: Clarendon Press, 1989.
Stern, F., *The Failure of Illiberalism. Essays on the Political Culture of
    Modern Germany*, New York: Columbia University Press, 1992.

Textual studies

1. Germaine de Staël, *Über Deutschland* (1813)

Vorwort: [. . .] Ein Gemälde der Literatur und der Philosophie
mag unter den gegenwärtigen Verhältnissen befremdend
erscheinen, vielleicht aber tut es dem armen, edlen Deutschland
wohl, wenn es mitten in den Stürmen des Krieges an seine
5 geistigen Reichtümer erinnert wird. Vor drei Jahren nannte
ich Preußen und die angrenzenden Staaten des Nordens das
'*Vaterland des Gedankens*'. In wie viele hochherzige Taten
hat sich dieser Gedanke umgesetzt! Was die Philosophien in
Systeme brachten, vollzieht sich, und die Unabhängigkeit des
10 Geistes wird die der Staaten begründen.
Dritter Teil, Elftes Kapitel: Über den Einfluß der neuen
Philosophie auf den Charakter der Deutschen.
Man sollte meinen, daß ein philosophisches System, das dem
von uns selbst abhängigen Willen eine allgewaltige Wirkung
15 beilegt, den Charakter stärken und von äußeren Umständen
unabhängig machen müßte. Es ist jedoch Anlaß zu dem
Glauben vorhanden, daß nur die politischen und religiösen
Institutionen den öffentlichen Geist gestalten können, und
daß keine abstrakte Theorie stark genug ist, um einer Nation
20 Tatkraft zu verleihen – denn leider muß man bekennen, daß
die Deutschen der Jetztzeit das, was man Charakter nennt,

nicht besitzen. Sie sind als Privatleute, als Familienväter, als
Beamte tugendhaft und von unbestechlicher Redlichkeit; ihr
gefälliger und zuvorkommender Diensteifer gegen die Macht
25 aber schmerzt, besonders wenn man sie liebt und sie für die
aufgeklärtesten spekulativen Verteidiger der Menschenwürde
ansieht. [...]

Wenn man nun aber auch anerkennt, daß die deutsche
Philosophie nicht ausreicht, eine Nation zu erziehen, so muß
30 man doch gestehen, daß die Jünger der neuen Schule dem
Ziel, Charakterstärke zu erlangen, weit näher stehen als alle
anderen: sie träumen, sie wünschen, sie begreifen sie – nur
fehlt sie ihnen noch oft. Es gibt nur wenige Männer in Deutschland, die überhaupt über Politik zu schreiben verstehen.
35 Die meisten, die sich damit befassen, sind Systematiker und
sehr oft unverständlich. [...]

(Germaine de Staël, *Über Deutschland*,
Reclam 1751–55, Stuttgart, 1973 [transl. by R. Habs,
S. Metken (ed.)]; pp. 45, 349)

Commentary: (numbers in parentheses refer to line numbers
in the text)
Mme de Staël (1766–1817), daughter of Jacques Necker, Louis
XVI's Finance Secretary, was a very emancipated woman
journalist and writer of inestimable influence on all the great
writers and philosophers of her time. Exiled from Paris by
Napoleon, she came to Germany in 1803. Acquainted with
Goethe, Schiller and Humboldt, she was closest to the
Romantic August Wilhelm Schlegel. Her book on Germany
is a somewhat biased attempt to interest her compatriots in
German literature and philosophy and suggests that a French
cultural rejuvenation could come from an opening towards
Germany.
(9f) Mme de Staël hopes that the cultural advances of the
previous generation will translate into political and economic
ones in the next.
(14ff) Here she seems to contradict the statement in (9): she
no longer believes that the philosophy of German idealism

(Kant, Fichte, Hegel) can develop a liberated German attitude. It is possible that she was influenced by Schlegel's own shift towards a more mystical, fatalistic philosophy.

Vocabulary:
befremdend = strange; in den Stürmen des Krieges = in tempestuous war-time; angrenzen = to border on to; hochherzig = high-minded; begründen = to establish; allgewaltig = omnipotent; beilegen = to attribute to; Anlaß (m) = cause, occasion; Tatkraft (f) = energy; unbestechliche Redlichkeit (f) = incorruptible honesty; gefällig = obliging; Diensteifer (m) = zeal; Jünger (m) = disciple.

2. Georg Herwegh: *Wiegenlied* [1843]

Schlafe, was willst du mehr? (Goethe)

Deutschland – auf
   weichem Pfühle
mach dir den Kopf nicht
   schwer!
Im irdischen Gewühle
schlafe, was willst du mehr?

5 Laß jede Freiheit dir rauben,
setze dich nicht zur Wehr,
du behälst ja den
   christlichen Glauben:
Schlafe, was willst du mehr?

Und ob man dir alles
   verböte,
10 doch gräme dich nicht zu
   sehr,
du hast ja Schiller und
   Goethe:
Schlafe, was willst du
   mehr?

Dein König beschützt die
   Kamele
und macht sie pensionär,
15 dreihundert Taler die Seele:
Schlafe, was willst du mehr?

Es fechten dreihundert
   Blätter
im Schatten, ein Sparterheer;
und täglich erfährst du das
   Wetter:
20 Schlafe, was willst du mehr?

Kein Kind läuft ohne
   Höschen
am Rhein, dem freien,
   umher:
Mein Deutschland, mein
   Dornröschen,
schlafe, was willst du
   mehr?

Bürger *and nation state*   167

Commentary: (numbers in parentheses refer to line numbers in the text)

In the tradition of the lullaby, a parody on Goethe's *Nachtgesang*. Contrasts the aspiration of freedom (liberalism) with the reactionary Christianity of the Holy Alliance (6), with a largely non-political neo-classical literature (12), with the administrative officialdom of the German *Beamte* (15) and with a rather restricted 'free' press (18). The final stanza contrasts reactionary Germany with the French revolutionary spirit, the 'ohne Höschen' (22) being a direct translation of French 'sansculottes'.

(14) Kamel = fool, ass, used here to describe the German civil servant.

(19) Sparterheer: the Spartans, fighting to preserve their political independence, fell to the vastly superior Persian army at the pass of Thermopylae.

(24) Dornröschen, fairy-tale figure of the Sleeping Beauty.

Vocabulary:

Pfühl (m) = cushion; Gewühl (n) = turmoil; Wehr (f) = defence; grämen = to grieve; pensionär machen = to pension off; Taler (m) = German silver coin; Blatt (n) = newspaper.

3. Badisches Wiegenlied

Schlaf, mein Kind, schlaf leis!
Dort draußen geht der Preuß.
Deinen Vater hat er umgebracht,
Deine Mutter hat er arm gemacht,

5 Und wer nicht schläft in stiller Ruh,
Dem drückt der Preuß die Augen zu.
Schlaf, mein Kind, schlaf leis!
Dort draußen geht der Preuß.

(H. Jessen, *Die deutsche Revolution 1848/49*
in Augenzeugenberichten, Munich: dtv, 1973; p. 344.)

Commentary:
M. Behnen quotes an additional couplet: 'Wir müssen alle
stille sein – als wie dein Vater unterm Stein' (M. Vogt (ed.),
Rassow Deutsche Geschichte, p. 427).
A satirical lullaby, based on a popular folk-tune 'Maikäfer
flieg, Dein Vater ist im Krieg'. The song suggests that Prussian military action enforces political abstention.

Vocabulary:
Preuß (m) = Prussian; die Augen zudrücken = to close one's
eyes [after death].

4. Friedrich Nietzsche, *David Strauß, der Bekenner und der Schrifsteller, [Erste Unzeitgemäße Betrachtung]* (1871)

Die öffentliche Meinung in Deutschland scheint es fast zu
verbieten, von den schlimmen und gefährlichen Folgen des
Krieges, zumal eines siegreich beendeten Krieges zu reden
[...]. Trotzdem sei es gesagt: ein großer Sieg ist eine große
5 Gefahr. Die menschliche Natur erträgt ihn schwerer als eine
Niederlage; ja es scheint selbst leichter zu sein, einen solchen
Sieg zu erringen, als ihn zu ertragen, daß daraus keine
schwerere Niederlage entsteht. Von allen schlimmen Folgen
aber, die der letzte mit Frankreich geführte Krieg hinter sich
10 dreinzieht, ist vielleicht die schlimmste ein weitverbreiteter,
ja allgemeiner Irrtum: der Irrtum der öffentlichen Meinung
und aller öffentlich Meinenden, daß auch die deutsche Kultur
in jenem Kampfe gesiegt habe und deshalb jetzt mit den
Kränzen geschmückt werden müsse, die so außerordentlichen
15 Begebnissen und Erfolgen gemäß seien. Dieser Wahn ist höchst
verderblich: nicht etwa weil er ein Wahn ist, [...] sondern
weil er imstande ist, unseren Sieg in eine völlige Niederlage
zu verwandeln: *in die Niederlage, ja Extirpation des deutschen
Geistes zugunsten des 'deutschen Reiches'.*

(K. Schlechta (ed.), *Friedrich Nietzsche, Werke in drei Bänden*, Band 1, Munich, 1962, p. 135.)

Commentary:
Nietzsche refers to the Franco-Prussian War of 1870/71 which led to the defeat of Napoleon III and to the subsequent unification of Germany. He warns the public that the sense of exuberance and superiority was not generally justified. Nietzsche's comments should be read in connection with the caution by Renan (Text 5). German unification diverted public attention from cultural matters; Nietzsche suggests that public opinion wrongly celebrated this war as a *Kulturkrieg*, with the victory of German culture over French civilisation.

Vocabulary:
öffentliche Meinung (f) = public opinion; zumal = in particular; Niederlage (f) = defeat; erringen = to gain; ertragen = to suffer; dreinziehen = to cause; weitverbreitet = common; Kranz (m) = wreath; gemäß = appropriate; Wahn (m) = delusion; verderblich = ruinous; segensreich = beneficial.

5. Ernest Renan, *Lettre à un Ami d'Allemagne* (Paris, 1879) (considerably abridged)

No-one has more love or admiration for your great German nation than I; a Germany of fifty or sixty years ago, personified by Goethe's genius and represented in the eyes of the world by this wonderful array of poets, philosophers, his-
5 torians, critics and thinkers who have truly added a new dimension to the riches of the human mind. Whoever we are, we owe a great deal to this vast, intelligent, deep-thinking Germany, a nation that gave us Fichte's idealism, Herder's faith in humanity, Schiller's poetry of moral sense and Kant's
10 abstract duty. [. . .]
Since 1848, a time when distinct questions began to be asked, we have always acknowledged that German political unity would come about, that such a revolution was just and

necessary. We saw Germany's national unity as fundamental
15 to world harmony. What naivety! [...] We built up great
hopes for the day when this nation of philosophy and rationality, friend of liberty, enemy of old superstitions, symbol of
justice and idealism, would take its place in the great European confederation. [...]
20   But things in this world never turn out as the learned might
hope. Hence, our thinkers were not too surprised to see
German unity declared at Versailles, over the ruins of a de-
feated France; this unity which they had imagined would be
favourable to France. [...]
25   To do great things in the manner of the German spirit –
such was the duty of Prussia when the curse of war put Germany's destiny in her hands. She could do anything for the
good of humanity since the condition for realising this is
strength. What was to be done? What did she do? She has
30 been the uncontested master of Europe for eight years [...].
What progress has been achieved in Germany and the world
to mark this period in history? [...]
   These great social issues that perturb our age can only be
resolved by a victorious nation, having at its disposal the
35 prestige of glory to impose concessions, sacrifices or amnesty
to all parties. Bringing peace, as far as is possible in this world,
and the greatest possible degree of liberty to a continental
Europe that has not yet found its balance; establishing permanent representative government; dealing positively with
40 social problems; elevating the lower classes without filling
them with envy of those necessarily superior; reducing suffering; alleviating unwarranted misery; solving the delicate
question of women's financial status [...]: this would have
justified victory; this would have maintained it. [...]
45   From this situation that fate seems to have imposed upon
you, what have you accomplished? Have your people become happier, more moral, more satisfied with their fate?
Clearly not. [...] Why is your government always preoccupied with measures that restrict freedom? [...] You have
50 become a nation organised for war; like those sixteenth-

century armour-clad cavaliers, you are overburdened by your arms. [...]

And on the political front, in realising this ideal of constitutional government which is so dear to us all and which
55 Europe has not yet achieved, what progress have you made? Has your parliamentary life been more outstanding, more free, more creative than that of other nations? [...] I find your statesmen preoccupied above all with restrictions, repression, coercive laws. No, I will say it again, you will not
60 win over the world like this. [...]

National glory is a great incitement for national genius. You have had an admirable literary movement for eighty years during which we have seen your writers flourish; writers who are amongst the greatest in the world. Why has this inspira-
65 tion dried up? [...] You certainly do not lack talent; but, in my opinion, two things have damaged your literary production: firstly, your excessive military costs and, secondly, your social state. [...]

Despite your strength, you have not created liberty. Your
70 campaign against ultramontanism, legitimate when confined to suppressing Catholic intolerance, has made no progress whatsoever towards solving the question of the separation of church and state. Your ministers continue to follow the old system of conferring state privileges to the church in return
75 for certain demands, but they fail to see that these demands, with their impression of tyranny, are outweighed by the privileges accorded to the church. [...]

[...] Humanity is frivolous; one must realise this if it is to be won over or governed.
80 To win over, one must please it; to please it, one must be amiable. Your Prussian statesmen are gifted in all areas but this one. Determination, implementation, restrained and unyielding genius have not proved to be lesser qualities than those of the great political minds of the past. But they are
85 mistaken if they believe that this is the way to please the world and win it over. The only way to leave one's mark on humanity is through love of humanity; through broad-minded,

172   *German thought and culture*

liberal attitudes and amiability which your new masters scoff
at so much, which they call a pretentious and sentimental
90 dream.

(Ernest Renan, *Lettre à un Ami d'Allemagne*, Paris,
1879; pp. 2–11, translated by Garry Tyrrell.)

Commentary: (numbers in parentheses refer to line numbers
in the text)
Ernest Renan (1823–92), French philosopher and Oriental
specialist, was influenced by the German Left Hegelian liberal theologian David Friedrich Strauß (1808–74), his 'German friend', whose *Das Leben Jesu* (1835/36) was of particular
influence on him. Also influenced by German idealism.
Ami d'Allemagne: his German friend Strauß.
(11) The German Revolution of 1848 and the debate on the
issue of German unification within a system of parliamentary
democracy.
(22) The Second German Reich was proclaimed during the
peace negotiations at Versailles (18th January 1871), the result of Prussia's defeat of France.
(33) 'the great social issues' are mentioned in this paragraph;
Renan thinks in particular of the effects of the industrial revolution and the emancipation of the working classes, to be
followed by the emancipation of women.
(49) 'measures that restrict freedom' refer in particular to the
Kulturkampf (cf. Chapter 2).
(56) 'parliamentary life': the German Constitution of 1871
was in fact far less liberal than the one envisaged in 1848. It
was the Kaiser's right to nominate his chancellor and to con-
vene parliament (*Bundesrat* and *Reichstag*).
(70) 'ultramontanism': a return to an extreme form of
montanism, an early Christian movement originating in the
second century.
(72f) The Protestant Church in Prussia was a state church;
the close relationship between throne and altar meant that
virtually the whole of Germany's elite was Protestant, with

the suppression of Catholics, at least during the period of the *Kulturkampf*.

(87f) 'Love of humanity' refers to the neo-classical German movement, returning the argument to Goethe and Schiller, with whom Renan's letter had begun.

Topics for further study

1. Try to give a definition of the German term *Sonderweg* and attempt to discuss how Germany, as a result of its history and geography, can lay claim to this position.

2. Describe the characteristics of the German 'middle classes' prior to 1848 and consider how they were affected by the rapid industrialisation of the second half of the century.

3. Attempt to explain why we witness the decline of liberal values after 1848 and to what extent this decline shaped the peculiar nature of the German Reich after 1871.

4. Compare the statements made by Mme de Staël with those of Ernest Renan (Texts 1 and 5). In how far do they represent a common perception of Germany at that time?

7

The decline of philosophical idealism and the road to inhumanity

The following points are discussed in this Chapter: literary images of the 'death of God' and of metaphysics. The dominance of philosophy over theology at the beginning of the nineteenth century as exemplified in Hegel and further illustrated in Goethe's Faust. The decline of metaphysical philosophy with Schopenhauer, Feuerbach and other 'Left-Hegelians' and its replacement by anthropology and economics. Nietzsche's pronouncement of the 'death of God' and its consequences: the critique of Christian ethics and the search for an Übermensch. The perversion of Nietzschean ideas at the turn of the century as illustrated in the ideologies of Spengler, Lagarde and other precursors of National Socialism.

Introduction

This Chapter differs slightly from the others in that it attempts to trace the philosophical developments of the nineteenth century, perversions of which led not only to Germany's alienation from Western civilisation, but also to a departure from its traditional stance. Since the Middle Ages Germany had established a strong lead in metaphysics, associated with the country's premier role in the Holy Roman Empire, birthplace of the Reformation. To keep this philosophical discourse within reasonable bounds, we will limit ourselves to the one theme: the 'death of God' and the consequent development of the *Übermensch*. Whilst our discussion will include the rise of racism and National Socialism, the decline of idealism should not be seen as a major attributive force in the rise of National Socialism, nor should connections be assumed between the philosophies of Hegel and

Nietzsche, and racism. Instead, the philosophical development should be seen as just one factor which can illustrate the proximity of culture and barbarism, or, as Thomas Mann put it, 'daß es nicht zwei Deutschland gibt, ein böses und ein gutes, sondern nur eines, dem sein Bestes durch Teufelslist zum Bösen ausschlug'[1] (that there are not two Germanies, a wicked and a good one, but only one whose best qualities were turned into evil through devilish cunning). We shall refer to just three aspects, all embedded in the Lutheran tradition of *Weltfrömmigkeit*.

The integration of religion into philosophy at the beginning of the nineteenth century

The Enlightenment not only achieved the individual's emancipation from the authority of aristocracy and the clergy, but also led to a fundamental critique of religion as superstition, summarised in Voltaire's 'écrasez l'infame'.[2] At the end of the eighteenth century, German literature was dominated by discussion of such metaphysical matters. Probably more than any other literature, German literature was in need of 'metanarratives' in order to preserve its cohesion, since it had not yet gained recognition as a national literature, nor was it associated with a stratum of society leading the struggle for emancipation.[3]

The notion of *Gottesferne* (God's alienation from man) and of man's separation from metaphysics was Schiller's theme in his philosophical poem *Die Götter Griechenlands* (1788). The ascent to heaven of the Christian God not only destroyed the earlier, joyous companionship of ancient gods with men, but also abandoned mankind in a joyless world, governed by the mechanical laws of cause and effect and void of true beauty.[4] Hölderlin's poem *Brod und Wein* (1801) approaches the same subject, but in a slightly more open way, taking the theme of endlessness instead of infinity, a cold objectivity instead of the sacred union of human beings and gods in 'blessed Greece':

Aber Freund! wir kommen zu spät. Zwar leben die Götter,
Aber über dem Haupt droben in anderer Welt.
Endlos wirken sie da und scheinen's wenig zu achten,
Ob wir leben, so sehr schonen die Himmlischen uns.
(But, my friend! We have come too late. Though the gods
are living,
Over our heads they live, up in a different world.
Endlessly there they act
and, such is their kind wish to spare us,
Little they seem to care whether we live or do not.)[5]

In his famous 'Rede des todten Christus vom Weltgebäude
herab, daß kein Gott sei'[6] (1796) (The dead Christ's speech
from the height of the cosmos, that there was no God), Jean
Paul anticipates the end of metaphysics. In the form of a
nightmare he experiences an utter heavenly void, but the
horror of a godless world disappears as he awakens and he
can return joyfully to his religion and the worship of God.
Jean Paul achieves only an emotional, not an intellectual volte-
face, and his prayer has become part of a religious insight.
The German Romantic movement was in particular opposed
to the French Enlightenment's one-sided logocentrism and
sought to re-establish the Christian faith. Schleiermacher's
famous *Reden über Religion* (Speeches on Religion) bear the
subtitle 'an die Gebildeten unter ihren Verächtern' (to the
educated among its detractors) and they define religion as a
feeling of *Wehmut* (wistfulness) for a once existing totality of
the individual in God.[7]

The early Hegel had been close to Schleiermacher's position in defining love as the binding force which would restore the lost totality of the human being and God, subject
and object. The more mature Hegel recognised that religion
had to be subordinated to philosophy in order to avoid
Schleiermacher's equation of religion with feeling. To this
end, religion and philosophy must be reconciled, religion
sublimated in philosophy, a process which would also give a

new impetus to the powers of reflection, no longer limiting reflective action to pure reason, but leading to a genuine realisation of the infinite.[8] Hegel distinguishes between a truly infinite life and a 'schlechte Unendlichkeit' (a spurious infinite).[9] The latter is only the 'endlessness which characterises the world of finite things', but the former is achieved by double negation and not by mere exclusion; it is a whole which is more than the sum of its parts.[10] This operation alone can bring about the reconciliation of faith and knowledge. Towards the end of his treatise *Glauben und Wissen* (Faith and Knowledge) Hegel accepts death as a necessary condition of life and of true infinity. In one of his most obscure passages he defines true infinity as 'der Abgrund des Nichts, worin alles Sein versinkt'[11] (the abyss of nothingness, into which all existence vanishes). This description encompasses the notion of the death of God, previously expressed only empirically in Pascal's *Dieu perdu*, but now philosophically defined as 'spekulativer Karfreitag' (speculative Good Friday). Hegel's term transfers the death of God from its dogmatic status as expressed in the second part of the Creed[12] via its historicity to philosophy. Out of the 'Härte und Gottlosigkeit [kann und muß] [...] die höchste Totalität in ihrem ganzen Ernst und aus ihrem tiefsten Grunde, zugleich allumfassend und in der heitersten Freiheit ihrer Gestalt auferstehen'[13] (harshness and Godlessness [can and must] rise up the most absolute totality in its utter earnestness and from the very depths of its being, at the same time all embracing and in the most joyful freedom of form). This reasoned understanding of the death of God is the necessary precondition for an infinity which encompasses death. Death thus becomes the necessary transition to life.

In the preface to *Phänomenologie des Geistes* (1807) Hegel further examines the importance of death, describing the life of the spirit ('Leben des Geistes') as the only force which can bear and sustain the notion of death.[14] It thus achieves 'die wahrhafte Substanz' (true substance) which is totally within itself, 'das Sein oder die Unmittelbarkeit, welche nicht die

Vermittlung außer ihr hat, sondern diese selbst ist'[15] (the essence or the immediacy which carries the mediation within it and is at one with it). Hegel's philosophy thereby achieved a totality which was essentially and comprehensively a concrete universal; it had overcome the separation of thought and life. He could pronounce with justification the identity of the real and the natural: 'Was vernünftig ist, das ist wirklich; / und was wirklich ist, das ist vernünftig'.[16] (The real is the rational and the rational is the real.) In philosophical terms Hegel achieved what Novalis in his *Hymnen an die Nacht* could express in poetic terms only, the all-in-one-ness of life and death, of man and God: 'Im Tode war das ewge Leben kund, / Du bist der Tod und machst uns erst gesund'.[17] (Only in Death did we gain knowledge of Eternal Life, / You are Death and you alone can make us whole'.) In all these instances the position of man *vis-à-vis* the anticipated death of God becomes crucial. Hegel employs philosophy and the reflective power of reason to go beyond mere feeling, but all writers mentioned here rely on a *Zauberkraft*,[18] a magic force, to turn the negation of God into its essence, into true life.

One particularly interesting case in point is Goethe's *Faust*, a work which occupied its author throughout his life. Faust's search for knowledge is absolute, it therefore leads to despair, to disillusionment with the inadequacy of the recognised disciplines of epistemology. Religion can no longer sustain him and in his desperate search for *Offenbarung* (revelation) he turns to St. John's Gospel, but cannot accept the translation of Greek *logos* as the Lutheran *Wort* and instead replaces it with *Tat*, action. Faust's emphasis on action further accentuates his challenge to the traditional metaphysical order; his 'great curse' not only rejects the finite world, but also declares war on the Christian virtues of Hope, Faith, and Patience and thereby on the Christian religion itself, for it withholds from him a fuller existence.[19] The ground is prepared for Faust's meeting with Mephistopheles, for a Satanic 'pact' in which Faust throws his spiritual well-being into the balance in order to secure super-human knowledge.[20] The pact or wager is based on Faust's conviction that he will never cease in his striving for knowledge, a striving which seems to define him as an *Übermensch*, as someone who is prepared to challenge the authority of a divine being.[21]

A brief recollection of the history of the term *Übermensch* will further illustrate this point: the word is recorded for the first time in 1527, when it was applied to Luther and his followers: 'Sie wandeln allein im geist und sind übermenschen und übermenschliche engel [. . .], dasz sie menschliche werke nicht mehr üben dürfen.'[22] (They wander alone in the spirit and are superhuman and superhuman angels [. . .] who are above the need for human deeds.) Within this context the term refers to men with above average moral qualities, to beings with quasi-angelic, spiritual attributes. As the term was introduced during the Renaissance, it can also be seen as indicative of medieval human being's rebellion against domination by priest and church, signalling a first emancipation from religious dogma. The word resurfaced 250 years later in Herder's generation, fluctuating somewhat between the exceptional *Außermensch* and the criminal *Unmensch*. Applied within the *Sturm und Drang* period, it gives an apt description of the genius or the new hero as *Tatmensch*. The adjective *übermenschlich* reinforces the divine qualities and suggests a human striving for divine omnipotence.

In Goethe's *Faust* the word is at first used in an ironical context by the *Erdgeist*, whose aid Faust had hoped to elicit. Having been scornfully rejected as an equal by this spirit of nature, Faust then seems to be reinstated in his super-human faculties, albeit by the mysterious *Geisterchor* who refer to him as *Halbgott*, accuse him of the destruction of the *schöne Welt* and urge him to rebuild it, if only in his own heart.[23] Faust's urge for knowledge has no ulterior motive, it can be compared with Adamic man's primeval thirst for knowledge, when the Serpent promises: 'your eyes shall be opened, and ye shall be as gods, knowing good and evil'.[24]

To refer briefly to the wider context of our discussion: Goethe cannot accept the Hegelian reconciliation of the real and the rational, cannot solve the death of God in philo-sophical terms. Instead, he seems to allude to Voltaire's dictum that 'Si Dieu n'existait pas, il faudrait l'inventer'.[25] Goethe's Faust has become a revolutionary in metaphysics, the Faustian *Übermensch* seeks omniscience. He rebels against the Christian *ordo* wishing to obtain divine omniscience for his own sake. However, Faust's revolution in metaphysics presented Goethe with another problem: the revolution had to remain open-ended, since it extended the all important human dimension. In later years Goethe was to recognise the futility of such a revolution and shied away from its nihilistic consequence. In Part Two of his great drama, completed during his classical phase, Goethe performed a 'U-turn': Faust returns to the Christian faith, receives a divine pardon and is commended for his honest striving: '*Wer immer strebend sich bemüht,/Den können wir erlösen*'.[26] (He who always endeavours to strive/Can find redemption.) With this affirmation, proclaimed by the angelic host, Faust's immortal soul returns to its Creator, reinforcing the Lord's statement in the Prologue, that while human striving will lead to error, remaining imperfect while man dwells on earth, God will lead the soul in its innate goodness from confusion to clarity.[27] Faust's deal with Mephistopheles is thus foreshadowed in the Prologue in the wager between the Lord and Mephistopheles. The transformed Faust of Part Two confines himself to this earthly world and replaces his former metaphysical aspirations with ethical considerations.[28] As a consequence, Faust, towards the end of his rich life, can confine himself to this world, can dismiss the supernatural assistance of Mephistopheles and can achieve self-reliance:

> Der Erdenkreis ist mir genug bekannt,
> Nach drüben ist die Aussicht uns verrannt;
> Tor, wer dorthin die Augen blinzelnd richtet,
> Sich über Wolken seinesgleichen dichtet!
> Er stehe fest und sehe hier sich um;
> Dem Tüchtigen ist diese Welt nicht stumm.

Was braucht er in die Ewigkeit zu schweifen!
(I've seen enough of this terrestrial sphere.
There is no view to the Beyond from here:
A fool will seek it, peer with mortal eyes
And dream of human life above the skies!
Let him stand fast in this world, and look round
With courage: here so much is to be found!
Why must he wander into timelessness?)[29]

The achievement of self-reliance, though accomplished here in only a very ironical manner – Faust has become blind and does not realise that the earth movements which he believes to be fortifications against the encroaching sea are actually the digging of his own grave – signals his return to ethical considerations. Faust seems to have recognised his own human limitations; he has forsaken his former, divine aspirations in favour of an ethical, humanitarian and humane attitude. The Faust of Part Two has embraced technology and economics, reclaiming land from the sea in order to sustain his fellow human beings.[30] This indicated Faust's rejection of the *Übermensch* concept, and although the new utopia associated with land reclamation might anticipate imperialism and the destruction of an idyllic world,[31] Faust is committed to life in the here and now, willing to forego any supernatural ties.

The transformation of theology into anthropology and the erosion of philosophical idealism

Completing his Faust drama a few days before his death, Goethe bequeathed it to a changed world. Philosophy had abandoned metaphysics; a further dismantling of theology in favour of anthropology and mythology was under way. Some forty years later Friedrich Nietzsche was to re-open this discussion, this time with unforeseeable consequences. However, before turning to Nietzsche's debate on the 'death of God' we must briefly review the intervening period and its rejection of metaphysics.

Whereas Hegel and most other representatives of German Idealism interpreted the world as an emanation from the divine spirit, the next generation of German philosophers turned against such a notion and either separated the metaphysical world entirely from the here and now, or transformed metaphysics into a function of the individual by perceiving it from an entirely anthropological viewpoint. Arthur Schopenhauer can be seen as the first anti-Hegelian philosopher. He derided Hegel as a charlatan and ridiculed his philosophy as *Kathederhanswurstiade*[32] (the armchair philosophy of a buffoon). He made similarly dismissive statements about the philosophies of the later Kant, of Fichte and Schelling and bitterly describes himself as a 'Kaspar Hauser' amongst philosophers,[33] as the unacknowledged stranger within the German school of philosophy. His rage against the philosophical establishment was partly the result of envy at being completely ignored by colleagues and students, but it also signals his abandonment of philosophical idealism in favour of an anthropological world view. His main opus, *Die Welt als Wille und Vorstellung* (1819/44), describes the world as *Gehirnanschauung*[34] (phenomenon of the brain), and defines the Kantian 'Ding an sich' (the thing in itself) as *Wille*[35] (volition) (Text 1a). Such a volition can only be of a very general nature; it precludes any form of individual willpower (Text 1b). Man is entirely defined within the *principium individuationis*, reduced to the categories of space and time. Whenever we conceive of ourselves as individuals, equipped with our own willpower, we delude ourselves. Schopenhauer's *Wille* is the will to live, but is not individual willpower. Whilst Fichte could still perceive of such a general willpower as action which achieved self-awareness in the individual,[36] Schopenhauer attacks this notion as absolute absurdity, since it is not directed towards an individual being. Its major manifestation within the individual is suffering and we can lessen this painful manifestation of volition through *Mitleid*, literally a 'joint suffering' or pity. Other modes of alleviating individual suffering lie in the enjoyment of art, particularly of

Philosophical idealism and inhumanity   183

music, since through this aesthetic enjoyment the individual can overcome the awareness of personal individuality and can gain some temporary cosmic comprehension. The most effective form of negating the realisation of willpower and individual suffering lies in Indian philosophy and religion, in particular in the notion of Nirvana.[37]

These few observations on Schopenhauer indicate his categorical opposition to German idealism; his atheism, born out of a fundamental pessimism, cannot conceive of a divine principle. We shall see later how Nietzsche has adopted some of Schopenhauer's ideas, but developed them in his own way. We also need to note in passing the tremendous impact which Schopenhauer had on Sigmund Freud; the latter's concept of the subconscious, of the 'Id', owes much to Schopenhauer's philosophy, as do his later cultural studies.

The philosophy of Ludwig Feuerbach (1804–72) presents in many respects the very opposite approach to Schopenhauer in that it focuses on the individual in a positive sense, regarding the abstraction of a general will with some scepticism. In a fragmentary statement in which he discusses Schopenhauer's philosophy, Feuerbach pledges to turn people into 'freie, selbstbewußte Bürger der Erde'[38] (free, self-confident citizens of the earth), thus rejecting any metaphysical demands and Schopenhauer's *Weltekel* (universal nausea). Like Hegel, Feuerbach began his scholarly career as a student of theology but, influenced by Hegel, moved over to philosophy. Studying under Hegel in Berlin, he realised to what extent Hegel's philosophy was still indebted to speculative theology and began to question Hegel's concept of the absolute spirit, describing his philosophy as 'drunk' and demanding instead a sober approach:

Der Atheismus, die Negation der Theologie, wird daher wieder negiert, d.h. die Theologie durch die Philosophie wieder hergestellt. Gott ist Gott erst dadurch, daß er die Materie, die Negation Gottes, überwindet, negiert. [...] Die Hegelsche Philosophie ist der letzte großartige Versuch,

das verlorene, untergegangene Christentum durch die Philosophie wieder herzustellen, und zwar dadurch, daß, wie überhaupt in der neueren Zeit, die Negation des Christentums mit dem Christentum selbst indentifiziert wird.[39]
(Atheism, the negation of theology, is negated again, i.e. theology is restored by virtue of philosophy. God becomes God only through his overcoming of matter, the negation of God. [...] Hegel's philosophy is the last grand attempt to restore the lost, perished Christendom through philosophy, and it does this, as is generally the case in modern times, by identifying the negation of Christendom with Christendom itself.)

The quotation illustrates some key points in Feuerbach's philosophy: it defines God in a negative manner, i.e. as the negation of matter whilst it assumes matter as given. It assumes moreover that 'Christendom' is a lost cause and that its very own negation is identified with it. From this quotation we can move to others which throw further light on Feuerbach's thinking. Feuerbach turns Hegel's philosophy on its head; instead of starting with Hegel's absolute principle he starts with the individual. In his main oeuvre, *Das Wesen des Christentums* (1841) we read: 'Das absolute Wesen, der Gott des Menschen ist sein eigenes Wesen'.[40] (The absolute being, the God of man is his own being.) God is, in other words, the result of the imagination of the human being. The individual is the measure of all things and must be the starting point for all philosophy. Theology has to be resolved and subordinated within anthropology.[41] Religion is defined as a product of the consciousness of the human being. The last chapter of *Das Wesen des Christentums* claims to demonstrate that the mystery and object of religion is of human origin, that the secret of theology lies in anthropology.[42] Surveying the development of religion, Feuerbach maps out a (negative) progression which has much in common with the literary debate from Schiller via Hölderlin and Jean Paul to the Romantics and beyond. Pagan religion was still firmly embedded in nature. Christianity alone removed the human being from nature into the freedom of the imagination. The concept of the divine now coincides with the concept of humanity. In a rather long-winded argument Feuerbach demonstrates that 'Gott ist der Begriff der Gattung als eines Individuums'[43] (God is the concept of the [human] species as an individual), for it is in the human species that we as individuals see all other human qualities present. His own philosophy vowes to break with this tradition by re-establishing the human being in nature and by basing all epistemology on anthropology.

In *Grundsätze der Philosophie*, the difference between the old and the new philosophy is sharply accentuated:

> Wenn die alte Philosophie zu ihrem Ausgangspunkt den Satz hatte: ich bin ein abstraktes, ein nur denkendes Wesen, der Leib gehört nicht zu meinem Wesen; so beginnt dagegen die neue Philosophie mit dem Satze: ich bin ein wirkliches, sinnliches Wesen; ja der Leib in seiner Totalität ist mein ich, mein Wesen selber.[44]

> (If the old philosophy started from the premise: I am an abstract, a solely thinking being, the body is not part of me; then by contrast the new philosophy begins with the sentence: I am a real, sensuous being; the body in its totality is me, my being itself.)

Feuerbach further underlined these sentiments in the memorable and often quoted sentence: 'Der Mensch ist, was er ißt'[45] (One is what one eats). This formula reduces all things to the laws of cause and effect and is firmly rooted in materialism. Little wonder then that the resurrection of Christ was explained as 'das befriedigte Verlangen des Menschen nach unmittelbarer Gewißheit von seiner persönlichen Fortdauer nach dem Tode – die persönliche Unsterblichkeit als eine sinnliche, unbezweifelbare Tatsache'[46] (the satisfaction of the need of humans for immediate certainty regarding their personal continuance after death – personal immortality as an undisputed physical fact). Having thus de-mythologised the philosophical concept of the death of God, he can, in an explanatory postscript to *Das Wesen des Christentums*, supply the formula: 'Der Mensch ist der Gott des Christentums, die Anthropologie das Geheimnis der christlichen Theologie.'[47] (The individual is the God of Christendom, anthropology the secret of Christian theology.) Or with reference to the main issue of our investigation: the human being is God, that is all, there is no need even for an *Übermensch*, for transcendence into mythology.

The scope of this Chapter does not permit a further exploration of Feuerbach's contemporaries. Feuerbach himself was greatly influenced by the theologian David Friedrich Strauß (1808–74) whose main oeuvre *Das Leben Jesu* (1835/36) attempted to demythologise the Gospel and approach religion through anthropology. Max Stirner (1806–56) took Feuerbach's philosophy to its logical conclusion by declaring the Self as the basis of all things and by introducing a radical form of philosophical egoism. In the vicinity of these philosophers stands Karl Marx (1818–83). He, too, was influenced by Feuerbach, but rejected the anthropological and individualistic approach in favour of a broader socio-historical interpretation, which saw the individual closely integrated into its material environment, so much so that it becomes the *homo economicus*, a being determined by economic processes.

By the end of the nineteenth century society experienced an ideological crisis. The materialism of the Left-Hegelian school had apparently led into a cul-de-sac; belief in the law of causation was shaken, the need for a new mythology was apparent and a new 'Reich der Jugend'[48] was proclaimed.

Nietzsche's radical departure from Western tradition
The notion of the 'death of God' gained a new and more radical interpretation with Friedrich Nietzsche. Whereas Hegel subsumed Christianity under the mantle of philosophy and the spirit of the absolute, the Left-Hegelian school from Feuerbach to Marx saw the death of God as a form of

emancipation, a liberation of the individual in the spirit of the Enlightenment. Nietzsche's own contribution led to a most radical and comprehensive questioning of our human tradition, almost from its historical foundations. Nietzsche refers frequently to the death of God throughout his work; the most memorable passage occurs in *Die fröhliche Wissenschaft* (1882) (Text 2). The passage is introduced by referring to a parable relating how after Buddha's death, his shadow was still visible in a cave, and going on to suggest:

> Gott ist tot: aber so wie die Art des Menschen ist, wird es vielleicht noch jahrtausendelang Höhlen geben, in denen man seinen Schatten zeigt. – Und wir – müssen auch noch seinen Schatten besiegen![49]
> (God is dead, but given the nature of man there may well be caves for a few thousand more years in which his shadow is on display. – And we – must also vanquish his shadow!)

The 'shadow' Nietzsche talks of is of a complex nature. It includes not only Christian morality with its notion of good and evil, but it also refers to the 'shadowy' existence of systems of whatever kind, in philosophy, religion and elsewhere. A new approach to life and to the meaning of life becomes necessary for the individual, signifying, in Nietzsche's opinion, the replacement of God by the *Übermensch*.

These ideas are evident in the passage referred to in Text 2, although the passage itself retains a deeply melancholic atmosphere of mourning, a cosmic awareness of the greatness of a deed of which human beings are – as yet – unworthy. The fifth book of *Die fröhliche Wissenschaft* bears the subtitle 'Wir Furchtlosen' (We, the fearless ones); and it strikes the reader as somewhat contradictory. Whilst Nietzsche fearlessly and optimistically proclaims a new age, 'the like of which has never before existed on earth', an age which will change our European morality and will afford humans the prospect of an entirely new beginning, he also suggests that we still maintain a certain piety because we cannot free ourselves of the last residue of a logocentric form of thinking and arguing. The death of God leads therefore not only to a life *Beyond Good and Evil* (1886),[50] the book which he saw as a prelude to a philosophy of the future, but also embraces the very possibility of such a projected philosophy. The magnitude of Nietzsche's undertaking was obvious to him, perhaps more so than to his later interpreters. Nietzsche is at his best in his analytical passages, attempting to question the totality of human thought and tradition; but one should also note that he often seems vague or 'poetic', even contradictory, when offering solutions. In his posthumously published writings, Nietzsche tries to explain his vagueness under the heading 'Mein neuer Weg zum "Ja"'[51] (My new approach to a 'yes'). Philosophy must not shy away from even the most 'despicable and heinous aspects of our existence' and, when facing the issue of how much truth an intellect can bear, it moves into the realms of psychology. The philosopher must not avoid any issues, even if his philosophy has to remain incomplete and of an experimental nature (Text 3). The only limitation Nietzsche sets for himself in such an 'experimental philosophy' is the acceptance of life now, of a life with no illusions, a life freed from the claims of historical and moral consciousness, from the Christian 'schlechte Gewissen' (guilty conscience). His maxim is *amor fati*, love of fate. Nietzsche seems to follow Schopenhauer here, except that the latter found no positive answer to this 'unconditional and honest atheism', whereas for Nietzsche it became a triumph of the 'European conscience', achieved after a struggle of 2000 years, which the final rejection of 'the *lie* of belief in God.'[52]

The problematic and often disturbing nature of Nietzsche's philosophy centres on two concepts which emerged particularly in his later work, the idea of an *Übermensch* and of a 'Wille zur Macht' (will to power). Both terms are used very frequently throughout his work and should be understood as part of his 'experimental' philosophy, as terms in the making, not yet fully operational. The term *Übermensch* is most closely allied to his *Also sprach Zarathustra*, an early twentieth century best-seller, but – I believe – much overrated, both as a philosophical discourse and as a literary work. It uses the Gospel as a paradigm, but fails to live up to it in terms of conviction and seriousness of intent. The relationship to the Gospel is important, since it suggests the possibility of a new logocentrism, a replacement for the dead God. As a result, it announces the advent of the *Übermensch*, but remains vague in defining this new creature. In the prologue to *Zarathustra* the *Übermensch* is defined as 'Sinn der Erde'[53] (the earth's essence), allowing us to live beyond good and evil. The individual is described as 'a rope' linking beast and *Übermensch*,[54] but is also seen as a transitional stage to be 'overcome'. We can only speculate as to the relationship between the human being and *Übermensch*, and Nietzsche himself occasionally fell victim to Darwinian concepts of evolution. The central message of the *Übermensch* occurs at the end of *Zarathustra*, part one: '"*Tot sind alle Götter: nun wollen wir, daß der Übermensch lebe*"'[55] ('All gods are dead; we now desire the *Übermensch* to live').

Modern and post-modern philosophers have criticised Nietzsche for his attempt to recreate a new meta-narrative, a new logocentric system.[56] It is not without irony that Nietzsche criticised Goethe's *Faust* on rather similar grounds, though his criticism seems, at first sight, to suggest the very opposite. Whilst praising the Faustian individual who challenges an untenable metaphysical world and sympathising with Faust's rejection of a theoretical, 'Socratic' approach to life, Nietzsche regrets Goethe's 'U-turn' and Faust's ultimate acceptance of a metaphysical order. Comparing Goethe with Rousseau, he states:

der Mensch Goethes weicht hier dem Menschen Rousseaus aus; denn er haßt jedes Gewaltsame, jeden Sprung – das heißt aber: jede Tat; und so wird aus dem Weltbefreier Faust gleichsam nur ein Weltreisender. [...] An einer beliebigen Stelle der Erde endet der Flug, die Schwingen fallen herab, Mephistopheles ist bei der Hand. Wenn der Deutsche aufhört Faust zu sein, ist keine Gefahr größer als die, daß er ein Philister werde und dem Teufel verfalle – nur himmlische Mächte können ihn hiervon erlösen.[57] (Goethe's concept of the human being shies away from Rousseau's man, for he hates everything forceful, every leap – and that is to say every action; and thus the world-liberator Faust turns, as it were, into a world traveller. [...] At an arbitrary point on earth his flight ends, his wings are shed, Mephistopheles is at hand. When the German ceases to be Faust then there is no greater danger than that he becomes a philistine and falls prey to the devil – only heavenly forces can save him from this.)

In retrospect, Nietzsche's own version of the *Übermensch* seems to fare little better; he too seems to seek for some form of metaphysics and it is questionable whether this *Übermensch* does not eventually occupy a similar position to that of God. For Nietzsche, the *Übermensch* is more of an Anti-Christ:[58] he rejects the Christian and humanist virtues of forgiveness, of humility, of restraint and endows his *Übermensch* with a 'will to power' which was finally to unleash the *Raubtier* and the *blonde Bestie*[59] with specifically racist implications. However, most Nietzschean scholars would not go as far in their criticism of this aspect of Nietzsche's philosophy and we must bear in mind his experimental style, the futuristic notion of his *Übermensch* concept.

As a formula, the 'will to power' is a most fascinating notion which has much in common with Schopenhauer's 'will'. Unlike the latter, Nietzsche gave it a positive, life-creating, life-enhancing nature, opposed to the Darwinian struggle for existence and Spinoza's self-preservation.[60] Emerging from his own Dionysian life-force, it is not an individualised will to live. Nietzsche's 'will to power' is in this respect synonymous with his desire for truth, for 'honest atheism'.[61] It is the living principle behind a conception of the world in terms of quanta and fields of force.[62] But as the will to power becomes an all-pervasive force which can explain all forces and every change as 'the encroachment of one power on another'[63] it is inevitable that Nietzsche should also employ the term in a political sense: democracy, in particular, is viewed as a form of decadence,[64] as a system that promotes weakness rather than strength. The product of such a system is the 'letzte Mensch' (lowest form of a human being), the opposite of the aristocrat and, to all intents and purposes, also of the *Übermensch*. This type of individual merely exists; it has sunk below self-criticism, belittling everything and seeking only material comfort and happiness.[65] Democracy, according to Nietzsche, encourages a slave mentality and the herd instinct. Seen in this context, Nietzsche is not free of racist ideas, even if these are not fully developed.[66] *Zur Genealogie der Moral* contains passages which speak of the Aryan race as a race of conquerors[67] and suggests that inferior races can stage a come-back under the cover of socialism, democracy and anarchism. While philosophical studies on Nietzsche tend to ignore or play down these statements, they have to be faced and ana-lysed in order to gain a full understanding of Nietzsche's impact on his followers and in particular on a Germany which had yet to experience democratic government and which, after the defeat of 1918, felt humiliated and vulnerable.

The perversion of philosophy and the rise of racist ideology

Much has been written in recent decades about the advent of National Socialism in Germany and especially about its vari-ous antecedents. Space permits only a very brief glance at those regarded as precursors of the 'Third Reich' and whose ideas can, almost without exception, be traced back to Nietzsche and his philosophy. Julius Langbehn is a case in point. His fame rests almost exclusively on one book, pub-lished in 1890 and into its 37th edition only one year later. *Rembrandt als Erzieher* was meant to bring about a new reformation. Rembrandt was celebrated as the perfect Ger-man, representing the antithesis to modern Western culture.[68] The book, written in an unsystematic, fragmentary and apho-ristic style, a 'rhapsody of irrationalism'[69] breathes Nietzsche's influence in style, character and theme. Langbehn cultivated Nietzsche's very life-style, almost down to Nietzsche's ill health. Lonely, eccentric, an unstable, homeless wanderer, he met the sick Nietzsche in Jena and resolved to rescue him, to rekindle his defunct intellect. His affinity with Nietzsche was, however, superficial: less interested in Nietzsche's analytical phase and in his profound atheism, he emulated instead Nietzsche's later attempts to reform his generation and to find a way forward. Rejecting the dominance of science and empiricism, condemning the intellectual penetration of life and the tradition of the Enlightenment which, by the turn of the century, manifested itself in modernism, Langbehn sought salvation for the perceived ills of his civilisation in secluded individualism. The true German combines within him or her talents of the original artist and warrior, predestined for the 'Zeitalter der kämpfenden und schaffenden Hand'[70] (the era of the martial and creative hand). His principle is 'Kunst und Krieg'[71] (art and war) (Figure 9).

Many of Langbehn's ideas share a hysterical contempt for democracy with those of the representatives of the Conservative Revolution, who wished for the return to a corporate state.[72] He advocates the destruction of the existing social order and the release of the individual's elementary passions, leading to a new Germany, based on artistry, genius and power. His venom is particularly directed at the spirit of 1848: instead of a liberal revival and reconciliation with Western views, Langbehn desires a return to folk-beliefs, 'Bindung des Volksgeistes'[73] (a bonding with the common spirit of the people). Here we see not only links to the German Youth Movement, but the foreshadowing of National Socialism: the bourgeoisie had become rootless, had turned philistine, had lost its innocence by straying from a folk-belief in nature and its origins. Racist tendencies became interwoven in such primitive Germanophilism, when a chapter on anti-semitism was added one year after the book's first publication.[74] The new Germany must return to values based on blood and soil, 'eine auf überlieferten geschichtlichen

Figure 9: 'Der deutsche Sieg' (1919)! by Fidus (Hugo Höppener). An example of the turn of the century Youth Culture (*Jugendstil*). Note the symmetry, the warrior's central position, in line with the rising sun, observe also the nudity of the figures, fashionable at the time; the raised hand of the central figure hails a new age. The picture symbolises the adoration of a *Führer*, of a messianic leader. For a detailed study on Fidus cf. Jost Hermand, 'Meister Fidus. Vom Jugendstil-Hippie zum Germanenschwärmer', in Hermand, *Der Schein des schönen Lebens. Studien zur Jahrhundertwende*, 1972. (Printed with kind permission of *Nymphenburger Verlag*)

Zuständen beruhende und darum mit den gesunden Elementen der niederen Volksklasse einige Sozialaristokratie'[75] (a social aristocracy, based on traditional historical conditions, united with those healthy elements of the common people).

Langbehn, who in his later years was to find a niche in Roman Catholicism, does not proclaim the death of God, but speaks instead of a rebirth of the nation, manifested in its youth movement. The new Germans must find their salvation in an artistic movement which is opposed to science and French modernity; it will fuse religion and art, truth and beauty in the incarnation of a German national genius. Langbehn's book ends with these words: 'Deutsch sein heißt Mensch sein; [...] es heißt individuell sein; es heißt ernst sein; es heißt fromm sein; es heißt Gott und dem Göttlichen dienen. Es heißt, leben.'[76] (To be German means to be human [...] to be individualistic; to be earnest, to be pious, to serve God and the divine. It means to live.)

Very similar ideas can be found in the oeuvre of Paul de Lagarde (1827–91).[77] Lagarde was an accomplished Orientalist and Old Testament scholar, but his real interest lay in the rebirth of Germany, in the spirit of Teutonic mythology. Nietzsche seemed interested in his work[78] and Langbehn regarded him highly. Lagarde, like Langbehn, was a very quarrelsome, lonely figure with a very low regard for his academic colleagues and a fanatical hatred of Jews. By 1850 he had broken with Prussian conservatism[79] and had become, as did Nietzsche two decades later, a vociferous critic of Prussia and later of the Second Empire. His anti-modernist sentiments exceeded those of Nietzsche and Langbehn; his venomous passion targeted liberalism, modern scholarship and philosophy and in particular every non-German influence, be it Semitic, Celtic or even Classical. He hated the cosmopolitan elements in the works of Goethe and Hegel, in liberalism and catholicism and hoped to free Christianity from the 'Jewish principle'.[80] Although a fundamental pessimist and prophet of doom, he believed in a rebirth of Germany and in a German national religion.

This combination of pessimism and the rejection of enlightened, modernist thought, so typical of Langbehn, Lagarde and, as we shall see presently, Spengler, led to the prophecy of a specific kind of *palingenesis*, based on *völkisch* principles and steeped in Teutonic mythology[81] (Text 4). The regenerated Germany was to be born out of a prehistoric Teutonic mythology, based on Siegfried and the Nibelungs, on Wotan and Baldur.[82] German religion, scholarship and art were to be purged of the modern spirit and returned to their *völkisch* origin. Lagarde advocated a national religion, a virtual deification of Germans: 'ein Leben auf Du und Du mit dem allmächtigen Schöpfer und Erlöser, Königsherrlichkeit und Herrschermacht gegenüber allem, was nicht göttlichen Geschlechts ist'[83] (an intimate relationship with the almighty creator and redeemer, royal magnificence and power over everything which is not of divine nature). The political demands of Lagarde anticipated those of Hitler: the borders of the new Germany were to be those of central Europe, Austria was to be returned to the Reich, together with all other territories inhabited by Germans; an 'ethnic cleansing' was to expel non-German elements to Russia in order to ensure more living space for true Germans.[84]

Oswald Spengler (1880–1936) became the most notorious writer to foreshadow the ideas of National Socialism. Not an original mind, he relied heavily on Nietzsche's philosophy, on the atmosphere created by the German Youth Movement and on the forces known collectively as instigators of the Conservative Revolution. Spengler's books, like those by Lagarde and Langbehn, became best-sellers, but he also enjoyed a considerable reputation beyond the German-speaking world. We shall refer mainly to his concept of the 'Faustian Man', the inhabitant of central and Northern Europe. Spengler was obsessed by simplistic biological ideas, based on the crude perception of life as a struggle for domination, a reductionist version of Nietzsche's will to power, infected by a fatalist vision of history, with each civilisation subject to the same laws of ageing as living organisms.[85] With such biological considerations in mind, Spengler had no time for humanist values. Central to Spengler's Faustian individual was the combination of Prussian discipline with an anti-Marxist socialism, as outlined in *Preußentum und Sozialismus* (1919). By demanding the liberation of Socialism from Marxist philosophy, he became the forerunner of Hitler and his National Socialism, as can be further illustrated from his appeal to the German youth:

> I call upon those who have marrow in their bones and blood in their veins. ... Become men! We do not want any more talk about culture and world citizenship and Germany's spiritual mission. We need hardness, a bold scepticism, a class of socialist mastermen. ...[86]

Commenting on Spengler's anti-intellectualism, his anti-rationalism and absolute fatalism, Thomas Mann called him a 'snob'.[87]

With oblique reference to the legendary Faust of the *Volksbuch* – who became a victim of his alchemist experiments – Spengler defines the Faustian individual as an inventor and discoverer, master of the twentieth century technological age, but eventually also its victim (Text 5). The technological thinking of the Faustian individual is of religious origin, likened to the individual's struggle with God for omniscience. Spengler's Faustian individual, knowing no morality, no tolerance towards other cultures, obeys only its inner will to power. Spengler accepts atheism as a form of decay, typical of a culture in decline and symptomatic of the Faustian individual's faith in the machine,[88] for there is no alternative solution for the Faustian culture. His answer to the Nietzschean death of God lies in fatalistic pessimism, far removed from Nietzsche's own *amor fati*. He compares the end of the Faustian individual with the death of a Roman soldier, engulfed by the eruption of Mount Vesuvius:

> Optimismus ist Feigheit. Wir sind in diese Zeit geboren und müssen tapfer den Weg zu Ende gehen, der uns

bestimmt ist. Es gibt keinen anderen. Auf dem verlorenen Posten ausharren, ohne Rettung, ist Pflicht. [...] Das ist Größe, das heißt Rasse haben. Dieses ehrliche Ende ist das einzige, das man dem Menschen nicht nehmen kann.[89] (Optimism is cowardice. We have been born into this age and must bravely continue on our predetermined path to its very end. There is no other way. It is our duty to remain at the doomed post without salvation. [...] This is greatness, this means to be of the true race. Such an honest end is the one thing which cannot be taken away from man.)

The passage is reminiscent of Hitler's 'final victory' call which spelt death to millions of civilians and could serve no conceivable purpose. Such attitudes betray an inhuman, anticivilising stance, inspired by a pre-historic, barbaric Germanic mythology to which the virtues of moderation, modesty and mercy were unknown.

We have attempted to demonstrate in this Chapter how the keen idealism of the early nineteenth century was repeatedly overturned. The hypothesis of a 'speculative' death of God was becoming increasingly taken for granted, the age of nihilism failing to provide a new, civilising morality so that, with the advent of National Socialism, Hegel's formula relating reason to reality was turned upside down, turning *Wirklichkeit* into *Unvernunft*, into madness. Goethe's essential humanity, which had shied away from the dangers of Faust's metaphysical revolution, was ultimately overturned by the satanic inhumanity of Nazism. Completed during the final days of the Second World War, Thomas Mann's novel *Doktor Faustus* is a most moving document. It exposes the satanic dangers of the Faustian individual and was conceived as a profound and tragic history of a Germany moving away 'from everything bourgeois, moderate, classical [...] sober, industrious and dependable into a world of drunken release, a life of bold, Dionysiac genius, beyond society. [...] Fascism as a Devil-given departure from bourgeois society which leads through adventures of intoxicatingly intense subjective feeling and super-greatness to mental collapse and spiritual death, and soon to physical death: the reckoning is presented'.[90]

Notes

1   Th. Mann, 'Deutschland und die Deutschen', in *Gesammelte Werke*, Vol. 11, p. 1146.
2   Quoted from G. Büchmann, *Geflügelte Worte*, 30th edn, Berlin: Droemer-Knaur, 1961; p. 395f.
3   cf. Chapter 3, p. 56.
4   F. Schiller, *Sämtliche Werke* (Säkularausgabe), Vol. 1, p. 160.
5   F. Hölderlin, *Sämtliche Werke*, F. Beißner (ed.), (Große Stuttgarter Ausgabe), Vol. 2, Stuttgart: Kohlhammer, 1951; p. 93. Transl. by M. Hamburger, *Friedrich Hölderlin, Poems and Fragments*, 3rd edn, London, 1994; p. 269.
6   Jean Paul, *Werke*, Vol. 2, Munich: Hanser, 1959; pp. 266–71.
7   F. Schleiermacher, *Über die Religion. Reden an die Gebildeten unter ihren Verächtern*, 7th edn, R. Otto (ed.), Göttingen: Vandenhoeck and Ruprecht, 1991; p. 198.
8   G. W. F. Hegel, *Werke*, Vol. 1 (Frühe Schriften), Frankfurt a.M.: Suhrkamp, 1986; p. 422.
9   Transl. by G. R. G. Mure, *The Philosophy of Hegel*, Oxford: OUP, 1965; p. 22, footnote 2. cf. also Hegel, *Werke*, Vol. 1, p. 427.
10 Hegel, *Werke*, Vol. 1, p. 427.
11 Hegel, *Werke*, Vol. 2 ('Jenaer Schriften'), p. 432.
12 The Creed of St. Athanasius seems to challenge the concept of the death of 'God', it accepts only the death of Jesus, as in the Catechism. Furthermore, it sees the Incarnation not as 'the transformation of the Godhead into flesh' but as that 'of the Manhood into God'.
13 Hegel, *Werke*, Vol. 2, p. 432f.
14 Hegel, *Werke*, Vol. 3 (*Phänomenologie des Geistes*), p. 37.
15 *ibid.*
16 Hegel, *Werke*, Vol. 7 ('Grundlinien der Philosophie des Rechts'), p. 24.
17 Novalis, *Schriften*, Vol. 1, Stuttgart: Kohlhammer, 1960; p. 147.
18 Hegel, *Werke*, Vol. 3, p. 37.
19 Goethe's *Faust*, verses 1605f. cf. also M. Beddow, *Goethe, Faust I*, London: Grant and Cutler, 1986; p. 51f.
20 Research literature on this topic is too vast for discussion here. Faust does, in fact, not enter into a pact with Mephistopheles in the narrower sense of the word, but rather challenges him: offering up his soul, should he ever surrender his active striving in favour of contentment and sensual pleasure.
21 On the complex nature of the wager cf. B. Bennett, *Goethe's Theory of Poetry. Faust and the Regeneration of Language*, Ithaca: Cornell University Press, 1986; p. 81: 'On the one hand, it is clear that Faust must eventually lose the wager; the alienation and frustration of our existence constitute our true unity with nature and [. . .] tempt us constantly toward a transcendent experience of unity, toward a perfect

Philosophical idealism and inhumanity   199

moment [. . .] But on the other hand, Faust can never lose the wager, for the perfect moment must automatically negate itself as soon as it occurs and drive us back into our hopeless alienation.'

22 J. and W. Grimm, *Deutsches Wörterbuch*, Vol. 11/2, Leipzig: S. Hirzel, 1936; col. 421.
23 Goethe's *Faust* verses 490 and 1607–1626. There have been many arguments as to the nature of the *Geisterchor*; recent research suggests that it refers to a host of devilish voices, even if their message is far from satanic. This seems in accordance with the generally rather 'human' and occasionally sympathetic character of Mephistopheles, an eighteenth century, enlightened devil.
24 Genesis book 3, chapter 5.
25 Quoted from G. Büchmann, *Geflügelte Worte*, p. 397.
26 Goethe's *Faust*, verses 11936f.
27 *ibid.* verses 317 and 309, possibly a reference to St. Paul, Corinthians I/13, verses 11f.
28 *ibid.* verse 4726, cf. E. Trunz (ed.), Goethe *Faust* (Hamburger Ausgabe), Munich: Beck, 1972; pp. 537–9 who relates the scene to Goethe's *Farbenlehre* and to the many other aspects of his oeuvre.
29 Goethe's *Faust*, verses 11441–11447. English translation by D. Luke, *Goethe Faust, Part Two*, World's Classics, Oxford: OUP, 1994; p. 219.
30 cf. E. Trunz (ed.), Goethe *Faust*, p. 612f.
31 A happy couple are being relocated from their idyllic home in order to serve Faust's reclamation plans.
32 Schopenhauer, *Sämtliche Werke*, Vol. 5, A. Hübscher (ed.), 2nd edn, Wiesbaden: Brockhaus, 1946–51; p. 143f.
33 *ibid.* p. 144
34 Schopenhauer, *Sämtliche Werke*, Vol. 1, p. 73.
35 Schopenhauer, *Sämtliche Werke*, Vol. 2, p. 131.
36 cf. Chapter 5, p. 112f.
37 Schopenhauer, *Sämtliche Werke*, Vol. 2, pp. 446–71.
38 K. Grün, *Ludwig Feuerbach in seinem Briefwechsel und Nachlaß*, Part 2, Heidelberg: Wintersche Verlagshandlung, 1874; pp. 253ff, in particular p. 294f.
39 Feuerbach, *Sämtliche Werke*, Vol. 2, F. Jodl (ed.), Stuttgart: Reclam, 1959; p. 276f.
40 Feuerbach, *Sämtliche Werke*, Vol. 6, p. 6.
41 Feuerbach, *Sämtliche Werke*, Vol. 2, p. 245.
42 Feuerbach, *Sämtliche Werke*, Vol. 6, p. 325.
43 Feuerbach, *Sämtliche Werke*, Vol. 2, p. 249.
44 *ibid.* p. 299
45 Feuerbach, *Sämtliche Werke*, Vol. 10, p. 22.
46 Feuerbach, *Sämtliche Werke*, Vol. 6, p. 163.
47 Feuerbach, postscript to *Das Wesen des Christentums*, *Sämtliche Werke*, Vol. 6, p. 406.
48 F. Nietzsche, *Werke in drei Bänden*, Vol. 1, p. 276.
49 Nietzsche, *Werke*, Vol. 2, p. 115.

50 Nietzsche, *Werke*, Vol. 2, pp. 565–760. The passage anticipates a further development in *Genealogie der Moral* (1887).
51 Nietzsche, *Werke*, Vol. 3, p. 834.
52 Nietzsche, *Werke*, Vol. 2, p. 227.
53 *ibid.* p. 280
54 Nietzsche, *Werke*, Vol. 2, p. 281.
55 Nietzsche, *Werke*, Vol. 2, p. 340.
56 cf. M. Heidegger, *Nietzsche*, Vol. 2, Pfullingen: Neske, 1961; p. 9ff. Further comments by Heidegger in *An Introduction to Metaphysics* (transl. by R. Manheim), New Haven: Yale University Press, 1979; p. 199. Also J. Derrida, *Of Grammatology* (transl. by C. Gayatri and C. Spivak), Baltimore: Johns Hopkins University Press, 1979; p. 19f.
57 Nietzsche, *Werke*, Vol. 1, p. 315f.
58 Nietzsche, *Werke*, Vol. 2, pp. 837, 1102.
59 *ibid.* p. 786
60 *ibid.* pp. 601, 215
61 *ibid.* p. 897
62 Nietzsche, *Werke*, Vol. 3, p. 777.
63 *ibid.* p. 750
64 Nietzsche, *Werke*, Vol. 1, p. 682.
65 Nietzsche, *Werke*, Vol. 2, p. 284.
66 *ibid.* pp. 687, 734
67 *ibid.* p. 776
68 A. J. Langbehn, *Rembrandt als Erzieher*, 50th edn, Leipzig: Hirschfeld, 1922; pp. 165–70.
69 F. Stern, *The Politics of Cultural Despair. A Study in the Rise of the German Ideology*, Berkeley: University of California, 1974; p. 98.
70 Langbehn, *Rembrandt*, pp. 170, 173.
71 *ibid.* p. 175
72 *ibid.* pp. 179, 223
73 *ibid.* p. 375
74 Stern, *Politics*, p. 110.
75 Langbehn, *Rembrandt*, p. 223.
76 *ibid.* p. 380
77 Born Bötticher, new name adopted in 1854 from his maternal great aunt in 1854.
78 Nietzsche, *Werke*, Vol. 3, p. 1091; cf. also Stern, *Politics*, p. 105f.
79 Stern, *Politics*, p. 8.
80 P. de Lagarde, *Deutsche Schriften*, Munich: Lehmanns, 1937; p. 237.
81 R. Griffin, *The Nature of Fascism*, London: Pinter, 1991.
82 Lagarde, *Deutsche Schriften*, p. 277.
83 *ibid.* p. 68
84 *ibid.* pp. 450, 452, 454f, 459
85 O. Spengler, *Der Untergang des Abendlandes*, Vol. 2, Munich: Becksche Verlagshandlung, 1922; p. 634f.
86 Quoted from H. Kohn, *The Mind of Germany*, p. 334.
87 Th. Mann, 'Über die Lehre Spenglers', *Gesammelte Werke*, Vol. 10, p. 179.

88 Spengler, *Untergang*, Vol. 2, p. 630.
89 Spengler, *Der Mensch und die Technik. Beitrag zu einer Philosophie des Lebens*, Munich: Becksche Verlagshandlung, 1931; p. 88f.
90 Quoted from T. J. Reed, *Thomas Mann, the Uses of Tradition*, Oxford: Clarendon Press, 1974; p. 364f.

Suggestions for further reading

Glaser, H., *Spießer-Ideologie. Von der Zerstörung des deutschen Geistes im 19. und 20. Jahrhundert*, Munich: Rombach, 1964.
Löwith, K., *From Hegel to Nietzsche. The Revolution in Nineteenth Century Thought* (transl. by D. E. Green), New York: Columbia University Press, 1991 [reprint].
Plessner, H., *Die verspätete Nation*, Stuttgart: Kohlhammer, 1959.
Stern, F., *The Politics of Cultural Despair. A Study in the Rise of the German Ideology*, Berkeley: University of California, 1974.

Textual studies

Arthur Schopenhauer, *Die Welt als Wille und Vorstellung*

1a. Da der Wille das Ding an sich, der innere Gehalt, das Wesentliche der Welt ist; das Leben, die sichtbare Welt, die Erscheinung, aber nur der Spiegel des Willens; so wird diese den Willen so unzertrennlich begleiten, wie den Körper sein
5 Schatten: und wenn Wille da ist, wird auch Leben, Welt dasein. Dem Willen zum Leben ist also das Leben gewiß, und solange wir von Lebenswillen erfüllt sind, dürfen wir für unser Dasein nicht besorgt sein, auch nicht beim Anblick des Todes. Wohl sehen wir das Individuum entstehen und vergehen; aber das
10 Individuum ist nur Erscheinung, ist nur da für die im Satz vom Grunde, dem *principio individuationis*, befangene Erkenntnis: für diese freilich empfängt es sein Leben wie ein Geschenk, geht aus dem Nichts hervor' leidet dann durch den Tod den Verlust jenes Geschenks und geht ins Nichts zurück.

(*Werke*, Vol. 3, Hübscher (ed.),
Brockhaus, 2nd edn, 1946–50; p. 127f.)

Commentary: (numbers in parentheses refer to line numbers in the text)

The passage describes the relationship between volition and individual: the latter is seen as a reflection of the former. Taking the image of body (volition) and shadow (individual) further, we can compare the death of the individual to the extinction of the shadow through lack of light; it does not change the character of the volition.

(10f) Satz vom Grunde = *principium rationis sufficientis*, causal nexus, principle of logical argument. Schopenhauer's doctoral dissertation was dedicated to this logical argument.

(11) *Principium individuationis*, the principle according to which individualism is possible. According to Schopenhauer, it seems synonymous with the 'Satz vom Grunde', it is defined by its existence in space and time.

Vocabulary:
Gehalt (m) = substance; Erscheinung (f) = appearance; besorgt = concerned; befangene Erkenntnis (f) = prejudiced knowledge.

1b. Sieh dich doch um! Was da ruft 'Ich will, ich will dasein', das bist du nicht allein, sondern alles, durchaus alles, was nur eine Spur von Bewußtsein hat. Folglich ist dieser Wunsch in dir gerade das, was *nicht* individuell ist, sondern allen
5 ohne Unterschied gemeinsam. Er entspringt nicht aus der Individualität, sondern aus dem Dasein überhaupt, auf welches allein er sich bezieht [...]. Was nämlich so ungestüm das Dasein verlangt, ist bloß *mittelbar* das Individuum; unmittelbar und eigentlich ist es der Wille zum Leben überhaupt, welcher
10 in allen einer und derselbe ist.
(*Werke*, Vol. 6, Hübscher (ed.), Brockhaus, 2nd edn, 1946–50; p. 299f.)

Commentary:
A graphic description of how the same will is reflected in the individual, but only as *Vorstellung* (imagination), not in reality. *Wille* is identified with life.

Vocabulary:
Spur (f) = trace; Bewußtsein (n) = awareness; sich beziehen
auf = to refer to; ungestüm = impetuously; mittelbar = indirectly.

2. Friedrich Nietzsche, *Der tolle Mensch*

Habt ihr nicht von jenem tollen Menschen gehört, der am
hellen Vormittage eine Laterne anzündete, auf den Markt lief
und unaufhörlich schrie: 'Ich suche Gott! Ich suche Gott!' –
Da dort gerade viele von denen zusammenstanden, welche
5 nicht an Gott glaubten, so erregte er ein großes Gelächter. Ist
er denn verlorengegangen? sagte der eine. Hat er sich verlaufen
wie ein Kind? sagte der andere. Oder hält er sich versteckt?
Fürchtet er sich vor uns? [...] so schrien und lachten sie
durcheinander. Der tolle Mensch sprang mitten unter sie und
10 durchbohrte sie mit seinen Blicken. 'Wohin ist Gott?' rief er,
'ich will es euch sagen! *Wir haben ihn getötet* – ihr und ich!
Wir alle sind seine Mörder! [...] Was taten wir, als wir diese
Erde von ihrer Sonne losketteten? Wohin bewegt sie sich
nun? Wohin bewegen wir uns? Fort von allen Sonnen? Stürzen
15 wir nicht fortwährend? [...] Ist es nicht kälter geworden?
Kommt nicht immerfort die Nacht und mehr Nacht? Müssen
nicht Laternen am Vormittage angezündet werden? [...] Gott
ist tot! Gott bleibt tot! Und wir haben ihn getötet! Wie trösten
wir uns, die Mörder aller Mörder? [...] Ist nicht die Größe
20 dieser Tat zu groß für uns? Müssen wir nicht selber zu Göttern
werden, um nur ihrer würdig zu erscheinen? [...]
(*Die fröhliche Wissenschaft, Werke in drei Bänden,*
K. Schlechta (ed.), Vol. 2, 2nd edn, Munich, 1960; p. 126f.)

Commentary: (numbers in parentheses refer to line numbers
in the text)
(1f) A reference to Diogenes who entered the market place
with a lighted lamp, searching for a true man.
(4f) It is important that the 'God-seeker' meets agnostics and
that it is they who ridicule him as the madman.

(11f) God has been killed by us. A reference to Good Friday, but beyond that also to the subjective nature of God: he is dead for us because we no longer believe in him.

(12ff) Describes the consequences of the death of God: a world without its centre, plunging into darkness. The death is seen here as disaster, a cosmic vision of nihilism, seen from a logocentric point of view.

(19ff) A first reference to the need for a replacement for God, a first indication of the need for an *Übermensch*.

Vocabulary:
toll = mad; anzünden = to kindle; unaufhörlich = incessantly; zusammenstehen = to be gathered together; erregen = to cause; sich versteckt halten = to be in hiding; durchbohren = to pierce; losketten = to unchain; stürzen = to plunge; Größe (f) = magnitude; würdig = to be worthy of.

3. Friedrich Nietzsche, *Mein neuer Weg zum 'Ja'*

[...] Eine solche *Experimental-Philosophie*, wie ich sie lebe, nimmt versuchsweise selbst die Möglichkeiten des grundsätzlichsten Nihilismus vorweg: ohne daß damit gesagt wäre, daß sie bei einer Negation, beim Nein, bei einem Willen
5 zum Nein stehen bliebe. Sie will vielmehr bis zum Umgekehrten hindurch – bis zu einem *dionysischen Ja-sagen* zur Welt, wie sie ist, ohne Abzug, Ausnahme und Auswahl – sie will den ewigen Kreislauf – dieselben Dinge, dieselbe Logik und Unlogik der Verknotung. Höchster Zustand, den
10 ein Philosoph erreichen kann: dionysisch zum Dasein stehn -: meine Formel dafür ist *amor fati*. [...]
(Nietzsche, *Werke* (Schlechta ed.), Vol. 3, 'Aus dem Nachlaß der Achtzigerjahre', p. 834.)

Commentary: (numbers in parentheses refer to line numbers in the text)
(1) Experimental-Philosophie: an – as yet – incomplete philosophy, a philosophy without its logocentricity. Nietzsche

frequently 'escapes' philosophical discourse with the aid of parables or makes use of fragmentary statements.

(6) The Dionysian force is for Nietzsche the will, the life-force, as opposed to the Apollonian force of individuality and shape.

(8) The eternal circle is possibly a reference to Nietzsche's philosophy of the 'ewige Wiederkehr des Gleichen' (eternal recurrence), a rather complicated concept which, however, rejects any teleological purpose in history and life.

Vocabulary:
versuchsweise = as an attempt; vorwegnehmen = to anticipate; Abzug (m) = allowance; Kreislauf (m) = circular course; Verknotung (f) = tying into knots.

4. Paul de Lagarde, 'Die Religion der Zukunft'

Das alte Deutschland ist mit nichten tot: aber es liegt viel tiefer und viel höher, als wo es der jetzige Reichskanzler und seine Freunde suchen. Was als klingendes Metall in den Glockenguß der Zukunft hineingeworfen werden wird, hat
5 mit der Presse, und vollends mit einer Regierungspresse, nichts zu tun: hinter dem Pfluge und im Walde, am Amboß der einsamen Schmiede ist es zu finden: es schlägt unsere Schlachten und baut unser Korn und [...] wird gut tun sich bald zu erinnern, daß in Deutschland nur Deutsche, aber nicht
10 deutschtuende Kosmopoliten und Parteigenossen zu gelten haben.

(Lagarde, *Deutsche Schriften*, München:
Lehmanns Verlag, 1937; p. 276.)

Commentary: (numbers in parentheses refer to line numbers in the text)
(1) Lagarde mentions J. Grimm's *Deutsche Mythologie* a few lines further on, the old Germany refers to the ancient Germanic tribes.
(2) Der jetzige Reichskanzler = Bismarck.

(3ff) Note the messianic style and the glorification of peasant life in the forest with faint allusions to the Germanic Siegfried myth. This type of 'blood and soil literature' was also produced by writers of the 'Conservative Revolution', cf. the *Bauer* in Hofmannsthal's *Salzburger Große Welttheater* (1922).

Vocabulary:
mit nichten = by no means; Glockenguß (m) = bell casting; Pflug (m) = plough; Amboß (m) = anvil; Schmiede (f) = smithy; deutschtuend = pseudo-German; Parteigenosse (m) = party member.

5. Oswald Spengler, *Der faustische Mensch*

Der faustische Erfinder und Entdecker ist etwas Einziges. Die Urgewalt seines Wollens, die Leuchtkraft seiner Visionen, die stählerne Energie seines praktischen Nachdenkens müssen jedem, der aus fremden Kulturen herüberblickt, unheimlich
5 und unverständlich sein, aber sie liegen uns allen im Blute. Unsere ganze Kultur hat eine Entdeckerseele. Ent-decken, das was man nicht sieht, in die Lichtwelt des inneren Auges ziehen, um sich seiner zu bemächtigen, das war vom ersten Tage an ihre hartnäckigste Leidenschaft. Alle ihre großen
10 Erfindungen sind in der Tiefe langsam gereift, durch vorwegnehmende Geister verkündigt und versucht worden, um mit der Notwendigkeit eines Schicksals endlich hervorzubrechen. [...] Wenn irgendwo, so offenbart sich hier der religiöse Ursprung alles technischen Denkens. [...]
15 sie [die faustischen Menschen] zwangen der Gottheit ihr Geheimnis ab, um selber Gott zu sein. Sie belauschten die Gesetze des kosmischen Taktes, um sie zu vergewaltigen, und sie schufen so die *Idee der Maschine* als eines kleinen Kosmos, der nur noch dem Willen des Menschen gehorcht. Aber damit
20 überschritten sie jene feine Grenze, wo für die anbetende Frömmigkeit der andern die Sünde begann, und daran gingen sie zugrunde, von Bacon bis Giordano Bruno. Die Maschine

ist des Teufels: so hat der echte Glaube immer wieder empfunden.

(*Untergang des Abendlandes*, Zweiter Band, Munich: Beck, 1922; p. 627f.)

Commentary: (numbers in parentheses refer to line numbers in the text)

(1–3) The chief qualities of the Faustian individual are will-power, vision, energy and practicality, modelled on the eighteenth century genius figure.

(4f) Of the eight prominent cultures discussed in the book only our own Western civilisation still exists. However, it is also viewed by Spengler as in the process of decline and this will inevitably lead to the rise of a new Caesar (cf. Mussolini as 'Duce' or Hitler as 'Führer' (cf. p. 634f)).

(6) 'ent-decken': spelling refers to the etymological origins of 'uncovering', of laying open.

(7) 'Lichtwelt': The youth-movement was preoccupied with sun-worship and Germanic mythology, Fidus (Hugo Höppener) being a major representative of this pre-fascist movement. cf. Jost Hermand, *Der Schein des schönen Lebens. Studien zur Jahrhundertwende*, 1972.

(14ff) Technology is seen to possess some divine quality which human beings have wrested from God, an oblique reference to the myth of Prometheus who stole the fire from Zeus. Note the violent language used here.

(22f) Faust's 'pact' with the devil is here modified into the Faustian individual's pact with the machine. Spengler's view is anti-modern, he expects our Western civilisation to be destroyed by technology.

Vocabulary:

Urgewalt (f) = primeval force; Leuchtkraft (f) = shining power; stählern = steely; Lichtwelt (f) = light world; sich bemächtigen = to gain a hold over; vorwegnehmend = anticipatory; verkündigen = to prophesy; abzwingen = to wrest from;

vergewaltigen = to do violence to; anbetend = worshipping; überschreiten = to transgress.

Topics for further study

1. Try to recapitulate the various stages in the German philosophy of the 'death of God' from Hegel to Nietzsche.
2. Examine the implications of Hegel's change from theology to philosophy with special regard to the 'death of God'.
3. Why did Goethe's *Faust* shy away from a 'metaphysical revolution'?
4. Distinguish between Schopenhauer's and Nietzsche's understanding of *Wille*.
5. To what extent can we find elements of National Socialism in the writings of Paul de Lagarde, Julius Langbehn and Oswald Spengler?

8

Germany today, a re-evaluation

Germany after the Second World War; the problem of coming to terms with National Socialism and German crimes against humanity. Attempts at preventing a recurrence of fascism: the Social Market Economy and West German integration into a united Europe. East Germany's development into a Socialist state and its path towards socialist humanism. The development in the Federal Republic of a democratic political culture, but some set-backs since the 1980s: the Historians' Debate and the re-emergence of xenophobia and racism. German unification and internal German difficulties over democratic and social values. A hesitant prognosis for the twenty-first century.

Introduction

This last Chapter is not intended to be a survey of cultural, political and social trends since 1945; many other, more comprehensive studies have dealt with these areas.[1] I wish rather to focus on some aspects covered in the preceding seven Chapters and attempt to demonstrate the relevance of some of our observations for today's Germany.

In brief, German history since 1945 can be divided into four phases: the material and political rebuilding of Germany and the country's separation into two opposing power blocks (1945–65); attempts to come to terms with its Nazi past and the country's re-entry into the international arena (1965–82); a post-modern, neo-conservative phase in reaction to earlier, progressive tendencies (since 1974); and the period since unification (since 1990). It is apparent that this division will reveal more emphasis on West Germany's development than on developments in the East and that there is a certain overlap between the individual phases. This Chapter will not exploit all four aspects equally; much emphasis will be placed on attempts at overcoming the fascist past, but will also focus on certain 'relics' of National Socialism or at least on those aspects of Germany's political culture which were responsible for its development and which seem to have resurfaced in recent years. The final part of this Chapter will focus on problems that have arisen since unification and will examine attitudes amongst East Germans to their newly experienced political culture within the enlarged Federal Republic of Germany (FRG).

Attempts at coping with the Nazi past

The Potsdam Agreement (August 1945) sought to eradicate 'the military tradition in Germany [. . .] in such manner as permanently to prevent the revival or reorganisation of German militarism and Nazism'. It also sought 'to convince the German people that they have suffered a total military defeat and that they cannot escape responsibility for what they have brought upon themselves. [In addition it attempted] to prepare for the eventual reconstruction of German political life on a democratic basis and for eventual peaceful co-operation in international life by Germany'.[2] This two-pronged declaration strove to eradicate any remnants of the Nazi administration, together with its ideology, but promised, at the same time, the re-integration of Germany into the family of nations, thus affording the country the opportunity for a new beginning. The policies formulated at Potsdam may help explain the term *Stunde Null* (Hour Zero) to describe the immediate post-war situation; such a description is only partly correct. The unconditional surrender of the German *Reich* had, indeed, led to its political and economic cessation. The process of denazification in the Western sectors, incorporated in the Potsdam Agreement and spearheaded by General Dwight D. Eisenhower, Supreme Commander of the American Forces, had set out to cleanse Germany of its 'brown' past. Subsequent events demonstrated, however, that such an undertaking was virtually impossible.

Initially, the newly emerging cultural and political elite was, on the whole, open to social issues. Even the newly constituted CDU, influenced by a group of Christian intellectuals, expressed the opinion, in its first political programme, that the capitalist economic system had failed to do justice to the vital social interests of the German people and that the new social order could no longer be based on a striving for capitalist gains.[3] These laudable attempts at a new start in Germany had little lasting effect, in the face of a number of factors working against them. The allies, particularly under the influence of the US government during the McCarthy era, were suspicious of any form of social ownership or anti-capitalist trends. The strengthening economy in the Western zones, especially after the Currency Reform of June 1948, changed the emphasis away from one of critical reflection and an understanding of national guilt, towards a *Leistungsfanatismus* (a fanatical will to achieve) and an 'entertainment culture', giving rise to a 'derealisierte Wirklichkeit'.[4] Such influences hindered a sincere and meaningful attempt to come to terms with the national guilt, to recognise the origins of the evil that led to National Socialism and to the acceptance 'daß in unserer Überlieferung als Volk etwas steckt, mächtig und drohend, das unser sittliches Verderben ist'[5] (that there is something powerful and evil in our tradition as a people which is our moral undoing).

Developments in the Eastern zone, though under immense material pressures and subject to much harsher deprivation, seemed to make a greater impact on coming to terms with the Nazi past. Even before the unconditional surrender, Soviet troops had co-operated with exiled German communists in an effort to establish a socialist republic. Contact with the working population was actively sought and in February 1945 the *Nationalkommittee Freies Deutschland*, was founded, which began to organise a new school system for the re-education of young people within its territory. In July 1945, the *Kulturbund* was established, under the direction of leading literary figures, with the aim of fundamentally destroying

Nazi ideology in all walks of life and re-establishing and promoting the 'freiheitliche, humanistische, wahrhaft nationale Tradition unseres Volkes'[6] (free humanist and truly national tradition of our people) (Text 1a). Many exiles, rather than settle in any of the Western zones, chose to return to the Eastern zone, where the rebuilding followed more closely a pattern which had its origins in the socialist tradition of the Weimar Republic.

The young German Democratic Republic (GDR) received its first setback with the uprising of East Berlin construction workers on 17th June 1953. Subsequent attempts at developing an ideology closely modelled on that of the USSR distorted the original aims of developing an indigenous German socialist model; the Cold War ideology deepened the estrangement between the two Germanies and further diluted the public debate on Germany's fascist past. Whilst much greater efforts were made by the GDR in this matter, the issue was inevitably subsumed into the wider anti-capitalism crusade and was thus sucked into the general ideological propaganda. Khruschev's disclosures of Stalinist atrocities, at the 20th Congress of the Soviet Communist Party in 1956, together with the Hungarian Uprising of the same year, weakened the political credibility of the increasingly hard-line GDR leaders. During a first 'thaw' of the Cold War they now found themselves increasingly at odds with their own dissident intelligentsia. This situation worsened with the building of the Berlin Wall (1961) and the suppression of the Dubček regime in Czechoslovakia (1968), significantly affecting the credibility of the GDR and contributing to its collapse in 1989. Western intellectuals were slow to recognise these developments, partly because they felt the need to react against their own country's political propaganda, partly in recognition of the genuine achievements of GDR cultural policy and the significant contribution of GDR authors to the new German literature. In the following we will therefore concentrate on developments in the FRG and will focus on the GDR only where issues of specific interest arise.

Vergangenheitsbewältigung through integration into the Western alliance

The economic stabilisation of West Germany brought in its wake little significant attempt at penetrating the fascist past, or much of a desire to remedy it. While some intellectuals believed that it would never again be possible to produce German art after Auschwitz, others hoped to make use of the incredible chance of turning Germany's total defeat into a complete transformation,[7] and yet others sought to return to a bygone 'better' Germany in order to build on its humanist traditions.[8] Those German writers who later became associated with Gruppe 47[9] fought against the general condemnation of all Germans, expressed in the formula of a collective guilt, and found support from philosophers such as Hannah Arendt and Karl Jaspers.[10] Jointly they hoped to lead their compatriots in a new direction, engaging literature into social commitment, fighting for social justice, for a planned economy and defining the humanist tradition as hunger for freedom.[11]

Karl Jaspers may stand as an example of the many critical voices amongst West German intellectuals: whilst recognising that the population did not wish to suffer any more, to be burdened with guilt, to ponder over crimes committed in their names, the emerging self-pity prevented a sincere analysis of Germany's guilt, which for Jaspers had become a vital issue for the German 'soul' which alone could achieve the fundamental change 'die uns zur Erneuerung aus dem Ursprung unseres Wesens bringt'[12] (which brings about the renewal from the origin of our nature). It took almost two decades before this vitally important renewal and a recognition of German failings could come about.

In the meantime, and under the guidance of Western leaders, a political and socio-economic reshaping of the public landscape was set in motion. Today's political parties were established or reconstituted, usually under the tutelage of pre-fascist politicians and emerging from within wider intellectual circles. The drafting of the Grundgesetz (Basic Law), the FRG's new constitution, followed allied recommendations, and was set in motion soon after the Currency Reform of 1948:

> The constituent assembly will draft a democratic constitution which will establish for the participating states a governmental structure of federal type which is best adapted to the eventual reestablishment of German unity at present disrupted, and which will protect the rights of the participating states, provide adequate central authority, and contain guarantees of individual rights and freedoms.[13]

These guidelines guaranteed the 'Westernisation' of the newly emerging FRG. Based on current neo-liberal economic concepts, they also incorporated the inherent tradition of German parliamentarianism of 1848 and 1919. The constituent assembly, some seventy politicians from the eleven *Länder*, with representatives from West Berlin as advisers, saw its main task as building up a defensive constitution, capable of withstanding any demagogic assault from unelected quarters. Surprisingly enough, the creation of the new constitution found little enthusiasm amongst the general population, despite the fact that it afforded the FRG entry into a future federation of Western European states, while retaining a number of features typical of the German tradition.

The *Soziale Marktwirtschaft* (Social Market Economy) is just one example. Often described as a neo-liberal concept, it was perhaps more firmly rooted in some typically German traditions, such as the integration of the individual into society, the obligation of the state to protect the citizen from ruthless exploitation and the Christian understanding of work as a process of self-fulfilment, values discussed in Chapters 2 and 3. One of its major aims was to prevent the reemergence of syndicates and cartels, which had played such a detrimental role in German politics since the 1880s, and to integrate the work-force fully into the decision-making process, both at their workplace and in relation to wider macroeconomic policies. Alfred Müller-Armack was of considerable importance in developing a new social and economic model for the budding FRG. A product of the CDU circle of Christian Socialists and a man of greater vision than his more pragmatic partner Ludwig Erhard, he became the main architect of the Social Market Economy. Deeply distrustful of state intervention, as experienced under the Nazi regime, he aimed at revitalising entrepreneurial activities for all strata in society, hoping to unite the entrepreneurial forces with a new spirit of responsibility and involvement on the part of the workforce (Text 2).

Critics of the new social market policy may suggest that the social measures did not go far enough, in that workers' co-determination was limited to social issues within their firm and that co-operation was accorded second place to free-market competition. However, subsequent developments proved that co-determination could be further strengthened,[14] becoming a meaningful instrument within the overall concept of economic democracy and that co-operation between state, capital and trade-unions functioned far better in Germany than in other Western countries. If viewed from our position in the mid 1990s, we can see how major aspects of the social market system have been integrated into the Maastricht Treaty, demonstrating the success of the German system of co-operation among all participants in the national economy. The development of the social market economy, with its potential for industrial co-operation and democracy at the workplace, has certainly played a crucial part in establishing a stable democracy in the FRG, stable enough to cope with various recessions and economic adversities.

The progressive integration of Germany into a European Union was another vital achievement, reinforcing not only economic success, but also democratic stability and leading to a reconciliation of aspects of German culture with Western civilisation. We have seen in Chapters 2, 4 and 5, how a typically German concept of *Kultur* assumed an increasingly anti-Western attitude.[15] The first steps towards closer European co-operation were established after the First World War with various intellectual initiatives to reconcile the French and German nations, such as the correspondence between Roman Rolland and Hermann Hesse. The total defeat of fascism in 1945 afforded a much greater opportunity for reconciliation. In 1948 Robert Schumann became French Foreign Minister, born in Lorraine, under German rule from 1871–1919 and again between 1940 and 1945. Schumann became the 'Father of Europe',[16] co-operating closely with Konrad Adenauer, the first Chancellor of the FRG (1949), himself born in the Rhineland, a territory with close affinity to France. Alcide De Gasperi, the Italian Prime Minister, born in the Tyrol and also German-speaking, was another leading figure during this gestation period that would bring forth the idea of the new Europe. These figures and others, such as the Frenchman Jean Monnet, Paul-Henri Spaak, the Belgian Prime Minister, Karl Arnold, Minister-President of North-Rhine-Westphalia, all pious Catholics, contributed to its success, and the Catholic element itself served to lead Germany away from its specifically Protestant brand of Christianity into a broader, cosmopolitan environment. Politicians such as these were responsible for the launch of the European Community of Coal and Steel, the cradle for the emerging European Community and the guarantor of peace within Europe. This organisation regulated European heavy industry, at least as far as the continent of Western Europe was concerned and thereby had control over any plans for re-armament.

However, it would be wrong to underestimate the interest of other groups in a European federation. The preamble to the FRG's *Grundgesetz*, approved by a vast majority of West German politicians, declared that it would safeguard its national identity as a state in a United Europe.[17] Even earlier, during the summer of 1946, European politicians from different parties joined in the *Union Européenne des Fédéralistes*, reaching from Paris to Warsaw to act as a bridge between East and West.[18] In his first programmatic declaration (October 1945), Kurt Schumacher, the SPD leader, stated his party's desire for a united states of Europe, albeit based on Social Democratic principles. After the outbreak of the Cold War, the emphasis was to shift towards Western Europe and away from any socialist solution. The SPD still maintained its preference for Europe, even if the new Europe would now have to be limited to the West, surrendering any hope of incorporating the Eastern zone. The retreat of Britain and the Scandinavian countries from the European movement in 1950 further weakened the Social Democratic base and plans to rearm West Germany and bring it into the North Atlantic Treaty Organization (NATO) alliance (1951) made it increasingly difficult for the SPD to agree to a Europe based on 'the 4 k formula' of a united Europe: 'zu allen konservativ-klerikal-kapitalistisch-kartellistischen Versuchen'[19] (to all conservative-clerical-capitalist-cartell-creating attempts). Only after the Bad Godesberg reform programme (1959) did the SPD accept the political reality of a West European Common Market and the FRG's membership of NATO. All the major political parties have since been loyal supporters of a federalist European idea, in marked contrast to France (De Gaulle) and Britain (Thatcher), where nationalist tendencies were more difficult to defeat.

It would clearly be misleading to suggest that the introduction of a social market economy and the FRG's integration into the West should be viewed as an effective atonement for Nazi crimes. However, it was perhaps unrealistic to believe, as Jaspers and other intellectuals did, that such an atonement could be undertaken by a whole nation, in the immediate aftermath of such horrors and in a political climate which already focused Western attention on a new threat at the Eastern fringe of West Germany's border. In terms of its changing political culture, the actual effect of the FRG's Western orientation, though more gradual and less spectacular, ensured a thorough and convincing rejection not only of her Nazi past, but also of the legacy of Bismarck's Empire. The traditional reactionary Prussian elites lost their base; the centre of the FRG shifted to the West, with Bonn a far more modest and amiable capital than Berlin ever was. Lutheran Protestantism lost its dubious political influence and the new military were integrated into civil society, with the soldier a citizen in uniform.[20] C. Graf von Krockow saw this development as a return to the liberal traditions of the nineteenth century *Bürger*[21] and Jürgen Habermas welcomed Western integration as the great intellectual achievement of the post war epoch, replacing the old Middle European German nationalism with a new commitment to the tradition of the Enlightenment:

> Der einzige Patriotismus, der uns dem Westen nicht entfremdet, ist ein Verfassungspatriotismus. Eine in Überzeugungen verankerte Bindung an universalistische Verfassungsprinzipien hat sich leider in der Kulturnation der Deutschen erst nach – und durch – Auschwitz bilden können.[22]
> (The only patriotism which does not estrange us from the West is a constitutional patriotism. A commitment based on a belief in universalist constitutional principles could, unfortunately, manifest itself in the German cultural nation only after – and through – Auschwitz.)

Such a constitutional patriotism developed only gradually and has since suffered several reverses. A survey of changes in the FRG's political culture would demonstrate that the unpolitical attitude, so prevalent in the 1950s and early 1960s and enshrined in the proverbial 'ohne mich Einstellung' (count me out attitude) and in the emphasis on economic development in preference to political achievement[23] gradually began to change. By the end of the 1960s, the student unrests, culminating in the 1968 student revolution, led to a new political commitment. Despite its strong theoretical base, which encouraged *Fundamentalkritik*[24] (fundamental criticism) and blindness towards political reality and led to the excess of political terrorism, the 1968 events also brought about a decisive and honest debate on National Socialism and on traditional German deficits in democracy. It fostered a high degree of political awareness and a conscious and decisive identification with those Western concepts and values of democracy which, it was felt, had been betrayed by successive govern-ments. Alexander and Margarete Mitscherlich's book, *Die Unfähigkeit zu trauern* (1967), became a best-seller and the student generation began to question the political past of their leaders and of the older generation in general.[25] Democracy was no longer seen as just a political veneer, but was accepted as *Lebensform*[26] (life form), essential for a civilised and mature society and symbolised in Willy Brandt's famous dictum that we must risk more democracy.[27]

A new confidence in the potential achievements of individual 'action groups' and extra-parliamentary opposition movements became evident. Party membership doubled and became comparable to that in other Western countries. 'Citizens' initiatives and localised action groups attracted some two million members and three in four West Germans declared that they might join, if a relevant issue were to arise within their personal environment.[28] The popularity of the Peace Movement in the early 1980s is proof of such developments, followed by protest movements against nuclear power stations and against politicians' reluctance to move towards a more open form of government. Perhaps the most lasting effects of this protest generation emerged in the ecology movement and in a new feminism. At last, it looked as if a move was under way, against the preponderance of private virtues towards an acceptance of public virtues, with public opinion accepting the pluralist modern *Streitkultur*.

Another modernising factor was the change from an all German, predominantly Christian society towards a multi-ethnic, open society. Although this development was perhaps less successful and more problematic than other developments, the growing influx of 'guest-workers' which started in the early 1960s meant an opportunity for the opening and the enrichment of the German mind. Compared with the experience of Britain and France, the move towards a multi-ethnic society in Germany happened at a faster pace, and without the legacy of any historical, colonial, linguistic or cultural dominance.

It occurred in a country which, with only a brief experience of colonialism, was perhaps more inward-looking than other Western countries. The process of integration was rendered more difficult in Germany because of the continuing existence of that 'disjunction between nationality and citizenship, between *ius soli*, which determines nationality by place of birth, and *ius sanguinis*, which determines it by descent'.[29] It is incredible that, in view of Germany's racist past, the old German Nationality Law of 1913 is still in place, only slightly amended in 1963 and still applying the *völkisch* principles of blood and soil. Nevertheless, the churches, charitable agencies and trade unions, as well as such writers as Günter Wallraff have taken an active part in attempting to overcome xenophobic trends and to help 'guest-workers' establish themselves in Germany.[30] We shall take up this issue later in the Chapter.

Relics of the past

The first part of this Chapter sought to map out various attempts in both German states at overcoming the fascist legacy. It was simply not realistic to cleanse a whole society from an experience which not only dominated the country for the twelve years of actual National Socialist rule, but had its origins far back in the nineteenth century. The establishment of a Western political culture and integration into an international network of alliances and organisations ensured the possibility of a permanent departure from the peculiarly German *völkisch* nationalism. Opinion polls in the late 1980s have demonstrated that Germans are less proud of their nationality than other European nations[31] and an analysis of attitudes among West Germany's young people indicated that their interest in other cultures, both abroad and at home, makes it unlikely that they will ever again fall prey to racist tendencies. In the main, a 'mature citizen', aware of civil rights, committed to equality of opportunity and tolerant of other views and life-styles, has entered the political landscape. At the same time, the German public seems more critical of established political parties and more vigilant of the occasional corrupt misuse of power.[32]

However, these trends were reversed by a general change of values, generated in the USA and popularised under the wide-ranging and complex term of 'Post-modernism', sometimes also referred to as 'Neo-conservatism'. By the mid 1970s the FRG had begun to register a *Tendenzwende*[33] (change of tendency) which, some eight years later, brought about Chancellor Kohl's much acclaimed political *Wende*. Some of the newly established values were now open to question; Ralf Dahrendorf proclaimed the 'end of the Social Democratic century' with growth, welfare and the right to work no longer guaranteed.[34] A commitment to 'melioration' was to replace an inflation-inducing growth. Others, more critical of this newly pronounced change of values, spoke of a 'neue Unübersichtlichkeit' (new obscurity) which had replaced the commitment to build on the normative values of the Enlightenment.[35]

We cannot possibly undertake a comprehensive analysis of post-modern value changes in Germany and will highlight the change in historical awareness to illustrate these trends. Kurt Sontheimer, examining general political attitudes in Germany and the West in the wake of the Second World War, spoke of *Geschichtsmüdigkeit* (history fatigue) and of a general anti-historical propensity which had taken over from the historicism fashionable well into the twentieth century.[36] He related the anti-historicism to four modernist tendencies: the expansion of a technological civilisation, a new search for security within a welfare state, the spread of egalitarianism post-1945 and, finally, a general universalisation of our world view. In addition, of course, Sontheimer registers the specifically German reluctance to delve into a murky, fascist past. However, these four major trends, under the general heading of modernity, applied to most Western countries. Taking hold in Germany much later than in other countries, this modernity became the driving force for the country's Western integration and for a general democratisation. The *Tendenzwende* brought about a further change of paradigm, the most prominent feature being a new historical awareness, a desire for *Bindung* (commitment). Golo Mann pleaded for a new understanding of history, for a return to old traditions, as opposed to the current dominant social history with its intellectual emancipatory drive.[37]

Since the mid-1970s, we have seen a steady increase in historical awareness in both German states. The Middle Ages were celebrated with a special Staufen Year (1979), Luther and Bismarck were commemorated (1984 and 1990), Frederick the Great's re-interment was conducted with considerable pomp and circumstance (1991) and the unification of Germany ushered in a new pride in her national history. Sontheimer's analysis and his four explanatory categories could, in a speculative and tentative manner, be reversed in order to highlight today's post-modern, neo-conservative trends and the new historical awareness: we witness a considerable scepticism towards technological innovation, a questioning of the ideal of the welfare state in favour of neoliberal concepts of self-reliance and of individual commitment to smaller, organically grown units such as one's family or region and we discover, not least with a reassessment of the proposed European Union, some aversion to European federalism and universalist federations. The eagerness to re-examine one's national past can, however, lead to a desire for normalisation and relativism.

The German *Historikerstreit* (Historians' Debate) is a case in point: it originated in the summer of 1986, as a consequence of President Reagan's visit to the military cemetery at Bitburg (1985), where German SS soldiers were buried. A group of neo-conservative historians, some of them associated with Chancellor Helmut Kohl, attempted a revision of our assessment of Nazi-Germany, comparing Nazi crimes to Stalinist massacres and to the Pol Pot terror regime and suggested that they were no worse than other crimes against humanity and should be seen as a response to the Communist Gulags of the 1920s. The leading representatives of this revisionist school were the historians Ernst Nolte, Michael Stürmer and Andreas Hillgruber; their opponents were loosely grouped around the social philosopher Habermas, but included social historians such as Eberhard Jäckel, Hans Mommsen, Martin Broszat and Jürgen Kocka.[38] The ensuing debate raged in German newspapers and journals and became perhaps the most spectacular event in German academic circles since the student unrest of 1968. We shall focus on some marginal aspects of this debate which illustrate important issues raised in previous Chapters.

Chapter 5 analysed the tradition of the German mandarin. Many historians belonging to this group of academics tried to legitimise their august position by acting as ideological defenders of the Wilhelmine Empire, rejecting, at the same time, Western values such as pluralism and democracy. Habermas suspects that, in the shadow of Kohl's revisionist, neo-conservative image of Germany's identity, a new school of revisionist historians may find their way back into the political limelight, to act as *Sinnstifter* (ideologues) of the newly united nation.[39] However, the return to a neo-conservative historiography is not a peculiarly German phenomenon, for Britain and the USA have experienced a similar shift to neo-conservative positions. Nevertheless, if seen in the context of other cultural and political issues, such as those associated with German unification, fears of a fundamental re-orientation of German policy, away from its Western dominated position, are justified.

Another marginal issue concerns the re-emergence of the *Sonderweg* debate, in particular the question of Germany's central European role. Habermas has attacked neo-conservative historians who suggest that Germany in 1945 was defending Western traditions against Bolshevism and that this historical circumstance anticipated Germany's current role within NATO.[40] A different version takes advantage of Germany's middle-European position in order to absolve it from any responsibility for two world wars. Apart from the fatalistic bankruptcy of such a vision which puts geographical factors above political skill and diplomacy, it cannot counter earlier historical theses which associate the cause of Germany's involvement in the First World War with her illiberal, non-parliamentary traditions.[41] The revival of this geo-political debate was related to the general change of paradigm, marginalising social historians and political scientists in favour of those historians who appear better suited to the new search for national identity.

It would be easy to dismiss the Historians' Debate as an example of academic eccentricity, were it not for this underlying basic change in direction, associated with neo-conservative policies, both before and after unification. The extreme right, at least on its intellectual wing, is profoundly influenced by France's *Nouvelle Droite* which itself adapted ideas picked up from representatives of the *Konservative Revolution*, discussed in Chapter 6. Of particular importance is the political scientist Carl Schmitt (1888–1985) who was promoted by *Nouvelle Droite* and is being publicised by the German New Right, in particular by the recently deceased Bernard Willms, by Manfred Lauermann and others.[42] Schmitt's position, particularly popular with the New Right since 1989,[43] is opposed to liberalism and the traditions of the Enlightenment. His followers support Schmitt's defence of totalitarianism and of the absolute power of the state, associating liberalism and pluralist societies with Western decadence and Jewish opposition to the concept of *Volksgemeinschaft* (community of the people). Schmitt was an enthusiastic supporter of Adolf Hitler, in particular of his *Röhm Putsch* (1934) and of the overthrow of democracy in the Weimar Republic. Disciples of Schmitt and early representatives of the political right in the FRG during the 1950s and 1960s were Arnold Gehlen, Helmut Schelsky and Ernst Forsthoff, whereas todays doyen of extreme neo-conservatism is Gerd-Klaus Kaltenbrunner and, slightly less extreme, Herrmann Lübbe, Robert Spaemann and Karl-Heinz Bohrer. Kaltenbrunner, in particular, advocates absolutist power and has paved the intellectual way for the radical new right and for new racist tendencies.[44] Echoes of such an acclamation for sacrifice, martyrdom and salvation from ethnic infiltration can also be found in the post-modern writer Botho Strauß (b. 1944) who explains racism and xenophobia as '"gefallene" Kultleidenschaften, die ursprünglich einen sakralen, ordnungs-stiftenden Sinn hatten'[45] (a passion for "lost" cults which originally had a sacral sense of orderliness). Strauß is strictly opposed to the tradition of the Enlightenment and especially to all claims for emancipation, 'da soziale Emanzipation stets nur Freigelassene und niemals Freie schaffen kann'[46] (since social emancipation cannot create free people, but only those released into freedom). Strauß's dangerously anti-rational position has recently led to an understandable, but regretta-bly vituperous response from the Chair of the Central Coun-cil for Jews in Germany, Ignatz Bubis, who accused Strauß of a right-wing radicalism which must accept a measure of re-sponsibility for the recent burning down of synagogues.[47] Within the wider context of this extreme conservative revival also figures the writer Ernst Jünger (b. 1895), renowned for his anti-democratic opus which glorifies war and absolute obedience. It seemed an act of unbelievable insensitivity for Helmut Kohl and François Mitterand to choose the 20th July 1993, the anniversary of the assassination attempt against Hitler, to visit Jünger. Kohl's critics have alleged that he is sympathetic to the new intellectual right and their anti-democratic tendencies, and he has been accused, even from within his own party, of supporting illiberal attitudes, reject-ing Germany's liberal tradition, forged in the Revolution of 1848.[48]

Germany since unification, a few concluding observations

The excitement and joy over the German *Wende* was felt everywhere in the Western world; the opening of the Berlin Wall was welcomed by millions as an act of liberation and the official unification ceremony in Berlin met with the approval not only of most governments, but also of their peoples. Opinion polls suggest that sixty per cent of Britons took a positive view of German unification, as compared to seventy per cent in France and even higher percentages in Spain, Italy and Hungary. Within Germany, the figure amounted to eighty per cent.[49] When Chancellor Kohl invoked the 'national' element, based on the Federal Constitution's commitment to unification, he met surprisingly little objection amongst the former occupation powers, since his ten point programme for unification was anchored in a commitment to the European Community and to NATO.[50] The first national elections since unification (December 1990) became a vote of confidence for Kohl, spelling defeat for his opponent, Oskar Lafontaine, whose attitude towards unification had been more hesitant and who had refused to play the 'national' card.

Many West German intellectuals, including Habermas, Claus Offe and Günter Grass have remained critical of Kohl's unification policy and fearful, in particular, of the creation of an artificially induced new German nationalism at a time when other Western democratic values seemed in some disarray.[51] The very act of unification has to be seen in its national and historical context (Text 3). If viewed as the celebration of a national rebirth, it would denigrate the liberal and demo-cratic achievements of the 'old' FRG and would give a new impetus to the political right, it would once more re-open the possibility of Germany's retreat to its *Sonderweg* position.[52] Demands for a specific re-affirmation of such concepts as parliamentary democracy, a republican spirit and the uphold-ing of values such as tolerance might seem exaggerated, were it not for the constant trickle of nationalist pleadings, for which the *Frankfurter Allgemeine Zeitung* and *Die Welt* have become mouthpieces.[53] At the height of the debate even *Der Spiegel*, under Rudolf Augstein's editorship, succumbed to the nationalist hysteria[54] and its supportive attitude to 'con-verts' to the new right such as Botho Strauß and Hans Magnus Enzensberger gives rise to some anxiety over the journal's traditionally liberal position.

In the light of these arguments, the policy of a *Beitritt*

(accession) was commendable, since it re-affirmed the commitment to the *Grundgesetz* 'Preamble'. Critics of the policy of a *Beitritt* have either maintained that it amounts to a lost opportunity, that a plebiscite on a revised, modernised constitution would have given the whole act some democratic credibility (Habermas) or have advocated the necessity for a new, more democratic constitution, based on some kind of 'third way', bringing together the different democratic attributes of the two German states. The latter position, voiced by *Bündnis 90* with its demand for a 'Totalrevision all dessen, was Demokratie und Demokratisierung gefährdet, aufhält, verengt'[55] (total revision of everything which endangers, arrests, constricts democracy and the process of democratisation) betrays profound ignorance of the system of pluralist democracy and must not be confused with Habermas's stance. *Bündnis 90* is reluctant to accept the political culture of liberal, Western attitudes, whereas Habermas wants to strengthen precisely this attitude by invoking the will of the people in accepting the *Grundgesetz* as part of Germany's liberal tradition, by transforming the unification process into a 'normative act of the citizens of both states' who are willing to join into a common nation of citizens (*Staatsbürgernation*).[56]

A broader analysis of the political culture in the former GDR since unification would suggest that the normative structures of a civil society have yet to evolve. Liberal principles of individual development, of personal and social responsibility could not flourish under a 'paternalistic regime of punishments, deprivations, rewards and general recognition [...] reinforced by the government's attempts at self-justification'.[57]

Matters are further complicated by an observed bifurcation in the political development of both German societies: whereas the West is entering a post-modern type of democracy, in retreat from state intervention and personal political involvement, disenchanted with the welfare state and increasingly subject to the demands of the free-market economy, East German society is still in need of a process of modernisation, has yet to experience the revolutionary fervour of 1968 and its expressed will of political participation.[58] The perceived 'peaceful revolution' of the autumn of 1989, led by the Protestant church, has come into question: having experienced a sixty per cent decrease in membership between 1950 and 1988 and remaining bound by the Lutheran edict of non-violence against authority, the churches functioned at best as 'pressure release valves or, as some have put it, as representative sites of modernisation for society at large'.[59] The strongest attack on the Protestant mentality of depoliticisation and revolutionary impotence is formulated by K. H. Bohrer:

> Diese Leute [protestantische Öffentlichkeitsfiguren der DDR] haben offenbar jenes protestantische Erbe, es komme nicht darauf an, was man tue (das sei katholisch), sondern darauf, was man denkt (das sei evangelisch) so sehr zum selbstachtenden Überleben gebraucht, daß sie nunnmehr selbst an den politisch fragwürdigsten Konsequenzen dieser Innerlichkeitstheologie nicht irre werden, sondern sie offensiv vertreten.[60]
>
> (These people [protestant public figures from within the GDR] have, for the survival of their own self-respect, been so much in need of that protestant inheritance [which states] that it is not what one does that matters (this being catholic), but what one thinks (this being protestant), that they themselves no longer question the most arguable consequences of their theology of inwardness, but aggressively promote it.)

Individual statements by intellectuals or politicians will serve to illustrate this absence of any liberal political culture. Jens Reich, a leading figure of the 1989 *Wende*-period, recognised the inevitable existence of two German traditions, one wedded to a Western, 'atlantic' tradition, the other to Eastern Europe.[61] However, his insistence on the 'Eastern tradition' as being the more German one reveals a somewhat naive attitude regarding the darker aspects of Germany's past, anticipating, no doubt unwittingly, the excesses of Hoyerswerda and Rostock:

Noch sind wir die ursprünglicheren Deutschen, und käme Heine aus dem Jenseits zu Besuch, dann, denke ich, würde er hier die verwitterten Fassaden wiedererkennen. Aber dort drüben? So viele Italiener, Griechen, Spanier, Türken, Dunkelhäutige?[62]

(We are still the more original Germans, and if Heine were to revisit us from the past, then, no doubt, he would recognise the weathered facades. But over there? [in the West] So many Italians, Greeks, Spaniards, Turks, dark-skinned people?)

While Reich may have a point, Heine would still have applied for political asylum in France, just as he did in 1831. And even if Reich's statement contains perhaps an element of irony, we still hear echoes of a typically German xenophobia, identified by Norbert Elias as *Fremddisziplinierung*, rather than *Selbstdisziplinierung*.[63] This habit of disciplining 'aliens', of expecting them to conform to the life-style of the *Volk*, is not only evident in xenophobia towards foreigners, it has also manifested itself at times in an exaggerated dislike of *Wessis*, West Germans.[64] Wolfgang Thierse, leader of the East German SPD, feels threatened by the West's openness to international influences which he reduces to the level of snack-bars, sex shops and video-libraries.[65]

The superiority felt *vis-à-vis* West Germans, apparent in such attitudes, is not only a case of an inverse inferiority complex or of simple jealousy towards their affluent, liberated Western neighbour, it is also based on a belief in their own ideological, democratic and cultural superiority. Brandenburg's Minister-President Manfred Stolpe, although not untainted by the suspicion of collaboration with the *Stasi* authorities, believes East Germans to be superior in matters of humanist value statements and Christian outlook, whilst West German thinking is dominated by economic materialism and consumerism.[66] This contempt for consumerism and its hedonistic life-style finds expression in a newly created *Trabi-Trotz-Kultur*[67] which may have its roots in a secularised form of Protestant *Weltfrömmigkeit.* Hans-Joachim Maaz, a Protestant psychotherapist from Halle, is a good example: fully aware of existing East German attitudes of 'kleinbürgerlichen lebensfeindlichen Erziehungsnormen' (petit bourgeois austere norms in education), he describes the transition from the old to the new political system as the change 'von der bösen Stiefmutter in die Arme der verführerischen Hexe'[68] (from the wicked step-mother into the arms of the seductive witch). Similar observations could be made with reference to the attempts at grassroots democracy in the autumn of 1989, which failed to resist the political and economic take-over by the West. Maaz, referring to former GDR citizens as the 'gestürzte Volk' (the toppled people), celebrates the peaceful 'revolution' as the great triumph of people power which, according to him, has been destroyed by party politics: 'die Macht des Volkes ist erneut und diesmal wesentlich effizienter denn je gestürzt worden'[69] (the power of the people has once more been crushed, and this time more spectacularly than ever before).

This peculiar form of secular protestantism (cf. Chapter 2) also influenced the debate over the site of the new German capital, involving intellectuals on both sides of the former wall. Whereas Bonn was seen to represent the Catholic Rhineland, associated with federalist, pro-Western policies in a frame of modest provincialism, Berlin stood for a more centralist capital with distinctly Protestant overtones. Journalists with a new found national mission even demanded a new Kulturkampf,[70] whilst one of their number, Sebastian Haffner, felt compelled to ask: 'Die Tradition Adenauers [...] war antipreußisch, westdeutsch, rheinisch. Will Kohl diese Tradition aufheben und in die Reihe der Wilhelminischen Reichskanzler einrücken?'[71] (Adenauer's tradition [...] was anti-Prussian, Western, of the Rhineland. Will Kohl abolish this tradition and step into the succession of Wilhelmine Reich chancellors?) Even from within the ranks of the CDU warning voices were heard, cautioning that the choice of Berlin as federal capital must not herald a return to 'Prussianism' and that the new-found German identity must not invoke a return to old political models, which could undermine the success of forty years of federalism.[72] References to Berlin as *Hauptstadt* in comparison to Bonn as *Bundeshauptstadt*, the restoration of the former *Reichstag*, the seat of the imperial parliament and the reinstatement of the 'iron cross' and Prussian eagle to the quadriga at the Brandenburg Gate, though only of symbolic value, give further rise to such fears. If seen in connection with persistent reference to Germany's middle-European position, voiced both by representatives of the former East and by associates of Helmut Kohl,[73] fears for the FRG's still rather young and untried democracy are not entirely unfounded.

However, in conclusion to this Chapter and as a verdict on our various excursions into Germany's rich and varied past, I feel confident enough to conclude with excerpts from a speech by the former Federal President, Richard von Weizsäcker, who recognised that while Germany cannot shake off its past, the country can correct past mistakes and can contribute to a peaceful, united new Europe. On the occasion of the fortieth anniversary of the end of the Second World War he stated:

Wir dürfen nicht im Ende des Krieges die Ursache für Flucht, Vertreibung und Unfreiheit sehen. Sie liegt vielmehr in seinem Anfang und im Beginn jener Gewaltherrschaft, die zum Krieg führte. Wir dürfen den 8. Mai 1945 nicht vom 30. Januar 1933 trennen. Wir haben wahrlich keinen Grund, uns am heutigen Tag an Siegesfesten zu beteiligen. Aber wir haben allen Grund, den 8. Mai 1945 als das Ende eines Irrwegs deutscher Geschichte zu erkennen, das den Keim der Hoffnung auf eine bessere Zukunft barg. [...] Es geht nicht darum, Vergangenheit zu bewältigen. Das kann man gar nicht. Sie läßt sich ja nicht nachträglich ändern oder ungeschehen machen. Wer aber vor der Vergangenheit die Augen verschließt, wird blind für die Gegenwart. Wer sich der Unmenschlichkeit nicht erinnern will, der wird wieder anfällig für neue Ansteckungsgefahren. [. . .] Der Neuanfang in Europa nach 1945 hat dem Gedanken der Freiheit und Selbstbestimmung Siege und Niederlagen gebracht. Für uns gilt es, die Chance des Schlußstrichs unter eine lange Periode europäischer Geschichte zu nutzen, in der jedem Staat Frieden nur denkbar und sicher schien als Ergebnis eigener Überlegenheit und in der Frieden eine Zeit der Vorbereitung des nächsten Krieges bedeutete. [. . .] Bei uns ist eine neue Generation in die politische Verantwortung hereingewachsen. Die Jungen sind nicht verantwortlich für das, was damalsgeschah. Aber sie sind verantwortlich für das, was in der Geschichte daraus wird.[74] (We must not seek in the end of the War the reason for expulsion, displacement and imprisonment. The reason is to be found in its beginning and in the beginning of the rule of violence which led to war. We must not separate the 8th of May 1945 from the 30th of January 1933. We have indeed no right to take part in today's victory celebrations. But we have every right to recognise the 8th of May 1945 as the end of that wrong turning in the history of Germany which contains within it the seed of hope for a better future. [. . .] We must all, whether guilty or not, whether old or young, accept the past. We are all affected by its consequences and bear our full responsibility for it. This is not a case for putting the past behind us. Such an attempt is not possible. We cannot change it in retrospect or pretend it did not happen. He who closes his eyes to the past becomes blind to the present. He who does not wish to remember such inhumanity, will once again become susceptible to new dangers of infection. [. . .] The new beginning in Europe after 1945 brought victory and defeat for the idea of freedom and self-determination. We must use the opportunity of putting an end to that long period of European history, in which peace for each state depended on its superiority and in which peace was only a period of preparation for the next war. [. . .] A new generation has grown up together with us to accept political responsibility.

The young are not responsible for what happened then. But they are responsible for what historically will be made of it.)

Weizsäcker's words, spoken before unification, exhibit the honesty and integrity for which he has always been admired. He also has the courage to recognise that Germany as a central European power will have to provide the cement necessary to keep the 'European house' together. Such a task need not lead to demands for a new mission or a new nationalism. Germany as an honest broker in a post-national phase can contribute to peace and better understanding in Europe. There is some hope that with renewed economic growth and the political will of the majority of the Republic's elite the recent nationalist xenophobia may be overcome. The Federal government's focus on Europe is welcome at a time of widespread 'Euro-scepticism', but it would be short-sighted for Germany to focus exclusively on this aspect, while failing to participate in the multi-ethnic culture of our global village and making its contribution to the human needs of a wider world. The leading position of Germany's economy has forced the country's people to look outward, to adopt a more cosmopolitan stance; let us hope this will lead to the urbanity, tolerance and humanism which we expect of a great and civilised nation.

Notes

1   Amongst the many studies on this topic see in particular: Christian Graf von Krockow, *Die Deutschen in ihrem Jahrhundert 1880–1990*, Reinbeck, 1990; and G. Smith *et al.* (eds), *Developments in German Politics*, London: Macmillan, 1992.
2   *Report on the tripartite Conference of Berlin* (Potsdam Agreement), quoted from I. von Münch (ed.), *Dokumente des geteilten Deutschland*, 2nd edn, Stuttgart: Kröher, 1976; p. 35f.
3   Ahlener Programm der CDU, February 1947, quoted from Krockow, *Die Deutschen*, p. 278.
4   A. und M. Mitscherlich, *Die Unfähigkeit zu trauern*, Munich: Piper, 1967; p. 81.
5   K. Jaspers, *Die Schuldfrage. Ein Beitrag zur deutschen Frage*, Zurich: Artemis [1947]; p. 56f.
6   Manifest of the *Kulturbund*, quoted from J. Berg *et al.*, *Sozialgeschichte*

der deutschen Literatur von 1918 bis zur Gegenwart, Frankfurt a.M.: Fischer, 1981; p. 472.

7   A. Andersch, introduction to first issue of *Der Ruf* (1946), quoted from J. Berg *et al.*, *Sozialgeschichte*, p. 571.
8   F. Meinecke in *Die deutsche Katastrophe*, quoted from Berg *et al.*, *Sozialgeschichte*, p. 571.
9   A group of writers who met annually under the stewardship of Hans Werner Richter and who significantly influenced the development of West German literature.
10 H. Arendt, 'Organised Guilt', in *Jewish Frontier*, Vol. 12 (1945), German version 'Organisierte Schuld', *Die Wandlung*, Vol. 4 (April 1946); pp. 337–44. K. Jaspers, *Schuldfrage*.
11 cf. H. A. Neunzig (ed.), *Hans Werner Richter und die Gruppe 47*, Munich: Nymphenburger, 1979; p. 54.
12 Jaspers, *Schuldfrage*, p. 8.
13 *Frankfurt Documents*, in Münch (ed.), *Dokumente*, p. 89.
14 cf. the additional co-determination laws: *Mitbestimmungsgesetz* (1951, revised 1965), *Betriebsverfassungsgesetz* (1972), *Mitbestimmungsgesetz* (1976), establishing parity in co-determination between employers and the work-force.
15 cf. this book, in particular p. 125.
16 R. Mowat, *Decline and Renewal. Europe Ancient and Modern*, Oxford: New Cherwell Press, 1991; p. 192.
17 *Grundgesetz für die Bundesrepublik Deutschland*, Präambel and Artikel 24, 2, in Münch (ed.), *Dokumente*, pp. 91, 96.
18 W. Lipgens, 'Europäische Integration', in R. Löwenthal und H. P. Schwarz (eds), *Die zweite Republik, 25 Jahre Bundesrepublik – eine Bilanz*, 2nd edn, Stuttgart: Seewald, 1974; p. 520.
19 K. Schumacher, *Reden und Schriften*, A. Scholz and W. Oschilewski (eds), Berlin, 1962; p. 246.
20 cf. *Soldatengesetz* (1956, revised 1975) gives soldiers the same basic political rights as other citizens; cf. also *Grundgesetz*, Artikel 17 and 17a.
21 Krockow, *Die Deutschen*, chapter 9, in particular p. 290.
22 J. Habermas, *Eine Art Schadensabwicklung. Kleine politische Schriften VI*, Frankfurt a.M.: Suhrkamp, 1987; p. 135.
23 G. Almond and S. Verba, *The Civic Culture*, Boston: Little Brown and Co., 1965; p. 64.
24 A typically German form of criticism, unwilling to enter into compromise and based on theoretical, fundamentalist positions.
25 For a comment on its reception cf. M. Mitscherlich, *Erinnerungsarbeit. Zur Psychoanalyse der Unfähigkeit zu trauern*, Frankfurt a.M.: Fischer, 1987; p. 40f.
26 cf. J. Habermas, *Theorie des kommunikativen Handelns*, 2 Vols, Frankfurt a.M.: Suhrkamp, 1981. Also R. Beck, *Sachwörterbuch der Politik*, 2nd edn, Stuttgart: Kröner, 1986; p. 217b.
27 Brandt's 'Regierungserklärung' 1969, in K. von Beyme (ed.), *Die großen Regierungserklärungen der deutschen Kanzler von Adenauer bis Schmidt*, Munich: Hanser, 1979; p. 281.

28   E. Kolinsky, 'Generation and Gender', G. Smith *et al.*, *Developments in West German Politics*, London: Macmillan, 1989; p. 253.

29   P. Pulzer, 'Unified Germany: A Normal State?', *German Politics*, Vol. 3 (April 1994), p. 12.

30   G. Wallraff, *Ganz unten*, Cologne: Kiepenheuer und Witsch, 1985; and most recently W. von Sternburg (ed.), *Für eine zivile Republik. Ansichten über die bedrohte Demokratie in Deutschland*, Frankfurt a.M.: Fischer, 1992.

31   cf. E. Noelle-Neumann and R. Köcher, *Die verletzte Nation: Über den Versuch der Deutschen, ihren Charakter zu ändern*, Stuttgart, 1987; and W. Weidenfeld, 'Am Pulsschlag der verletzten Nation: Was die Bundesbürger hoffen und fürchten', *Die Zeit*, 10th April 1987.

32   G. Smith *et al.*, *Developments in West German Politics*, pp. 83, 136ff.

33   H.-J. Hahn, 'The Concept of *Tendenzwende* as seen in the Sontheimer-Habermas Controversy', H.-J. Hahn and E. Kolinsky (eds), *Germany in the Eighties*, *AMGS*, Vol. 2, Birmingham: Aston University Press, 1986; pp. 1–19.

34   R. Dahrendorf, *Die Chancen der Krise. Über die Zukunft des Liberalismus*, Stuttgart: Deutsche Verlagsanstalt, 1983; pp. 16–24.

35   J. Habermas, *Die neue Unübersichtlichkeit. Kleine politische Schriften V*, Frankfurt a.M.: Suhrkamp, 1985; in particular pp. 141–66.

36   K. Sontheimer, *Deutschland zwischen Demokratie und Antidemokratie*, Munich: Nymphenburger, 1971; in particular pp. 10–37.

37   G. Mann, 'Die alte und die neue Historie', in C. Graf Podwelis (ed.), *Tendenzwende? Zur geistigen Situation der Bundesrepublik*, Stuttgart: Klett, 1975; pp. 41–58.

38   R. Augstein *et al.*, *'Historikerstreit'. Die Dokumentation der Kontroverse um die Einzigartigkeit der nationalsozialistischen Judenvernichtung*, Munich: Piper, 1987.

39   J. Habermas, 'Eine Art Schadensabwicklung', in *'Historikerstreit'*, in particular pp. 63, 72f. cf. also K. Sontheimer, 'Maskenbildner schminken eine neue Identität', *ibid.*, p. 276f.

40   Habermas, 'Eine Art Schadensabwicklung', p. 71.

41   J. Kocka, 'Hitler soll nicht durch Stalin und Pol Pot verdrängt werden', *'Historikerstreit'*, pp. 138–40.

42   B. Willms, 'Die politische Theorie von Carl Schmitt. Ein Fragment aus dem Jahre 1960' and M. Lauermann, 'Editorische Nachbemerkungen zu B. Willms . . .' in V. Gerhardt *et al.*, *Politisches Denken Jahrbuch 1991*, Stuttgart, 1992; pp. 120–46.

43   J. Habermas, 'Das Bedürfnis nach deutschen Kontinuitäten. "Unser aller Avancierriese": Carl Schmitt in der politischen Geistesgeschichte der Bundesrepublik', *Die Zeit*, 3rd December 1993.

44   cf. Th. Assheuer und H. Sarkowicz, *Rechtsradikale in Deutschland, die alte und die neue Rechte*, Munich: Beck, 1990; pp. 143–9, 175–9.

45   B. Strauß, 'Anschwellender Bocksgesang', *Der Spiegel*, 8th February 1993; p. 205.

46   Quoted from M. Schmitz and T. Assheuer, '"Wir sind enttäuscht genug": Die Befreiung des Menschen vom Staatsbürger. Botho Strauß

und die Überwindung der (Post)Moderne', *Frankfurter Rundschau*, 10th July 1993.

47 I. Bubis, 'Wegbereiter wie Nolte', *Der Spiegel*, 16 (April 1994); p. 170. cf. also U. Greiner, 'Der Seher auf dem Markt. Botho Strauß, Ernst Nolte, die *FAZ* und der Rechtsintellektualismus: Auf der Suche nach dem richtigen Rechten', *Die Zeit*, 22nd April 1994.

48 G. Hofmann and W. A. Perger (eds), *H. Geißler im Gespräch mit Gunter Hofmann und Werner A. Perger*, Frankfurt a.M.: Eichborn, 1993; p. 35.

49 G. J. Glaeßner, 'German Unification and the West', G. J. Glaeßner and I. Wallace (eds), *The German Revolution of 1989*, Oxford: Berg, 1992; p. 223.

50 J. Breuilly, 'Conclusion: nationalism and German reunification', in J. Breuilly (ed.), *The State of Germany*, London: Longman, 1992; p. 226.

51 G. Grass, 'Kurze Rede eines vaterlandslosen Gesellen', *Die Zeit*, 9th February 1990; J. Habermas, 'Der DM-Nationalismus. Die deutsche Einheit braucht einen Volksentscheid', *Die Zeit*, 30th March 1990; C. Offe, 'Vom taktischen Gebrauchswert nationaler Gefühle. Warum die Beschwörung des "Glücks" der deutschen Einheit den dringend notwendigen demokratischen Konstitutionsprozeß nicht ersetzen kann', *Die Zeit*, 14th December 1990.

52 G. Hofmann, 'Links und Rechts. Und Gorazde', *Die Zeit*, 29th April 1994.

53 Most recent developments seem to suggest, however, that both papers have distanced themselves somewhat from the excesses of right wing positions such as those by the historian E. Nolte and R. Zitelmann, editor of *Die Welt*. cf. U. Greiner, 'Der Seher auf dem Markt', *Die Zeit*, 22nd April 1994.

54 cf. R. Augstein, 'Adieu, DDR – zu früh oder zu spät?', *Der Spiegel*, 1st October 1990.

55 Quoted from W. Herles, *Geteilte Freude, Das erste Jahr der dritten Republik*, Munich: Kindler, 1992; p. 59.

56 J. Habermas, 'Die normativen Defizite der Vereinigung', *Vergangenheit als Zukunft*, Zürich: Pendo, 1990, p. 59.

57 C. Offe, 'German Reunification...', p. 5.

58 C. Koch, 'Zwischen östlichem Staatsbedürfnis und westlicher Marktgesellschaft: Experimentierfeld Deutschland', *Merkur*, 2 (1991); pp. 97–111.

59 G. Lease, 'Religion, the Churches and the German "Revolution" of November 1989', *German Politics*, Vol. 1 (August 1992), p. 269.

60 K. H. Bohrer, 'Deutsche Revolution und protestantische Mentalität', *Merkur*, Nr. 9/10 (Sept./Oct. 1992), p. 961.

61 Quoted from Herles, *Geteilte Freude*, p. 31.

62 J. Reich, *Rückkehr nach Europa. Zur neuen Lage der deutschen Nation*, Munich/Vienna: Hanser, 1991; p. 169.

63 N. Elias, *Über den Prozeß der Zivilisation*, Vol. 2, 2nd edn, Bern/Munich: Suhrkamp, 1969; p. 432.

64 H.-J. Hahn, 'Ossis, Wessis and Germans: an inner-German Perception

of National Characteristics', *Journal of Area Studies*, Nr. 2 (1993), pp. 114–28.

65 Quoted from Herles, *Geteilte Freude*, p. 40.
66 M. Stolpe, *Die Zeit*, 22nd February 1991.
67 *Der Spiegel*, 46 (17th August 1992), p. 36.
68 H. J. Maaz, *Das gestürzte Volk, die unglückliche Einheit*, Berlin: Argon, 1991; p. 13.
69 *ibid.* p. 27
70 R. Augstein, 'Kulturkampf, anders', *Der Spiegel*, 13th May 1991, p. 21.
71 S. Haffner, *Der Stern*, 22nd August 1991.
72 Hofmann and Perger, *H. Geißler im Gespräch*, pp. 35, 41f.
73 H. J. Veen, 'Die Westbindung der Deutschen in einer Phase der Neuorientierung', *Europa-Archiv*, Vol. 2 (1991), p. 34.
74 R. von Weizsäcker, 'Der 8. Mai 1945. Ansprache bei einer Gedenkstunde im Plenarsaal des deutschen Bundestages'. [Given in excerpts.]

Suggestions for further reading

Augstein, R. *et al.*, *Historiker-'Streit', Die Dokumentation der Kontroverse um die Einzigartigkeit der nationalsozialistischen Judenvernichtung*, 7th edn, Munich: Serie Piper, 1989.

Breuilly, J. (ed.), *The State of Germany. The National Idea in the Making, Unmaking and Remaking of a Modern Nation-State*, London/New York: Longman, 1992.

Hahn, H.-J. (ed.), *Germany in the 1990s. A Symposium*, special edition of *German Monitor*, January 1995.

Krockow, C. Graf von, *Die Deutschen in ihrem Jahrhundert 1890–1990*, Reinbeck bei Hamburg: Rowohlt, 1990.

Smith, G. *et al.* (eds), *Developments in West German Politics*, London: Macmillan, 1989.

Smith, G. *et al.* (eds), *Development in German Politics*, London: Macmillan, 1992.

Textual Studies

Zur Kunst des Volkes

1a. *Neues Deutschland* Nr. 139, 4th October 1946: ... Die Gesellschaftsart der Zukunft wird sozialistisch sein. Und darum auch die Kunst. Es ist etwa seit der zweiten Hälfte des vorigen Jahrhunderts viel davon gesprochen worden, daß das Kriterium der Kunst nicht mehr die Schönheit, sondern nur noch die Wahrheit sein könne. Die echte Kunst muß wahr sein, daran ist nicht zu zweifeln, und gerade darum erwarten wir eine kommende sozialistische Kunst. Aber die künstlerische Wahrheit des Geistes und nicht des Verstandes.

10 [...] Die künstlerisch wahre Ansicht des Menschen ist nicht
die anthropologische, sondern die humanistische. Und die
sozialistische Kunst malt die Welt der Arbeit und des Arbeiters
nicht in der alltäglichen Plackerei, sondern in ihrer inneren
Kraft und Sinnhaftigkeit, in ihrer echten Freude und Not.
15 Ja, auch Not und Leid, nur nicht in ihrer oberflächlichen
Richtigkeit, sondern eben in ihrer Grundwahrheit. Diese
Wahrheit, die hier die geistige Wahrheit genannt wurde, ist,
sichtbar, anschaulich gemacht, nichts anderes als die Schönheit.
(E. Schubbe (ed.), *Dokumente zur Kunst-, Literatur- und
Kulturpolitik der SED*, Stuttgart: Seewald, 1972; p. 56.)

Commentary:
The passage refers to the social responsibility and commitment of literature; the writer is opposed to formalist, avant-
garde aestheticism and instead harks back to the humanism
of Goethe and Schiller. The belief in a normative truth is
significant for the socialist programme mapped out here.

Vocabulary:
zweifeln = to doubt; Plackerei (f) = toil; Sinnhaftigkeit (f) =
meaning; oberflächlich = superficial; anschaulich gemacht =
made visible.

**1b. Wolfgang Weyrauch, *Fünf Modellgeschichten*, Nach-
wort:** ... Unsre Literatur kann unsrer Existenz helfen. Denn
unsre Literatur, ich wiederhole es, ist öffentlich. [...] Die
zukünftige deutsche Literatur wird eine verpflichtende
Literatur sein, oder sie wird nicht sein. [...] Wo der Anfang
der Existenz ist, ist auch der Anfang der Literatur. Wenn der
Wind durchs Haus geht, muß man sich danach erkundigen,
warum es so ist. Die Schönheit ist ein gutes Ding. Aber
Schönheit ohne Wahrheit ist böse. Wahrheit ohne Schönheit
ist besser. Sie bereitet die legitime Schönheit vor, die Schönheit
hinter der Selbstdreingabe, hinter dem Schmerz.
(W. Weyrauch (ed.), *Tausend Gramm. Sammlung neuer
deutscher Geschichten*, Hamburg/Stuttgart/Baden-Baden/
Berlin: Rowohlt, 1949; p. 216f.)

Commentary:
Observe the similarity of this statement by a young West German writer with the previous text. In both instances we find a commitment to 'truth', to the public function of literature. Both passages are written in simple German.

Vocabulary:
verpflichtend = demanding commitment; erkundigen = to inquire; Selbstdreingabe (f) = self-sacrifice.

2. Alfred Müller-Armack, 'Die Anfänge der Sozialen Marktwirtschaft'

Wir sind überzeugt, daß die Gesundung unserer Wirtschaft nicht durch Wiederholung überwundener Wirtschaftsformen erfolgen kann. [...] Was wir verlangen, ist eine neu zu gestaltende Wirtschaftsordnung. Eine solche kann nie aus dem
5 Zweckdenken und überalterten politischen Ideen allein hervorgehen, sondern bedarf der tieferen Begründung durch sittliche Ideale, welche ihr erst die innere Berechtigung verleihen. Zwei großen sittlichen Zielen fühlen wir uns verpflichtet, *der Freiheit und der sozialen Gerechtigkeit*. [...]
10 Um den Umkreis der sozialen Marktwirtschaft ungefähr zu umreißen, sei folgendes Betätigungsfeld künftiger sozialer Gestaltung genannt:
a) Schaffung einer sozialen Betriebsordnung, die den Arbeitnehmer als Mensch und Mitarbeiter wertet, ihm ein
15 soziales Mitgestaltungsrecht einräumt, ohne dabei die betriebliche Initiative und Verantwortung des Unternehmers einzuengen. [...]
c) Befolgung einer Antimonopolpolitik zur Bekämpfung möglichen Machtmißbrauches in der Wirtschaft.
20 d) Durchführung einer konjunkturpolitischen Beschäftigungs-politik mit dem Ziel, dem Arbeitgeber im Rahmen des Möglichen Sicherheit gegenüber Krisenrückschlägen zu geben. Hierbei ist außer kredit- und finanzpolitischen Maßnahmen auch ein mit sinnvollen Haushaltssicherungen versehenes
25 Programm staatlicher Investitionen vorzusehen.

e) Marktwirtschaftlicher Einkommensausgleich zur Beseitigung ungesunder Einkommens- und Besitzverschiedenheiten, und zwar durch Besteuerung und durch Familienzuschüsse, Kinder- und Mietbeihilfen an sozial Bedürftige.

30 f) Siedlungspolitik und sozialer Wohnungsbau. [...]
i) Ausbau der Sozialversicherung [...]
k) Minimallöhne und Sicherung der Einzellöhne durch Tarifvereinbarungen auf freier Grundlage.
(Quoted from R. Löwenthal und H. P. Schwarz (eds), *Die zweite Republik*, Stuttgart, 2nd edn, 1974; p. 146f.)

Commentary:
The emphasis on a new beginning, based on ethical concepts, is typical for the post-war period. The two pillars for Müller-Armack are freedom and social justice. The seven principles mentioned refer to the introduction of democracy in the firm (a); opposition to traditional German monopolies in industry (c); Keynesian market policy with state intervention to secure employment (d); a policy of social balance to achieve an even spread of wealth in society (e); affordable housing with state intervention (f); a system of social security (i); a minimum wage policy, based on the principle of free collective bargaining (k).

Vocabulary:
überwunden = outdated; Zweckdenken (n) = utility thinking; Umkreis (m) = vicinity; Betriebsordnung (f) = regulations in industry; Mitgestaltungsrecht (n) = right of co-determination; Krisenrückschlag (m) = critical set-back; Haushaltssicherung (f) = budgetary safeguards; Einkommensausgleich (m) = fair distribution of income; Tarifvereinbarung (f) = collective bargaining agreements.

3. Jürgen Habermas, 'Die Last der doppelten Vergangenheit'

[...] Die Historiker sind als Geschichtsschreiber daran gewöhnt, für ein Publikum von gebildeten Laien zu schreiben.

Insbesondere im 19. Jahrhundert hatten literarisch anspruchsvolle Darstellungen der Nationalgeschichte Einfluß auf Ausbreitung und Prägung des Nationalbewußtseins. Dieser Zusammenhang von Historismus und Nationalismus hat sich inzwischen aufgelöst. [. . .] Im Interpretationsstreit der politischen Öffentlichkeit gibt es nur Beteiligte, die sich engagiert, nämlich im Lichte konkurrierender Wertorientierungen, darüber auseinandersetzen, wie sie sich, sagen wir nach 1990, als Bürger der erweiterten Bundesrepublik und als Erben jener 'doppelten Vergangenheit' verstehen sollen. [. . .] Seit der deutschen Vereinigung ist der Kampf um die Interpunktion der Zeitgeschichte voll entbrannt. Wer etwa den Zeitraum von 1914 bis 1989 zu einer einheitlichen Epoche, sei es der Ideologien, des Weltbürgerkrieges oder des Totalitarismus, zusammenzieht, wird der NS-Periode einen anderen Stellenwert zuschreiben als jemand, der aus deutscher Sicht die Zeit zwischen 1871 und 1945 als eine Periode des Nationalismus versteht, während der Siegeszug des demokratischen Rechtsstaates erst nach 1945 eingesetzt hat.

Aus einer anderen Interpretation ergeben sich andere Zäsuren. Wer beispielsweise die Sonderwegthese kurzerhand umkehrt und die Bundesrepublik zum mehr oder minder pathologischen Interim erklärt, gewinnt freie Hand, um die Zäsur von 1945 als 'antifaschistische Umgründung' zu bagatellisieren und stattdessen 1989 als eine Zäsur zu begreifen, welche 'die Räson der alten Bundesrepublik erledigt' und die Rückkehr zu Traditionen des Bismarckreichs eröffnet.

Wer hingegen den Untergang der Weimarer Republik als Zäsur betrachtet, wird, wenn er an einer demokratischen Kultur interessiert ist, aus der 1990 wiedergewonnenen 'nationalstaatlichen Normalität' weniger Hoffnung schöpfen als aus dem Stand der politischen Zivilisierung, der in der alten Bundesrepublik bis dahin erreicht worden war.

(J. Habermas, 'Die Last der doppelten Vergangenheit', *Die Zeit*, Nr. 20, 13th May 1994; p. 54.)

Commentary:
Jürgen Habermas, a representative of the 'Frankfurt School' and eminent social philosopher, discussed the general understanding of history and, in particular, that of the different German states, leading to different understandings of a German identity. The text can be seen as a further response to the Historians' Debate: he contests the position of historians as the only interpreters of our time and illustrates how different attitudes to various periods of Germany's past can lead to dramatically different political value statements on democracy and on the importance of the democratic order of the FRG. The 'doppelte Vergangenheit' refers to the Nazi past (1933–45), but also to the dual past of the two German societies from 1945–90. His own preference is to see the period from 1871–1945 as one of nationalism and the period since as one of democracy.

Vocabulary:
anspruchsvoll = ambitious; Öffentlichkeit (f) = public; Wertorientierung (f) = value judgement; zusammenziehen = to condense; kurzerhand = simply; Umgründung (f) = re-evaluation; bagatellisieren = to belittle; erledigen = to finish.

Topics for further study

1. List the three aspects which contributed significantly to (West) Germany's democratisation after 1945 and discuss to what extent they have also upheld the 'German' tradition.
2. Give a brief synopsis of the *Historikerstreit* and examine to what extent this debate represents the difficulties of coming to terms with Germany's past.
3. List the themes and issues in this Chapter which relate to previous Chapters. Examine their specifically 'German' nature and compare them with traditions in your own country.
4. Scan several British and some German newspapers as well as TV reports and examine their attitude to Germany. In how far do these reports reflect the various issues discussed in this book and where do you detect significant differences in bias?

A brief survey
of major historical data

Numbers in [brackets] refer to page numbers

476 Collapse of West-Roman Empire. Invasion of Germanic tribes under Odoacer [1]. Tacitus' account of Germanic tribes [1].

800 Proclamation of Holy Roman Empire as successor to ancient Roman Empire by its first Emperor 'Karl der Große' (Charlemagne 742–814) [2]. Note: intervening period is age of Germanic/Teutonic tribes [3ff].

843 Treaty of Verdun: Holy Roman Empire divided amongst Charlemagne's grandchildren: (1) East-Frankish Empire, (2) West-Frankish Empire and (3) Lothar's Empire [3].

955 Battle of the Lechfeld, defeat of the Huns, Otto the Great (936–73) declared Saviour of the Empire [5f].

962 Otto crowned in Rome as the Emperor of 'Holy Roman Empire of the German Nation'. Note: this definition became familiar in the 11th century but was never the official title of the 'Holy Roman Empire'. This event could be seen symbolically as the birth of Germany [5f].

1070–1122 Investiture Contest (*Investiturstreit*) between Emperors and Popes [7, 11]. Henry IV in Canossa (1077) [11f].

8th–13th century Period of feudalism (*Lehenswesen*) [9].

12th/13th centuries Zenith of Holy Roman Empire, especially during period of Staufen dynasty (1138–1254) [9–11]. Most famous Staufen emperor 'Barbarossa' (*Rotbart*) (1121–1190) drowned in River Saleph whilst on third crusade to the Holy Land [11, 13ff, 22ff, 38, 98]. Last Staufen prince Konradin beheaded in Naples 1268 (aged 26), by Charles of Anjou, whilst attempting to reassert imperial power throughout Italy [11].

(1254–1273) *Interregnum* Period of internal strife, no acceptable emperor emerged, period of decline for Holy Roman Empire [11].

1273–1806 (with some interruptions) Dynasty of the Hapsburgs (*Habsburger*), beginning with emperor Rudolf (1273) and ending with Franz II who resigned Imperial Crown, thus bringing to a close the tradition of the Holy Roman Empire (1806).

Most important amongst the Hapsburgs were Kaiser Maximilian ('der letzte Ritter') and Charles V, under whom Reformation started and Empire saw its greatest expansion (Germany, Austria – including Bohemia and Hungary – northern parts of Italy, Burgundy, the Low Countries and Spain.)

Most important events during Hapsburg period

1356 Golden Seal (*Goldene Bulle*), limits imperial power through introduction of Electors (*Kurfürsten*) [12].

1453 Conquest of East Roman capital Byzantium by Turks [2]; symbolic end of Middle Ages with removal of Platonic Library from Byzantium to Italy.

***c*.1468** Invention of mechanical printing by Johannes Gutenberg [33].

1517 Martin Luther (1483–1546): 95 Theses presented at Wittenberg. 1520: *Address to the Christian Nobility of the German Nation* [35f] and *Letter on a Christian's Freedom* [36, 48f]. 1521: Diet (*Reichstag*) at Worms. 1522–34 saw translation of Bible into German. 1525: *Against the Murdering, Thieving Hordes of the Peasants* [37, 49f]. 1530: Augsburg Confession. Other contemporary reformers: John Calvin (1509–64) [30f]; Thomas Müntzer (1490–1525) [38f]; Ulrich Zwingli (1484–1531) [38].

1524/5 Peasants' Rebellion [37f, 51f].

1525 'Birth' of Prussia: Grand Master of Brandenburg Teutonic Order adopts new faith and creates secular Dukedom of Brandenburg [40ff].

1555 Peace of Augsburg, settles religious conflict [40].

1618–48 Thirty Years War (*Dreißigjähriger Krieg*), effectively destroyed Holy Roman Empire, led to secession of Low Countries, annexation of Alsace-Lorraine by France and emergence of Prussia and Austria as the two major German states [12, 27, 56f].

The ascendency of Prussia

1806 Battles of Jena and Auerstedt and Peace of Tilsit humiliated Prussia [103] and Austria and resulted in Napoleon's hegemony over Germany [104, 115] and dissolution of Holy Roman Empire [68, 115]. Southern German states formed *Rheinbund* in coalition with France and were rewarded with territorial gains, also emergence of liberalism in Germany (Constitutional Monarchies) and modernisation of Prussia [142].

1813–49   Period of German liberalism [43], beginning with Wars of Liberation (*Befreiungskriege* [111, 115]) against Napoleon and ending with failed German Revolution against illiberal monarchies (Austria, Prussia) and ill-fated attempt to establish a democratic nation state [143, 148–52].

Important events during this period: Foundation of Holy Alliance (*Heilige Allianz* (1815)) [115f] and of German Federation (*Deutscher Bund* [114f, 116, 153]). Liberal opposition to *Deutscher Bund* at *Wartburgfest* (1817) [114] and elsewhere [146].

1834   *Deutscher Zollverein* [116, 157]; start of German industrialisation [116f].

1848   German Revolution and unsuccessful attempt at forming a nation state [117f, 143f, 148–52].

1849–1919   Period of Prussian ascendency under *Hohenzollern* dynasty, beginning with Prussian supremacy over Austria [149, 152ff] and ending with First World War.

1870   Franco-Prussian War [154f].

1871–1919   *Deutsches Reich* [152–62] with Otto von Bismarck as *Reichskanzler*: a period of immense industrial and financial growth [157–9], but also of internal strife against Social Democrats [120, 158f], Catholic Church (1870–8: *Kulturkampf* [42f, 52–4]), Liberals [153f] and of external anxieties, leading to an arms race [154–7] and eventually to First World War [124f, 156f] (Britain, France, Russia, Japan, Italy, Rumania, Greece, USA against Germany, Austria, Turkey, Bulgaria).

Concept of a German *Sonderweg* [141, 224ff].

1919–33   *Weimarer Republik*. First effective democratic constitution, mainly supported by Social Democrats, Liberals and Catholics, but unpopular with Nationalists, nobility, bourgeoisie and academic circles. Rocked by inflation, civil war, unemployment, leading to strife between Communists and Fascists, culminating in Adolf Hitler's election to power.

1933–45   *Drittes Reich* with Adolf Hitler as *Reichskanzler*.

1933   Concordat with Vatican [43]. Formation of (Protestant) *Deutsche Christen* [43, 54f] and of *Bekennende Kirche* (1934) [43f].

German expansion with annexation of Austria and *Sudentenland* and invasion of Poland leads to Second World War and destruction of Third Reich and of German nation state.

1945   *Stuttgarter Schulderklärung* [44f].

Germany to the present (1945-94)

1945 (August) Potsdam Agreement: Allies' decision on the future of Germany [211]. *Stunde Null* [211], Denazification process [211]. Formation of early social policies and their disruption by the Cold War and McCarthyism [212].

1948 Currency Reform [212f] and beginning of Cold War [212, 215] with Berlin blockade.

1948 Foundation of European integration with European Community for Coal and Steel [215-18]; its predecessor *Union Européenne des Fédéralistes* (1946) [217].

1949 Division of Germany into two states, the Federal Republic (*Bundesrepublik Deutschland*) and the German Democratic Republic (*Deutsche Demokratische Republik*). Attempts in East Germany at coming to terms with Nazi past [212f]. *National-kommittee Freies Deutschland and Kulturbund* [212].

Major events since 1949

1949 Drafting of *Grundgesetz* (Basic Law) [214f].

1949 Introduction of *Soziale Marktwirtschaft* (Social Market Economy) [215f, 240f].

1951 First attempts by FRG to join NATO [218].

1953 (17th June): Uprising in East Berlin [213].

1961 Building of Berlin Wall [213].

1968 Student unrests [219f].

1974 *Tendenzwende* [222].

1990 German Unification [226ff].

A brief survey of major
cultural periods/events

Antiquity with Germanic tribes (Vandals, Franks, Lombards [1, 2f]). Middle Ages: approx. 500–1492 [1–13]. Philosophy of St. Augustine [4, 13, 28, 36].

Development of German language from various Germanic dialects with Old High-German (*althochdeutsch*) 9th–11th century, mainly religious and ecclesiastical texts. Concept of *deutsch* < 'theodisk' = Latin *sermo vulgaris* = language of the (common) people [6f].

Middle High-German (*mittelhochdeutsch*) 11th–15th century, texts include German troubadour songs (*Minnesang*), courtly romance (*Ritterepen, höfische Epen*) and later on also more common or trivial stories. Most famous writers: Walther von der Vogelweide (*c.* 1168–1228) [10, 21f], Wolfram von Eschenbach, Hartmann von der Aue, Gottfried von Straßburg and the author/s of the *Nibelungenlied* [97f]. Also first period of German mysticism [28f].

New High-German (*neuhochdeutsch*), beginning with *Prager Kanzleisprache*, decisively influenced by Luther [28] and basis of today's German.

Renaissance period with discovery of individualism [33–5], Luther's concept of freedom [35–7], *Kultur* versus *Zivilisation* [31f] and concept of *Weltfrömmigkeit* [30–3]. Main figures: Luther, Erasmus von Rotterdam (1467–1536) [33–5], Melanchton, Albrecht Dürer [34].

Major cultural periods since the Thirty Years War

Baroque (Late 16th and 17th century)
Mainly ecclesiastical and courtly, main theme: *vanitas* (the vanity of life), interest in a standard German language [92], influenced by events of Thirty Years War.

German Enlightenment (*Aufklärung*) (1720–85)
[57–9, 87, 92f, 109, 176]
Less influential than in France or Britain, major figures were Wieland [87, 92, 95] and Lessing in literature [60f, 87, 90, 94, 103f] and Leibniz and Kant in philosophy. Kant's essay 'Was ist Aufklärung' (1784) [57–9, 103].

Pietism (*Empfindsamkeit*) (1740–80)
A second mystical period, emphasis on psychic energies (*Innerlichkeit, Seele*) [28f, 32].

German Storm and Stress (*Sturm und Drang*) (1767–85)
The literature of the young Goethe and Schiller, of Lenz, Klinger and many others, establishing a typically German element in literature, harking back to the Middle Ages [93], to nature and in opposition to French literature and thought. Of particular importance Herder and his concepts of *Volk* and *Sprache* [57, 60, 61–6, 76–9, 85, 90].

German Classicism (*Deutsche Klassik*) (1786–1832)
The literature of the mature Goethe [83ff, 87–91, 93, 95, 107f, 143, 179–82], Schiller [57, 87, 88, 93, 94f, 99, 101–3, 104f, 176] and Hölderlin [70, 80f, 87, 90, 176f]: period of *Weltliteratur* [83–92, 100], discovery of Greek classicism for a German literary tradition (Winckelmann [87, 100, 108]), but also leading to formation of the ideas of *Weltbürgertum* and *Kulturnation* [95, 105]. Flourishing period of German lyric poetry (*Lied, Erlebnisgedicht*) and of drama (*Bürgerliches Trauerspiel*). With Wilhelm von Humboldt foundation of modern German education system [95, 105, 107–111, 115, 130–3], also influenced by Pestalozzi's ideas [109, 112, 117].

German Romanticism (*Romantik*) (1795–1835)
The literature of Tieck [90], Novalis [67, 90, 179], Brentano [96], Eichendorff and Kleist. Together with Classicism established Germany's role in literature and thought and introduced the concepts of *Nationalliteratur* [92ff] and *Germanistik* [96] under the influence of J. Grimm [96f, 143] and others. Romantic philosophers were Fichte [57, 66–70, 92, 111–115, 117, 119, 133–5], Hegel [41f, 57, 70–4, 113, 141, 128, 177–9], Schelling, Schleiermacher [69f, 79f, 177]. Romantics tried to unite the typically German, Christian [177f] and Classical strands, aimed to bring about a Golden Age with humankind's reconciliation with God and Nature. Mme de Staël pro-

moted German Classical and Romantic ideas in France [85, 143, 165–7], but some of the more patriotic Romantics indulged in xenophobia against France and Western civilisation [69, 96f, 103f, 111, 113f]. Although outside this period, Richard Wagner is often seen as a late Romantic [96f, 98f].

German/Austrian *Biedermeier* (1820–50)

The literature of Grillparzer [99], Stifter [144], Mörike, the philosophy of Schopenhauer [183f, 202–4]. A typically *bürgerliche* and conservative-liberal period in Germany, as illustrated in education, cf. *Stiehlsche Regulative* [118, 136f]. The rise of the German *Bürger* [141ff, 144], the image of the *deutsche Michel* [146f], the position of women [147f].

Vormärz/Junges Deutschland (1830–50)

A 'Left-Hegelian', progressive literature, critical of Holy Alliance, anticipating the social and industrial revolution. Main figures Heinrich Heine (1779–1856) [15f, 58f, 69, 142, 143, 146], Georg Herwegh [167f], the young Karl Marx and Friedrich Engels.

German Realism (*Realismus*) (1850–90)

Relatively insignificant within Germany with major German writers outside Germany: G. Keller, Th. Storm, Th. Fontane [160f], F. Hebbel. Strong impact of Marxist ideas (K. Marx [91, 149, 187], F. Engels [91, 149], L. Feuerbach [184–7] and F. Nietzsche [160, 169f, 187–92, 204–6]). Rise of the 'bourgeoisie' during *Gründerzeit* [143f, 159f]. Impact of industrialisation on education [115f] with reform movement by G. Kerschensteiner [119f, 137f] and on officialdom ('Mandarine' [122ff, 160]). Developing tension between *Gymnasien* and newer, more vocationally biased schools [120–2], emergence of a cultural crisis [122ff, 161f, 187], of the concept of *Geisteswissenschaft* [123], of racism [124] and anti-western sentiments [125].

The Weimar Republic (1919–33)

German Expressionism (*Expressionismus*), another revolutionary period in German literature, major contributions to drama and poetry, attempts to develop the concept of 'der neue Mensch' and of the *Übermensch* [175, 180ff, 182, 188–92]. Of particular importance for political and literary developments were Heinrich and Thomas Mann [91, 125f, 162, 176, 197, 198f] and other liberal republicans such as Max Weber [29f, 125, 159], Friedrich Meinecke *et al.* [95f, 105f, 125]. A dangerous counter movement became known as *Konservative Revolution* [126, 225].

National Socialism (1933–45)

Racism and its origins in German culture [126, 192f]. J. Langbehn, P. Lagarde and O. Spengler as precursors of National Socialism [192–9, 206–9].

Germany since 1945

Reactionary trends in education [126f], concept of *Stunde Null* [140, 211], intellectuals and the Nazi past [214f, 238–40], *Gruppe 47* [214]. Hannah Arendt and Karl Jaspers on guilt [214], changes in Germany's political culture with increasing Westernisation [219f, 221]. Alexander and Margarete Mitscherlich, *Die Unfähigkeit zu trauern* [220]. The *Tendenzwende* [222f] and a general change towards post-modern values [223ff], emergence of *Historikerstreit* (Historians' Debate) (1986) [140, 223f] and the re-emergence of the *Sonderweg* debate [224f] and of a new right (Kaltenbrunner, Botho Strauß) [225f]. West German intellectuals' attitude towards unification [226–8, 241f], compared with those of East German intellectuals [228–31].